Market-driven Politics

Market-driven Politics

Neoliberal Democracy and the Public Interest

COLIN LEYS

V

VERSO

London • New York

First published by Verso 2001
© Colin Leys 2001
All rights reserved

1 3 5 7 9 10 8 6 4 2

Verso
UK: 6 Meard Street, London W1F 0EG
USA: 180 Varick Street, New York, NY 10014–4606
www.versobooks.com

Verso is the imprint of New Left Books

ISBN 1-85984–627–0

British Library Cataloguing in Publication Data
A catalogue record for this book is available from the British Library

Library of Congress Cataloging-in-Publication Data
Leys, Colin.
 Market-driven politics : neoliberal democracy and the public interest / Colin Leys.
  p. cm.
 Includes bibliographical references and index.
 ISBN 1–85984–627–0
 1. Great Britain—Economic policy—1997–2. Great Britain—Politics and government—1997–3. Public television—Great Britain. 4. National Health Service (Great Britain). I. Title.
HC256.7 L49 2001
338.941—dc21
                                    2001045570

Typeset by SetSystems Ltd, Saffron Walden, Essex
Printed by Biddles Ltd, Guildford and King's Lynn

Contents

Preface

In 1993 I was asked to consider undertaking a new revision of my book *Politics in Britain*, which was first published in 1983 and then revised for Verso in 1987. But by 1993 I felt that the advent of economic globalisation meant that national politics had to be analysed in a new way, focusing on the causal chains linking global market forces to national politics. This in turn meant being willing to trace in some detail the way those forces operate in specific markets. The needed shift of approach took some time. The result is a book with a double agenda: while the empirical focus is on Britain, the analysis should apply everywhere.

An immediate consequence of this way of thinking about politics is to make one dependent on the expertise of people who work in and on particular markets. I have had invaluable tuition about television broadcasting and the National Health Service from many people, but especially the following: on broadcasting, from Steven Barnett, Peter Goodwin, Mathew Horsman, Tony Garnett, Paul Styles and Granville Williams, and above all James Curran; and on health care, from Declan Gaffney and Jean Shaoul, and above all Allyson Pollock. They have undoubtedly not been able to save me entirely from error, but they have tried very hard and I am extraordinarily grateful, while absolving them from all responsibility. The empirical data used in the book are as far as possible those available in December 2000.

I have also had invaluable help in thinking about economic globalisation from Greg Albo, Sam Gindin, Leo Panitch and Alan Zuege; and about markets and commodification from Ursula Huws and, especially, Barbara Harriss-White, who kept insisting that the project was worth while when I felt most disheartened. I thank them all very much. I was also generously helped to think more systematically about the politics of markets by the late Gordon White, and I owe another debt to the efficiency and courtesy of the librarians at the Independent Television Commission and the King's Fund.

I am grateful to the Killam Program and the Social Science and Humanities Research Council in Canada, and the Lipman–Miliband Trust in England, for financial support at various times while I was working on this book. Last but not least I want to thank Leo Panitch, John S. Saul, Adam Leys and Nancy Leys Stepan for constant encouragement and practical help and good advice; Ginny Hobart for doing so much to try to improve my prose; Tansy Huws for preparing the index; and the members of CUPE Local 3903 at York University in Toronto for inspiring me to finish the book during the long autumn of 2000.

Colin Leys
March 2001

1

Introduction

Politics used to be thought of as an autonomous field of activity, and the management of the national economy was seen as one of the most important tasks of government. Now, however, it is generally agreed that capital mobility across national borders means that national governments can influence the domestic economy only by controlling inflation and trying to facilitate the competitiveness of locally-based companies through 'supply-side' measures. But political analysis has still to come to terms with the implications of this change, with the result that there are big differences of opinion about the significance of what has happened. Highly generalised books with titles like *The End of the Nation State, False Dawn, Empire, The Lexus and the Olive Tree* – or, more soberly, *Internationalization and Domestic Politics* – conclude either that the nation state has been consigned to the rubbish-bin of history or that, on the contrary, the constraints within which it operates have merely been rearranged, with no profound political implications.[1] Very few studies have examined empirically the extent to which politics and policy in any particular country are conditioned, or even determined, by global economic forces, and what this implies for democracy and the collective values on which it depends.

The aim of this book is to try to explore this question by a multi-level study of British politics, sticking as closely as possible to the facts and moving from global economic forces down through national politics to the changes occurring week by week in two fields of public life that are both fundamentally important and familiar to everyone – public service television and health care. The book's central argument is that politics everywhere are now *market-driven*. It is not just that governments can no longer 'manage' their national economies; to survive in office they must increasingly 'manage' national politics in such a way as to adapt *them* to the pressures of transnational market forces. These pressures take several forms, including tight constraints on macro-economic policy, the demands made by investors for favourable regulatory arrangements, the direct impact of global economic forces in specific markets, and the continuous 'deep' reshaping of social relations and ideas by a great variety of market forces operating with increased force thanks to globalisation. For reasons outlined below, British politics are more 'market-driven' than most, but the logic that shapes them now operates everywhere.

Public sector activities like health services and broadcasting, to which people are attached historically, and as citizens rather than consumers, play an important role here, because they affect the legitimacy of the government of the day. In market-driven politics these domains become political flashpoints because they are also targets for global capital. As we follow the evolution of policy in these spheres from the 1980s onwards we become aware that what has been happening to them is not primarily explicable in terms of the initiatives of this or that politician or entrepreneur but flows from a new political dynamic resulting from economic globalisation. It is not that the state has become impotent, but that it is constrained to use its power to advance the process of commodification.

In outline, the argument runs as follows. What is novel about the global economy that took shape from the 1970s onwards, compared with the years before 1914, is, first, the much wider choice of locations for capital investment; second, the weight and omnipresence of global financial markets; and, third, the importance of transnational manufacturing and service corporations (TNCs), and the advanced communications technology on which both financial markets and TNCs depend. Capital mobility has not just removed the 'Keynesian capacity' of national governments – their ability to influence the general level of demand. It has made all policy-making sensitive to 'market sentiment' and the regulatory demands of TNCs. Governments can try to reduce these pressures through various kinds of protectionism, through participating in global or regional institutions to regulate market forces, and through shedding responsibilities downwards (devolution and 'subsidiarity'), but they can't escape them. States are obliged to become more and more 'internationalised', adapted to serving the needs of global market forces.

How big a change this reversal of power involves for any particular country depends on what existed before. Britain lacked market-coordinating, trust-based institutions of the 'Rhineland', 'Nordic' or 'East Asian' types – banks with long-term equity in companies, state-backed national training systems, 'families' of corporations doing business with each other like the Japanese *keiretsu* or South Korean *chaebols*. In Britain there were no domestic mechanisms with which the necessary economic restructuring could be undertaken. Instead, the Thatcher governments of the 1980s actively promoted global capital mobility with a view to exposing the economy as much as possible to global market forces, and entering frankly into competitive deregulation to attract investment to Britain. State institutions were also radically restructured, with three main aims: to make the state serve business interests, to remodel its internal operations on business lines, and to reduce the government's exposure to political pressures from the electorate.

These changes and the logic behind them were accepted by the incoming New Labour government in 1997. Labour's 'modernisers' were also keenly aware that the social basis of politics had changed. The institutional legacy of Thatcherism had gained general acceptance (if little affection) as a result of accompanying social changes – rapid income growth, consumerism, the erosion of traditional class and caste boundaries, the intense 'mediatisation' of politics and the penetration of everyday life by commercial values. The working-class voters in Labour's traditional 'heartlands' were now a minority. They could only be helped if Labour formed a long-term coalition with elements of business, secured the approval of the markets and permanently attached middle-class voters to the party. To be able to do these things the Labour leadership needed to insulate itself from pressures from its own membership. The party constitution was rewritten and the Leader's inner circle assumed unprecedented control over not only the making of policy, but also its day-to-day interpretation. And after the Conservatives' defeat in 1997 their new leader William Hague tried to follow Labour's example.

The effect of these changes is that in Britain the pressures of market forces on national politics are unusually open and efficacious. Both party leaderships are highly attuned to responding to them and exceptionally free to do so. To appreciate the importance of this fully we must study specific markets, a fascinating but seriously neglected field. Contrary to the impression given by neoliberal ideology and neoclassical economics textbooks, markets are not impersonal or impartial but highly political, as well as inherently unstable. In the search for survival, firms constantly explore ways to break out of the boundaries set by state regulation, including the boundaries that close non-market spheres to commodification and profit-making. This is a crucially important issue, since it threatens the destruction of non-market spheres of life on which social solidarity and active democracy have always depended. For a non-market field to be successfully transformed into a market, four requirements need to be met. First, the goods or services in question must be reconfigured so that they can be priced and sold. Second, people must be induced to want to buy them. Third, the workforce involved in their provision must be transformed from one working for collective aims with a service ethic to one working to produce profits for owners of capital and subject to market discipline. Finally, capital moving into a previously non-market field needs to have the risk underwritten by the state. Both public service television and the National Health Service show these processes strongly at work, and the way the state facilitates them.

Once the process of commodification is under way a further dynamic comes into operation – the transformation of the commodity under the pressures of competition. Industrialised production involves 'Taylorism' – the substitution of cheaper for more expensive labour – and standardisation of the product in the search for scale economies.[2] In the case of services, the ultimate phase in commodification is the substitution of mass-produced material goods for the sale of services, and the transfer of all remaining labour to the consumer. This too is in evidence in television and health care. What begins as the provision of a service to fulfil collectively determined socio-political purposes ends up as a drive to find mass-produced goods that can be sold profitably. The collective needs and values that the service was originally created to serve are gradually marginalised and finally abandoned.

While every commodity has some specific characteristics that influence the way these basic mechanisms work on it, none seems immune, and what is true for television and health care is also at work in education, personal social services, public transport, and so on. The facts suggest that market-driven politics can lead to a remarkably rapid erosion of democratically-determined collective values and institutions.

Those students of 'comparative politics' who have come closest to asking the central questions posed in this book have mostly arrived at much more optimistic conclusions. In the view of these authors, relatively little has changed for European social democracy.[3] The difference between us arises, it seems to me, partly from their methodology and partly from their politics. Their methodology combines the so-called 'new institutionalism' with very large-scale cross-country statistical comparisons. Without going into detail here, it seems to me that these methodological commitments divert attention from the *tendencies* at work, in different ways and to different degrees, in the various countries studied, tendencies whose cumulative social and political effects are not picked up by relatively short-term and large-scale macro-economic statistics. These authors, too, while sympathetic to social democracy, are essentially liberal in their politics. They treat global capitalism as inevitable; the idea that its social and political consequences may be intolerable is absent from their work. My view, by contrast, is that what is happening is incompatible with democracy – and in the long run, with civilised life – and that the point of trying to understand it is to be able eventually to change it.

The analytic task involved has become more complex. The main causal links no longer converge conveniently – in the case of Britain – in Westminster and the City of London, but run off the edge of the national map to Washington, Brussels, New York and Tokyo, not to mention manufacturing hubs like Detroit, tax havens like the Bahamas, and innumerable other places abroad. Bringing out the connections between seemingly (though not really) remote market forces and the changes occurring in people's everyday lives is harder work than it was when a great deal of effective power over the economy still rested with governments. On the other hand it is more important than ever to undertake it. Otherwise cause and effect are dangerously confused. 'Brussels' is blamed for 'taking away British sovereignty' when both British sovereignty and that of the EU have increasingly been surrendered to private capital. Foreigners are blamed for 'taking away' jobs when job losses are a normal consequence of globalised capitalist production. The BBC is threatened with the loss of its licence fee both for having too low ratings and for not being serious enough, when audiences have been handed over for fragmentation (and 'dumbing down') by global market forces. The NHS is seen as an inefficient provider of commodities and exposed to competition (on a very uneven 'playing field') with global market forces, rather than championed as a highly efficient means of sharing risk by avoiding the commodification of health care. If we are to reassert our collective needs against the interests and logic of global capital, it is essential to understand the way national politics and global market forces are now connected.

No theoretical ambitions are attached to the term 'market-driven politics'. It refers simply to the political dimension of the shift of power from voters to capital that results from trans-border capital mobility. It has some affinity with Karl Polanyi's term 'market society', which he coined to refer to a society in which market forces, i.e. capital, had escaped political control. 'Market society' was actually inconceivable, Polanyi thought:

> To allow the market mechanism to be the sole director of the fate of human beings and their natural environment, indeed, even of the amount and use of purchasing power, would result in the demolition of society. . . . Robbed of the protective covering of cultural institutions, human beings would perish from the effects of social exposure; they would die as the victims of acute social dislocation through vice, perversion, crime and starvation. Nature would be reduced to its elements, neighbourhoods and landscapes defiled, rivers polluted, military safety jeopardized, the power to produce food and raw materials destroyed.[4]

In 1944, when Polanyi published *The Great Transformation*, he clearly believed that the most destructive war in human history had shown that the social costs of allowing capital to escape from political control were too great ever to be risked again. By the 1970s, however, after three decades of prosperity, people had forgotten the costs of 'deregulation' and voted for a new instalment of it. We shall soon have to measure the social costs once again, and the question will then be whether a sufficient number of states acting together want to reassert the control over market forces that was abandoned in the 1980s. What the British case shows is that party politics and state policy-making are themselves now powerfully market-driven and less and less likely to defend, let alone renew and revitalise, the prerequisites of democracy. We need to understand this in order to develop an effective alternative politics.

The organisation of the book is as follows. Chapter 2 considers how the global economy was formed and the main ways in which the market forces operating in it tend to determine national government policy and – in the end perhaps even more importantly – shape the basic social relations that national politics express. Chapter 3 looks at British politics: first in terms of the 'deep' continuing impact of global market forces on British society and culture; then in terms of the ways in which political institutions and the political parties have been transformed in the course of both initiating and then adapting to economic globalisation; and finally in terms of what this means for policy-making. Chapter 4 narrows the focus down from the nation to specific policy sectors. It discusses the nature of markets and commodities, the processes involved in converting non-commodified services to commodities, and the social significance of the transformations that commodities undergo as a result of capitalist competition. Chapters 5 and 6 then use this framework to analyse what has happened to public service television and health care, respectively, in the era of economic globalisation – how the collective values or 'goods' that were served by public services in these fields have been progressively undermined and look destined to disappear. Chapter 7 very briefly considers some of the implications of market-driven politics, and what needs to be done about them.

2

The global economy and national politics

Since this book is about the impact of global market forces on British politics it must begin by setting out as clearly as possible what those forces are – how the global economy came into being, what its chief characteristics are, who the chief actors in it are and where their strengths lie, how national governments respond, and – in the barest outline – how global market forces shape and reshape the underlying social structures and cultures that national politics reflect. This is not an essentially difficult or complex matter, but it needs disentangling from the much wider and looser topic of 'globalisation'. At the turn of the century public discussion was saturated with this term: like rain falling on the waterlogged British soil, not a drop more of it could be retained. So it is worth stressing that this chapter is not about globalisation, in the sense of the increased inter-connectedness of everyone and everything, from the 'new mediaevalism' in international relations to 'space-time compression' and the internet. It is just about the particular kind of global economy that had been put in place by the year 2000, and its implications for national politics.

The formation of a global economy

The international trading regime established in 1944 at Bretton Woods succeeded brilliantly in its aim of permitting global trade to expand without risking more world-wide depressions like the one that had culminated in the Second World War. The unprecedented expansion of output and trade that the Bretton Woods system made possible, however, gave rise to new developments by which it was eventually undermined.

First, sustained world-wide growth led to a steady increase in the number of countries in which capital could be profitably invested. As material and legal infrastructures and urbanised low-wage workforces became available in more and more places, one industry after another found it profitable to invest there. Labour-intensive industries such as textiles and the assembly stages of secondary manufacturing were usually the first to move, then capital-intensive industries such as automobiles and chemicals, then higher technology-based industries like consumer electronics, and finally – by the 1990s – information-based industries like financial services. By the 1990s capital had many more options than in 1944.

Second, scientific and technological advances in both production and transport greatly reduced the cost of moving production from one place to another. Between 1930 and 1990 sea freight costs fell by 50 per cent, and air transport costs by 80 per cent.[1] Production could also now be divided up in new ways, with different stages distributed among sites in different countries – the most labour-intensive in low-wage countries, those most dependent on sophisticated technology in high-wage countries, those showing the highest profits in low-tax countries, and so on. On the other hand, the capital-intensity of new technologies, and the rapidity of technological change, meant that producers of relatively high value-added products (including services) could not hope to recoup their costs quickly enough unless they sold them on an international scale. This, coupled with the fear of reviving protectionism, led to a growing surge of foreign direct investment (FDI) from the mid-1980s onwards, especially in the form of acquisitions and mergers, as companies based in Western Europe, the USA and Japan sought to secure access to each other's markets. Throughout the 1990s about 27 per cent of all such transactions were transnational, and in the first half of 2000 a record $1.88 trillion of acquisitions and mergers were recorded world-wide.[2]

Third, dramatic advances in information and communications technology allowed a growing number of TNCs to begin treating the whole world not just as a single market, but also as a single production site – or, rather, as a limited number of linked regional sites, co-producing broadly similar products.[3] Research, development and production itself could now be coordinated almost as effectively across the globe as across a country or even a city in the past. The fact that this involved operating in many different national jurisdictions meant that TNCs established large legal and technical departments to negotiate with governments and engage in 'regulatory arbitrage', getting the greatest possible advantage out of the differences between national regulatory regimes.

Fourth, with the recovery of the Axis countries after the Second World War, and intensifying international competition, the United States, which had been a major creditor country in the late 1940s, became the world's largest debtor, causing President Nixon to abandon the convertibility of the US dollar in 1971. This was followed in 1973 by the abandonment of fixed exchange rates between the world's leading currencies, and a corresponding explosion of activity on the currency exchanges, driven partly by companies' attempts to hedge against the risks of future currency fluctuations in their foreign operations, and partly by speculative activity. By the middle of 2000 about two trillion dollars' worth of currency was being exchanged world-wide every day, dwarfing not only the value of the currencies needed for the exchange of goods and services, but even more the foreign exchange reserves of any national central bank. This meant that governments could no longer influence the exchange rate for their currencies by intervening in the currency markets. The British government discovered this the hard way on 'Black Wednesday', 16 October 1992, when, after spending £10 billion of the country's foreign exchange reserves to prop up the value of the pound, it saw sterling driven by speculators out of the European Exchange Rate Mechanism and was forced to devalue it by 15 per cent.

Fifth, and closely connected to the end of fixed exchange rates, effective control over the movement of capital was progressively abandoned with the rise of 'offshore' banking. Beginning in the 1950s, owners of US dollars who wanted to keep them outside the jurisdiction of the US government started depositing them in special dollar accounts in banks in Paris and London that were not subject to US government regulation. These so-called 'Eurodollars' were later joined by other currencies (which also came to be called Eurocurrencies, even though they were also increasingly deposited in non-European banking centres); and so many interests were served by the practice that both the US and other governments acquiesced, until by 1987 the combined value of all these 'offshore' accounts totalled $4 trillion.[4] Deposits on this scale meant that borrowers could borrow large sums in major currencies outside the regulatory jurisdiction of the governments that had issued them. In 1981 the US government belatedly tried to rein in the Eurodollar market but found that foreign banks would not cooperate.[5] Instead, it settled for a wholesale deregulation of US domestic banking, forcing other governments with major financial sectors to follow suit. As a result all national controls over capital movements quickly became less and less effective and by the late 1980s had been mostly abandoned, leading to the formation of a single global capital market and permitting the surge of FDI mentioned above.[6]

Sixth, successive rounds of negotiations had progressively liberalised the General Agreement on Tariffs and Trade. By 1990 average import tariff levels had fallen to less than 5 per cent;[7] and in the Uruguay Round of negotiations, concluded in 1994, agricultural products and 'intellectual property' (i.e. the increasingly important information and media industries) were brought within the scope of the Agreement.

Seventh, in 1989 the communist regimes of the USSR and Eastern Europe collapsed, while reforms were also opening up China to foreign investment. By the late 1990s North Korea was virtually the only country in the world still fenced off from global capital.

This list of the factors leading to globalisation on neoliberal lines includes most of those usually cited, but in one respect it shares a crucial weakness with those popular accounts of globalisation that portray it as driven by autonomous technological changes and 'impersonal' market forces: it omits the crucial political dimension. For governments had it within their power to try to resist these changes, or to try to change their direction; but they rarely tried. One reason was that once the trend to financial deregulation was under way there was at least a temporary avantage to be had in deregulating *ahead* of other countries.* The main driver, however, was the initial commitment to

---

* Trade liberalisation (the reduction of national tariffs and non-tariff barriers) requires collective action (countries seek reciprocal treatment), but states can gain from reducing their financial regulations unilaterally, so that 'states would be tempted to derive the benefits of a closed financial order (such as increased policy autonomy and more stable exchange rates), while "free riding" by unilaterally liberalizing their markets to gain advantages for their national financial systems' (Eric Helleiner, *States and the Reemergence of Global Finance*, [Cornell University Press, 1994] p. 197). Helleiner also cites the common training, experience and outlook of the world's main central bankers; the fact that the USA and Japan had interests as lenders of last resort that made them give leadership in financial matters that had no equivalent in trade; and the fact that 'trade liberalization is generally controversial because the costs in terms of lost jobs are readily visible and they are borne by concentrated populations, whereas the benefits in terms of lower consumer prices are less tangible and more dispersed. Financial liberalization arouses less controversy because the kinds of costs

deregulation by the USA (accounting for about 20 per cent of the world's GDP) and the UK with its major financial services sector, which immediately made it more and more costly for other countries not to conform.

Even this way of putting it, however, makes the neoliberal domestic policies adopted almost everywhere in the 1980s and 1990s look like a rational – if not unavoidable – response to a primarily economic externally imposed imperative. But globalisation was also a political project to defeat 'socialism'. Both the US and the British economies had experienced slow growth and declining international competitiveness in the 1960s. In both countries politics became polarised, between defenders of the post-war 'settlement' (the British term) or 'national bargain' (the US term) – in which the state played the role of both manager of the economy and provider of social services and social security – and those who feared that private capital risked losing its power and authority. One side of the New Right's successful campaign to 'roll back socialism' (or in the USA, 'liberalism') was to attack its domestic base in the labour movement through anti-union measures and higher unemployment, privatisation and reduced taxes on capital. The other side was to end controls over capital movements and reduce trade barriers, exposing the domestic workforce to competition from lower-paid workers in countries with weaker regulatory regimes – at the same time making it hard, if not impossible, for any future government to reverse these changes. The result of capital mobility was thus the rapid formation of a global economy that quickly generated market forces which impinged on national states and governments much more powerfully, and led to domestic deregulation in response. But business leaders and right-wing parties throughout the OECD also supported deregulation for domestic political reasons as well as economic ones, i.e. to weaken the political power of organised labour and the left.[8]

By 1990 a new global economy clearly existed. Any company could sell its goods or services virtually anywhere, production could take place

discussed at Bretton Woods are dispersed at the macroeconomic level, whereas it provides direct benefits to specific individuals or groups operating at the international level' (ibid., p. 205). Of course the fact that cooperation between states is needed to liberalise trade does not mean that the results are equally beneficial to all, since their bargaining powers are highly unequal. The failure of the WTO's Seattle summit reflected this.

almost anywhere, capital could be invested more or less anywhere, profits could be remitted from anywhere. This did not mean there was a single, homogeneous world-wide market, or that foreign capital could be invested, or foreign goods sold, as easily in Japan as in Canada. Non-tariff barriers of all kinds remained, and distinctive national tastes did not change overnight, although international sales of US-made films and television programmes, and the penetration of foreign markets by firms like Toyota, McDonald's and Blockbuster Video were quite rapidly homogenising tastes. Firms could treat all the countries of the world as just parts of a single market, and more and more were beginning to do so; moreover, advances in production technology had made it much easier to vary the product to suit particular regional or even national 'niches' in the world market. As Eric Hobsbawm put it, 'for many purposes, notably in economic affairs, the globe is now the primary operational unit and older units such as "national economies" . . . are reduced to complications of transnational activities'.[9]

The new global economy

In relation to the global economy, 'globalisation sceptics' have argued that trade remains predominantly regional rather than world-wide; that the proportion of world output that is traded internationally only returned to its 1914 level in the early 1990s; that most large companies have heavy investments and roots where they are headquartered, and are still owned largely by nationals, whether institutions or individuals; and that nation states remain crucial to the operation of the global economy.[10] This is true, yet it really misses the point. There are fundamental differences between the global economy of 1914, and that of the early 1990s, and they do not lie in the ratio of transnational trade to global production, although that has long since greatly surpassed the 1914 level. They lie in a series of developments in the new global economy that have led to the 'internationalisation of the state' – i.e. the acceptance on the part of states of a new world-wide economic order, driven by global market forces, which they must help construct.[11]

The three most significant differences between 1914 and the late twentieth-century global economy lie in the scale and power of contemporary global financial markets, the global production and marketing of manufactured goods and services by TNCs, and the transnational structures for regulating the new global order.

Global financial markets

By the end of the 1980s 'deregulation' and computerisation had resulted in the elimination of most significant geographic barriers in all kinds of financial activity. Besides the phenomenal growth of the currency markets, the securities and bond markets had also been globalised; shares in companies in Japan could be traded as easily in Frankfurt as in Tokyo, and bonds issued by Volkswagen or the city of New York could be bought as easily in London. When the London Stock Exchange closed, the New York exchange was already open, and when it closed, Tokyo took over until London opened again.[12] Although there were some important hold-outs against free capital movements, including India and China, speaking generally the owners of capital were now free to move it more or less anywhere; and through satellite-based information technology they were also acquiring the capacity to evaluate with greater accuracy and speed more and more alternative ways of investing or banking it world-wide. Net international bank loans rose from 0.7 per cent of world output in 1964 to 16.3 per cent in 1991; bond issues grew at about three times the rate of world output between 1973 and 1995; the volume of derivatives – tradable instruments designed to hedge against risks, especially fluctuating exchange rates, but in the process, taken together, heightening risk – expanded 'astro-nomically', to a total value in 1996 of $321 trillion, more than world GDP.[13]

According to Gowan, in 1999 a small number of highly secretive US-based 'hedge funds' – firms speculating in foreign exchange deriv-atives – had between them access to something like $30 trillion of bank loans to bet against national currencies. Gowan reasons convinc-ingly that their successive attacks on foreign currencies must have had the tacit approval of the US government; in effect they were financial privateers, a modern version of the pirates licensed by the British government in the eighteenth century to raid enemy merchant ship-ping.[14] The scale of the funds they could borrow explains why the notorious collapse in 1998 of the Long Term Capital Management fund, with its Nobel laureate directors, necessitated the mobilisation of

$3.5 billion by the US government to bail out banks that would otherwise have collapsed.

TNCs and global production

By the end of the 1980s TNCs were responsible for more than half of all the world's trade in manufactures, and perhaps three-quarters of all trade in services: according to one estimate, in 1994 the 500 largest TNCs controlled three-quarters of all world trade. TNCs also controlled 80 per cent of all land under export crops, and the marketing channels for a large number of primary commodities.[15] FDI also made TNCs omnipresent; by the mid-1980s the value of production by TNCs' foreign affiliates had overtaken the value of world exports. At the same moment, FDI in service industries overtook FDI in manufacturing, and for the first time FDI as a whole expanded faster than financial flows.[16]

A high proportion of the assets of both the manufacturing and the service sectors in most OECD countries thus came to be owned by big transnational companies. By the late 1990s about a third of all international trade consisted of intra-firm transactions (and of course more in the case of major industrial exporters – over 50 per cent of the trade of the USA and Japan).[17] Large TNCs are, moreover, by definition oligopolists, with considerable market power. The most significant indicators of concentration have become world market shares rather than national ones, and 'in a wide range of industries and product groups the world market is shared by 10–12 firms, and often fewer'.[18]

Yet such data tend to understate the scale of TNC dominance of the global economy, because they do not take into account the growth of corporate networks. A firm may derive substantial profits from a country without owning any plant or employing a single worker in it, through franchising, licensing and similar contractual relationships.[19] 'Network' firms, consisting of webs of legally independent units linked by cross-ownership or contracts, have become increasingly common, as have alliances of a looser kind between companies on the lines of the Japanese *keiretsu*, with no cross-ownership or standing contractual links.[20] A statement, therefore, to the effect that 'the world's top 300 industrial corporations now control . . . 25 per cent of the world's $20 trillion stock of productive assets' has become hard to interpret.[21] Their power to determine the use of the world's productive assets may well be larger. The UN estimated in 1994 that 'overall, as much as one-third of world output may now be under the direct governance of TNCs, with the indirect influence certainly much greater'.[22]*

The need to operate globally in order to survive has in any case enormously expanded the number of TNCs, from 7,000 in 1970 to 60,000 by the late 1990s, with 508,000 affiliates;[23] and this means, from the perspective of national politics, that even a quite small company by world standards may be fulfilling specific tasks in a tightly integrated global production and marketing strategy directed from overseas. The most important directing centres are the headquarters of a limited number of very large TNCs; in 1990 fewer than 300 American firms accounted for three-quarters of all transnational activity by US companies, and about 150 British firms accounted for four-fifths of all British FDI.[24] In 1997 Britain was 'host' to the parent firms of ten of the world's 100 largest multinationals, and host to over a thousand TNCs in all. Conversely there were 2,525 affiliates of foreign-based TNCs operating in Britain; of the major OECD countries, Britain in 1997 was far the most 'transnational' (i.e. it had much the largest proportion of its GDP produced by foreign TNC affiliates, the largest foreign TNC share of gross fixed capital investment, and so on).[25]

The significance of TNCs in national politics can be summed up in two broad generalisations. First, since they are often very large organisations – in 1997 the largest 100 TNCs had total sales of $39 billion and assets of $42 billion – they often have larger negotiating resources than do national states, as well as having considerable economic leverage, regularly borrowing and spending more than the states of quite large

---

* These UN figures naturally do not cover transnational criminal organizations, although some of these function in many respects like legal TNCs and have comparable assets. Louise Shelley notes that the Medellin syndicate, the less successful of the two Colombian drug cartels, was said to have at least $10 billion worth of assets in Europe, Asia and North America in the late 1980s, equal to the average assets of the four Swedish TNCs included in the UN's top 100 list in 1992. Barnet and Cavanagh report estimates of between $100 and $300 billion as the annual world-wide profits from the drugs trade, implying the existence of numerous powerful transnational enterprises. (See Louise I. Shelley, 'Transnational Organized Crime: An Imminent Threat to the Nation-State?', *Journal of International Affairs* 48/2, 1995, pp. 480–1, and Richard J. Barnet and John Cavanagh, *Global Dreams: Imperial Corporations and the New World Order* (Simon and Schuster, 1994), p. 389.) The growing significance of organised crime in the global economy, and the parallels between it and both TNCs and states, were noted by Susan Strange in 'The Limits of Politics', *Government and Opposition* 30/3, 1995, pp. 305–7.

countries. In January 2000, for example, America Online raised $160 billion to take over Time Warner, four times the GDP of Nigeria. A country like Britain has a larger GDP than the gross revenues of most TNCs, but TNCs are free to deploy their resources single-mindedly in pursuit of their limited goals in a way no government can. George Monbiot quotes an officer who had been assigned by the Office of Fair Trading to report on predatory pricing by the big supermarket chains as admitting that, 'including myself, there will be only four of us working on this – and that's along with the other cases we look at. We have to do this on a shoestring while the companies we look into have a hundred times more resources than we have.'[26] US banks – now heavily represented in London – spent $15 billion on information technology in 1990, while as late as 1996 the annual expenditure on information technology by the entire British government was estimated at about $3 billion.[27] In general, states have long since lost whatever communications advantage they may once have had over companies.

Corporations are also sophisticated lobbyists at the supranational as well as national levels of power, often with diplomatic backing by their 'home' states.[28] The chief executive of a major TNC seldom has to wait long for an appointment with a minister: Monbiot's painfully revealing study of the corporate penetration of the British state is full of examples.* In short, Susan Strange was right to insist that 'transnational corporations should now be put centre stage' in any realistic analysis of domestic politics, not just in the analysis of international relations.[29]

The second politically significant feature of TNCs is that they are profitable in large part precisely because of their political capacity, especially in their negotiations with host or prospective host governments. They can get regulations altered (or maintained) to their advantage; Monbiot, again, has documented numerous examples of TNCs in Britain using their huge lobbying and financial power to get

---

* See George Monbiot, *Captive State: The Corporate Takeover of Britain* (Macmillan, 2000), *passim*. The supermarket chain Tesco, after donating £12 million to the British government's ill-fated Millennium Dome, succeeded in getting the government to drop plans to impose a tax on out-of-town parking, which formed part of its efforts to prevent the decline of town centres. Monsanto, whose representatives met ministers and officials from the departments of Agriculture and the Environment on twenty-two occasions in the twenty months following the 1997 election, succeeded in getting the government to refuse to have GM food labelled as such, among many other achievements. And so on.

the regulatory environment they want. A good example is that of
SmithKline Beecham (now GlaxoSmithKline) the world's tenth largest
pharmaceutical company, which spent 30 millon ecus in the mid-1990s
on the biotech companies' successful joint campaign to get the European Parliament to allow the commercial patenting of genes.[30] Alternatively they can exploit the existing pattern of regulatory differences
between countries, getting labour-intensive work done where unions
are weak and wages low, declaring taxable profits where taxes are lowest
through 'transfer pricing', and so on.[31]

The phenomenon of 'network' firms – consisting of many legally
separate companies, but with complex interlocking shareholdings allowing for unified overall control – is to a significant extent about reducing
regulatory costs. It is usually justified in terms of the 'positive externalities' this can yield from specialisation, greater flexibility, and so on; but
'dissolving' itself into a network can also allow a TNC to escape taxes
and other costs. 'Because the firm determines its own size [in deciding
what bit of a network, legally speaking, it will 'be'], it also chooses the
limits of its legal responsibilities, which in turn provides an open
invitation for the evasion of mandatory legal duties.'[32]

Liability to taxes is especially significant, since the power to tax is the
foundation of national sovereignty; yet the complexity of contemporary
TNC financing, combined with the network form of organisation,
enables them to limit the bite of all but the biggest and most determined national tax authorities. Picciotto notes that

> TNCs . . . have opposed attempts at strengthened regulatory cooperation
> [between states]. Instead, they have developed legal structures for trans-
> national corporate capital which take advantage of the ambiguities, dis-
> junctures, and loopholes in the international tax system. Indeed, the
> growth of the TNC, in the characteristic form of an international network
> of related companies carrying on businesses in different countries in a
> more or less integrated way, is to a significant extent attributable to the
> opportunities it has to take advantage of regulatory differences, or 'regu-
> latory arbitrage'.[33]

As a result both corporate tax rates and marginal personal tax rates for
high income investors fell in almost every OECD country from the mid-
1980s to the mid-1990s;[34] and 'perhaps half of the industrialized world's
stock of money resides in or passes through tax havens'.[35] It is sobering

to reflect how far the political salience of personal taxation in the OECD countries in the 1980s and 1990s, and the devastating impact on public spending of voters' 'tax aversion', were due to the fact that so much corporate income was escaping tax altogether.

In short, we have to recognise how far the balance of power between governments and corporations has shifted. Perhaps the best comparison is between most states today and municipalities in the past. In the era of national economies, corporate investment decisions were made on the basis of variations between different locations in the country in terms of labour supplies, infrastructures, proximity to markets, local taxes, and the like. Today, in the neoliberal global economy, national 'regulatory regimes' themselves have become part of the pattern of local conditions (or 'complications', as Hobsbawm says) that transnational corporations take into account, and are constantly working to change.

Institutions of global regulation and discipline

A diverse range of supra-national organisations make up what is often optimistically called an evolving system of global economic 'governance'. Many of the organisations – like the EU, NAFTA, ASEAN, MERCOSUR and the rest – are regional, and exist primarily to promote trade liberalisation. These intergovernmental bodies, being regional, and especially when they have a representative element such as the European Parliament, are close enough to the populations concerned to have to try to balance the concerns of citizens with those of corporations, however uneasily, and however much they are in fact dominated by corporate interests.* International bodies, such as the IMF and the Bank for International Settlements, are much more remote, and the USA inevitably tends to dominate them. Cable describes them as being a response to 'a demand for international public goods that neither markets nor nation-states will provide and . . . externalities they cannot capture'. But the public goods they provide

---

* NAFTA is a notable exception, due to the massive imbalance between its members in terms of economic and political power. The USA was able to impose a structure in which decision-making was entrusted largely to unaccountable bodies dominated by US corporations, and the Canadian and Mexican governments do not have the influence over it that the larger EU member governments, for example, have in EU institutions.

are invariably those that chiefly concern capital: 'systemic financial stability, the rule of law and dispute settlement needed for an open system of trade and investment; common standards for weights, measures and interconnection; management of global communications networks . . .; management of environmental concerns like Antarctica, the atmosphere, and oceans . . .'[36]

Of course financial stability and the rule of law and telecommunications are important to everyone, but public goods like stable employment, freedom from crime, and an environment free from pollution – which are today just as 'global' as financial stability but which, while very important to ordinary people, are either less important to capital, or positively opposed by it – are much less well provided for. In terms of effectiveness alone, the international regulatory institutions set up by and for capital, such as the Bank for International Settlements, are much more effective than, for example, the agencies set up, and the treaties made, to reduce pollution.[37] A case that proves the rule by *not* being the exception one might expect is the International Labour Organisation (ILO), all of whose decisions must be based on a consensus between organised labour, employers and governments, and whose conventions are not binding.

A third category of supranational organisations that is even more indicative of the character of the new global economy consists of bodies which are in effect instruments for formally replacing national states as economic regulators. Following the defeat of the OECD's proposed Multilateral Agreement on Investment in 1998, this political project became focused instead on the World Trade Organisation (WTO); and when the Seattle meeting of the WTO ended in failure, the strategy shifted to securing more limited, regional agreements that could gradually be linked together into an eventually global system.[38] The central idea is to get the states concerned to agree to (a) mutually recognise each other's regulatory regimes and (b) make the general rules on trade and investment agreed between them legally enforceable. The effect is to give corporations the right to sue the states concerned for damages arising from any state action that is held by a tribunal to breach the agreement and adversely affect their profits – including their anticipated profits.

The authors of these plans are the chief executives of the largest TNCs and their staffs, organised in bodies like the European Round Table, the International Chamber of Commerce and the Transatlantic

Business Dialogue (TABD), working closely with officials of the European Commission and the US Department of Commerce, and strongly supported by some states, notably Britain.[39] As Monbiot notes, NAFTA is a regional prototype of what is intended, and shows clearly what is involved: for example a US company successfully sued the Canadian government for banning a carcinogenic fuel additive and forced the lifting of the ban, while another successfully sued it for banning the export of dangerous chemicals to the USA. The ultimate goal of these initiatives is clear, and the success rate so far is impressive: according to the US Under-Secretary of State for Commerce in 1997, 'virtually every market-opening move undertaken by the United States and the EU in the last couple of years has been suggested by the TABD'.[40] How far other states will be induced to surrender their sovereignty to TNCs in as wholesale and humiliating a way as Canada and Mexico have done under NAFTA remains to be seen.

Global market forces and national policy-making

Financial and productive market forces affect national state policy in different ways.

Financial market forces

Taken together, the global financial markets are supposed to register the collective judgement of the owners of capital about how profitable it is to operate in a given country when all factors, including the risk of adverse government policies, are taken into account. 'With instantaneous communication and information flows among all the major markets, passive capital and unexploited investment opportunities will not long be kept apart by national borders. . . . If there is a viable futures or options market to be made, it is of little relevance where it is made.'[41] Global markets are thus supposed to ensure that holders of financial assets receive roughly the same risk-adjusted real return everywhere; any country that offers significantly lower returns is likely to experience capital outflow and a depreciating exchange rate.   This means that governments' spending and fiscal policies are tightly constrained, at least in the short term, by the markets' judgement of what they should be. 'The power of the bond market has forced discipline on to governments everywhere', and Keynesian macro-economic policies are no longer an option for the government of one country acting alone.[42]

If the option of devaluing the currency is given up, whether through monetary union with other countries, or by tying the currency to a stronger one (or even adopting it, as in 'dollarisation'), then no cushioning by devaluation is possible, and virtually no scope remains for traditional macro-economic policy-making at the national level. Cerny summed up the consensus as follows:

> Governments have all found their capacity to intervene in the domestic economy significantly altered, reducing their power to pursue comprehensive economic strategies and differentiating and complicating the kind of market interventions which they are led or forced to adopt. The interaction of changing financial market structures on the one hand and states on the other has done more than production, trade or international cooperative regimes to undermine the structures of the Keynesian welfare state and to impose the norms of the competition state, while at the same time narrowing the parameters of competition still further.[43]

But this loss of 'Keynesian capacity', important though it is, has tended to divert attention from the tendency of financial markets to constrain all areas of policy, not just macro-economic policy; and this they do continually, with the help of the grades awarded to governments and public organisations by the credit rating agencies. Plans that the experts employed by these agencies dislike, whether or not they affect public spending, have an automatic negative effect on interest rates.[44] Nothing is excluded from consideration. Their surveillance of social and political change, as well as economic indicators and policies, becomes more and more comprehensive, and whether or not it gives rational signals or leads to rational responses by investors, governments increasingly feel its constraining influence. Even matters that might once have seemed purely the province of politics, such as professional training and qualifications, or the protection of the national language, can turn out to be of concern to 'the market', not to mention matters as vital to investors as proposals to tighten the regulation of money markets or to impose new obligations on the managers of pension funds.[45]

More generally, market analysts routinely estimate a 'political risk factor' for every country, expressed as a premium on the current interest rate on government bonds, which discounts the possibility of future political changes unfavourable to capital. Any proposed increase in taxation, especially on capital, or any increase in the budget deficit, necessitating increased public borrowing, will tend to result in increased interest rates, and 'left-labour' governments in the 'north' have consistently had to face a risk premium of 1 or 2 per cent.[46] All public spending plans are therefore highly sensitive to market opinion. In Britain, the former Labour leader John Smith was said to have arranged an immediate 2 per cent interest rate increase by the Treasury in the event of a Labour victory in the 1992 election – a victory that, in the end, eluded them – and the pre-election policy commitments of Gordon Brown, as Labour's Shadow Chancellor in 1996–97, were heavily (and successfully) directed to avoiding a large interest rate penalty for winning the 1997 election.

Market forces in goods and services

Non-financial capital differs from financial capital in being committed in the relatively long term to particular lines of production of goods or services. The pressures it brings to bear on national governments can be examined in relation to, first, non-tariff barriers to trade and, second, non-tariff barriers to investment.

As tariff barriers to global trade grew steadily lower under the Bretton Woods arrangements, non-tariff barriers (NTBs) of various kinds came more clearly into view, affecting an estimated 18 per cent of world trade in 1992.[47] Some of them, such as state purchasing rules that confine bids for government contracts to domestic companies, serve national interests in defence, food security, and so on; others, like complex bureaucratic customs procedures, or safety or health tests not applied to domestically-produced goods, are essentially protectionist measures. A third category consists of domestic social practices or arrangements, sometimes reinforced by law, that express long-standing and cherished national values – sensitive issues of national culture and social practice, from national conceptions of safety and hygiene and environmental conservation to the national language, culture (films and magazines) and tastes. Such embedded social practices were famously defined by the Americans, in their efforts to open up Japanese markets to US exports, as 'structural impediments [i.e. to free trade]'.[48]

The main pressure to lift NTBs to trade comes from foreign companies anxious to break into local markets, predominantly (though not exclusively) TNCs. Governments also get involved, through lobbying and diplomatic efforts, in trying to reduce other states' non-tariff barriers and defend their own. This is especially likely if they have balance-of-payments difficulties, and if their ability to influence their balance of trade in other ways has been reduced by the weight of intra-firm transactions in their country's foreign trade. The member states of the EU initially aimed at eliminating such barriers through 'harmonisa-tion' – i.e. adopting common standards and rules; but when this proved too difficult it was dropped in favour of 'mutual recognition' – i.e. subject to certain grounds of exception, any product or service that could legally be sold in one country could be sold in them all. 'Mutual recognition' legitimated the least onerous regulations and gave all the EU states an incentive to adopt them.

But TNCs are almost by definition concerned less with access for exports than with productive investment, which makes them interested in a much wider range of policy issues than the regulations specifically applying to their products. John Dunning, a pioneer of TNC studies, summarised their outlook as follows:

> . . . if the government of one country imposes too high a corporation tax, firms – be they domestic or foreign – may decide to relocate their value-added activities in another country where taxes are lower; or, in consider-ing where to site their new plants, firms may choose that country with the least burdensome environmental constraints, or whose government pur-sues the most favourable industrial policy, or which offers the most advanced telecommunications facilities or the most attractive tax breaks for R and D activities. Indeed . . . anything and everything a government does which affects the competitiveness of those firms which must have some latitude in their cross-border locational choices must come under scrutiny.[49]

The scope of the 'regulatory regimes' that states compete to 'lighten' for non-financial TNCs may, then, like the scope of the capital markets' concerns, be very wide. What is more, states may often be 'outgunned' by the legal and technical expertise that TNCs can command.*

---

* Yves Dezelay has pointed out that the huge global firms of corporate lawyers that have emerged since the 1980s do not just supply a demand created by regulatory arbitrage, and by regulatory competition between states; they also play an important role in driving the whole process: 'One of the main factors disrupting the national

Yet the tendency of 'regulatory competition' to cause a 'dive to the bottom' is offset by political pressures on states to prevent the lowering of standards, whether to protect some special interest or one more widely shared. The result is not so easy to predict as many advocates of deregulation imply. Even under the favourable influence of the EU's Single Market Act, which obliges states to recognise each other's standards, effective resistance is mounted and outcomes are determined by complex combinations of reason, interest, the relative strengths of the participants, and so on, and do not always end in lower standards.[50]

Nonetheless, it is clear that states no longer have the last word; indeed there is no last word, since there is always a potentially lower standard than the prevailing one that some country may choose to adopt. Corporations constantly return to the attack on standards they want to lower, eventually wearing out the usually poorly resourced and frequently amateur public opposition. Further regional trade and investment agreements, or treaties, of the NAFTA type can also be expected, and new global agreements will be taken up again at the WTO. TNCs still look to these regional and global agreements to force open some important domestic markets, especially in services (including health services, as we will see in chapter 6).

To sum up this discussion: the power of 'market forces', whether affecting macro-economic policy generally through the financial markets, or micro-economic policy through pressure from TNCs and their home governments, has greatly increased, and the autonomy of most states – except, perhaps, the USA, or oil-rich states like Saudi Arabia – has greatly declined.* National policy-making is now pervasively influenced by this new circumstance.

---

systems of regulation results from the competitive pressure exerted by the forum-shopping for regulatory regimes to which multinationals of expert services incite their clients.' ('Professional Competition and the Social Construction of Transnational Regulatory Expertise', in Joseph McCahery, Sol Picciotto and Colin Scott (eds), *Corporate Control and Accountability* [Clarendon Press, 1993], p. 203.)

* There are obviously big differences between states, in terms of the scale of their internal market, the extent of their economy's exposure to global market forces, their possession of strategic resources, and so on, which affect their capacity to resist external pressures. I would argue that these pressures always operate at the margin and affect even the most powerful states over time, but what is said here about states in general is meant to refer to states roughly like Britain's, i.e. states with medium-sized industrial economies and no unique economic or political leverage vis-à-vis TNCs or other states.

The options for national governments

There is an obvious conflict between the logic of capital accumulation, which drives the global economy, and the logic of legitimation, which drives politics in all states with free elections. The former gives priority to the needs of capital at the expense of labour, and at the expense of public sector funding on which most public goods and almost all social services depend; the latter depends on catering to these other needs as well as ensuring economic growth – or at least economic stability. In the era of national economies, the conflict between these two logics was contained, however erratically, by capital's relative immobility. Globalis-ation has for the first time separated the fields of operation of the two logics. Can this last? It is too early to say. Meantime national states that want to moderate the impact of market forces on their citizens have limited resources available to them.

First, states can still try to pursue macro-economic strategies to reduce unemployment, which is the single most important determinant of welfare, and of government popularity. The scope for doing this is often greater than it seems in theory, at least in the short run. Capital markets will tolerate pre-election 'give-away' budgets if they think the government in power is a more reliable defender of their general interests than the opposition. Governments may also take protectionist 'anti-dumping' measures with strong public support, and may get away with them for quite a while by bending or simply ignoring the rules, or by relying on deeply 'embedded' non-tariff barriers that hamper invest-ment by foreigners and protect domestic firms from foreign takeover. Most states do what they can in this line, however contradictory it may be to their general support for global liberalisation: 'There is . . . an underlying tension and contradiction in the policies of most govern-ments: embracing certain aspects of globalization and loss of sover-eignty while resisting others in the name of the sovereignty of the nation-state.'[51] This does involve costs, however, in terms of taxes, prices and profitability, and in the long run there will be resistance from those who have to pay them.

Second, states can cooperate to try to establish a global state, or something approximating one, with the capacity to regulate global market forces. Conflicts of interest between the world's 180 countries – not to mention American resistance to the loss of its *de facto* control of the global economy – would make this difficult, even if the owners of capital did not mobilise strongly to prevent it. For example, while all countries will ultimately suffer disastrous consequences if the ozone layer is destroyed, a global agreement on banning production of CFCs could only be obtained by allowing the late industrialising countries to go on producing them after production has ceased in the advanced industrial countries.[52] But capital also strongly resists the establishment of anything resembling effective global regulation in the interests of anyone but 'investors', including even the long-canvassed 'Tobin tax' on speculative capital movements (arguing that it is not only undesirable but also technically impossible).[53] For the foreseeable future a global state capable of regulating the global economy on behalf of global citizens is a utopian dream.

Third, if it is not practicable to create a global state capable of regulating capital, a group of reasonably compatible partner states can try to create a regional one. This was one of the impulses behind the EEC and remains a reason for the continuing push by left-leaning European federalists for closer political union, reflected in (among other things) the Social Chapter of the Maastricht Treaty, which was supposed to lay down minimum standards of employment. The weakness of the Social Chapter's final provisions, however, and the lack of interest on the part of most EU states in upholding them, are also significant: the EU has always reflected the interests of capital much more than those of labour.[54]

A fourth option is to pass the buck downwards – devolution or 'subsidiarity'. In effect, local political authorities are left to do what they feel they can within the constraints set by the market in their areas. Provided it is done in such a way that local people feel they have an appropriate share of whatever national resources there are, this option has the merit of relieving the central government of some of the responsibility for decisions that are in any case more and more severely constrained. It is also a useful response to the popular misconception (assiduously fostered by neoliberal politicians and newspapers) that power has been 'taken away' from people and transferred to regional authorities ('Eurocrats' in Brussels), when in reality it has been ceded, with EU help, to capital.*

---

*Whether subsidiarity is a useful option seems likely to depend on the extent to which there is an embedded culture of coordinated production and distribution

Meanwhile national governments have had to pursue whatever economic policies global market forces permit, or demand, that are thought likely to boost 'national competitiveness' and sustain economic growth and employment, while if possible compensating – or alternatively neutralising – those who lose out in the process. As capital controls were dismantled throughout the OECD, national exchange rate, monetary and fiscal policies and interest rates all increasingly converged. This remained true throughout the 1990s, even after social-democratic parties had taken office in twelve of the fourteen EU countries; by then these parties had all accepted the inevitability of a global economy based on the free movement of capital, and were adjusting their economic policies and ideologies in a neoliberal direction. Most of these same social-democratic parties also agreed to the establishment of a common European currency, giving up exchange rate flexibility as a cushion against the social costs of adjustment to global market forces. A further general trend was that taxes on capital and personal incomes declined and taxes on consumption rose, exacerbating the rise in after-tax income inequality caused by the globalisation-driven decline in demand for low-skilled workers in the OECD countries, while average levels of social security provision and welfare spending were reduced.[55]

The fact that the European social-democratic parties pursued these policies does not mean, of course, that they were forced to pursue all of them, or all of them to the same extent. The experience of France in 1980–82 – when the Socialist government's attempt to reflate the economy by redistributive spending and expanding the public sector was definitively defeated by a collapsing trade balance and capital flight

---

(discussed below, pp. 30–32). An already existing culture of trust and reciprocity in the economy may perhaps be strengthened by the devolution of policy-making, choice and implementation, sharing more widely the dilemmas of trying to preserve group cohesion in face of global market pressures. In France and other 'Rhineland'-type European countries substantial devolution to sub-national levels of elected government took place in the 1980s. The fate of devolution in the individualistic, privatised climate cultivated by successive British governments offers an instructive contrast. Margaret Thatcher's neoliberal governments held power in the 1980s with a minority of electoral support, thanks to the peculiar effects of the first-past-the-post electoral system. At the local council level, however, the voting system produced majorities opposed to neoliberalism, so powers were not devolved to them but on the contrary withdrawn and centralised in Whitehall. The 1999 devolution of powers to a Scottish Parliament and a Welsh Assembly was by contrast significant. Its potential for reducing, or aggravating, the tensions caused by globalisation remains to be seen.

– had convinced everyone that it was no longer possible to run national macro-economic policy independently of the rest of the world. Many social-democratic politicians may also have been convinced of the need to move towards market-oriented social and economic policies for a variety of reasons – because they were frightened of the bond markets, or convinced of the electoral unpopularity of income tax, or persuaded of the intellectual merits of 'post-classical endogenous growth theory'. But it did not necessarily follow that no other economic policy packages except those advocated by neoliberals could be adopted, and there were in fact some marked variations within the general trend; some countries continued to spend much more than others on social security and welfare, to take a much higher share of GDP in taxation, to maintain much more protective labour legislation, and so on. How should this be explained? Were the pressures less than has been suggested here, or does the answer lie in important differences in the way they affected individual countries?

Explaining national responses

Country-specific ideas, anxieties and dreams, reflecting each country's history and current preoccupations, clearly play an important part; for instance French support for the Euro, and British opposition to it, have a lot to do with the two countries' different experiences of war, and their different historical relationships to the USA. But important as such factors are, they do not lend themselves easily to reduction to 'institutions', to which most of those involved in this field of research – the 'new institutionalists' – have been committed.[56] These researchers also look upon globalisation as something positive, and are interested in identifying the factors that tend to facilitate a country's adaption to it. For these reasons they have concentrated on the degree to which (a) constitutional arrangements and (b) the kind of capitalist economy a country has may slow down or even block a country's adaptation to global market pressures. One does not need to share these authors' politics to find some of their analysis useful, so it needs to be briefly summarised.

Broadly speaking, they suggest three kinds of distinction between constitutional arrangements, which have some interest for the British case: the nature of the electoral system (proportional vs winner-takes-all); the number of 'veto points' provided by the constitution, at which policy changes can be resisted (federal constitutions, with numerous checks and balances between the branches of government, are contrasted with unitary constitutions and dominant executives); and the degree to which important executive bodies such as central banks are 'insulated' from the party-competitive process altogether. The hypothesis is that proportional representation, many 'veto points' and few 'insulated' executive organs will tend to prevent policy being adjusted to global pressures for change, because these institutional arrangements give those who will suffer most from the changes more opportunities to resist. Conversely the government of a unitary state, with an electoral system that tends to produce a large single-party majority, and which confronts few constitutional checks and balances, is freer to respond to the globalising pressures.

A second line of explanation concerns the distinction between two types of capitalist economy: 'institution-rich' or 'co-ordinated market economies' (CMEs), and 'liberal market economies' (LMEs) – often also called economies of the 'Rhineland' or 'Anglo-Saxon' types.* The ideal-typical CME is distinguished by strong and 'encompassing' trade unions, with a central leadership able to speak for and deliver cooperation from the whole workforce. This gives employers confidence that wage bargains will be kept, and in return they can make investments that they know will be profitable over the long term, and which will also raise productivity and keep the firms in question internationally competitive. A model CME also has banks that hold equity shares in companies and therefore take an informed and long view of their prospects, and it has a government that ensures the constant reskilling of the workforce, and taxes employers to fund it.

The idea is that the government of a country with proportional representation, facing multiple veto points and with few if any executive institutions insulated from political pressures, is least able to make rapid adaptations to global market forces. On the other hand, if, as in

---

* The coordinated market economies or CMEs are further divided into two variants: 'state' or 'centrally' coordinated and 'sector'-coordinated, referring to the European (especially German and Swedish) and East Asian (Japanese and Korean) models respectively. In the European model the state coordinates the financing of industry, the training of the labour force and the wage-bargaining between capital and labour. In the East Asian model coordination occurs within the *keiretsu* or *chaebol* networks of firms.

Germany or Sweden, the government presides over a CME, it can leave companies to make the necessary adaptations themselves, since the coordinating institutional structure makes this possible. A government in a country with a LME, however, is more likely to turn to maximum exposure of the economy to market forces as the only way of ensuring that domestic producers stay competitive. If, like Britain, it happens to have a majoritarian electoral system, a unitary constitution and a powerful executive, it will be that much freer to do so.

What is not possible, even in the medium term, is to create a CME in a country where one does not already exist, because the coordination involved must by its nature be deeply 'embedded' in the social structure and culture; it must rest on expectations and trust that are the product of an organic evolution over decades, if not generations. That is why the call for a country like Britain to 'adopt' a 'stakeholder' strategy (as Will Hutton notably did in Britain in 1995), rather than a strategy based on 'shareholder value' alone – seen as requiring maximum exposure to market forces – is unlikely to be realistic in the short term.[57] The logic of the two situations is summed up by David Soskice as follows:*

---

* A third case is where effective adjustment to global market forces is blocked by a country's institutional structures and there is no CME. Then a remedy – from the point of view of the new institutionalists, that is – will typically be provided by one of the shocks that global economic integration sends throughout the world. The 'new institutionalist' school sees shocks as creating opportunities for 'political entrepreneurs' to 'fundamentally reorganise domestic politics' – i.e. to permit economic deregulation. Major shocks, of course, also create openings for external capital – chiefly in the shape of the IMF – to insist on deregulation as a condition of financial rescue, as happened most dramatically in East Asia. The scale of the shocks, however, their frequency, and their social and political consequences have grown to potentially catastrophic proportions. In 1982, when Mexico defaulted on its national debt, the international banking system was suddenly threatened with collapse. In 1994, when the Mexican neoliberal bubble burst and the peso collapsed, the international rescue effort coordinated by the US government consumed $48 billion. Ordinary Mexicans' living standards fell overnight by 20 per cent, and it was estimated that repairing the damage would consume the net growth of the whole of Latin America until the year 2002. A much more modest example, but nonetheless typical of the knock-on effects of crises in a globalised economy, involved the UK. The Kohl government brought about German reunification by pumping funds into East Germany, with inflationary consequences. The Bundesbank, concerned to meet the criteria for entering the European Monetary Union, raised interest rates, which raised the exchange value of the Deutschmark. This squeezed the profits of the German firm Daimler-Benz, and led it to terminate its financial support for the ailing Dutch aircraft company Fokker, in which it had a controlling interest. Fokker collapsed, with the loss of 5,000 jobs in

in the coordinated economies . . . business representatives . . . [including] leading multinationals [have] sought not deregulation but re-regulation in order to face up most effectively to global markets. The reason for this has been the need of businesses to preserve for their companies long-term financial frameworks, cooperative skilled work forces, and research networks in order to remain competitive. . . . Thus thoroughgoing deregulation, generally believed to imply greater risk of closure or takeover, is not a rational choice for business if alternative regulatory systems can provide international competitiveness with greater security for preexisting top managers.

In Anglo-Saxon economies in which business was not organized so effectively, this lack of business coordination meant that the institutional capacity necessary for re-regulation along similar lines was missing, as was political power. In these liberal market economies, governments – both left and right – were forced or chose to implement a wide-ranging deregulation as the only available framework in which companies could remain or become internationally competitive.[58]

The case of Britain

To the 'new institutionalists', then, Britain is a good example of a country undergoing radical reforms in the interest of international competitiveness – reforms that, because British industry had no capacity to coordinate change, had to be government-led and in the direction of the most fully deregulated economy possible. The Thatcher government was able to push through these reforms thanks to an exceptional combination of reasons. The shock caused by the balance of payments crisis and the IMF loan of 1976, which resulted from the 'stagflation' of the 1970s and finally discredited the Keynesian policies of the post-war era, created an opportunity for Thatcher to win an election with the claim that 'there was no alternative' to deregulation. The electoral system exaggerated her parliamentary majority, while the division of the anti-Thatcher vote between Labour, the Social Democrats and the

---

the Netherlands, but also 1,500 at Short Brothers in Belfast, which made wings for Fokker. This example is only unusual in that the origin of the crisis was so explicitly political; in a world of 60,000 TNCs with 500,000 foreign subsidiaries, employing an estimated 86 million people, virtually every local economic crisis has significant transnational effects.

Liberals after 1981 allowed her to continue in office for a decade. Britain's unitary system of government (and one must add, though the new institutionalist literature curiously omits it, the lack of a written constitution) afforded few 'veto points' for opposing forces. On top of all this was the fact that Mrs Thatcher was unusually willing to risk unpopularity.[59]

Whether there really was no alternative, as Mrs Thatcher insisted and Soskice seems to imply, is not the point at issue here; nor do we have to decide whether Thatcher's deregulation strategy, and its continuation by New Labour after 1997, has in fact made British firms more internationally competitive. Both positions are strongly contested.[60] What is relevant here is only the way these analysts explain how this strategy came to be adopted by the Conservatives under Thatcher (and continued by Labour under Blair) as a logical outcome of Britain's distinctive constitutional and industrial history. Up to a point, there is no reason to disagree.

We can also agree that states that are relatively 'insulated' from popular pressures are best able to make the ongoing adjustments to global market forces. This applies to parties as well as to states. Kitschelt argues that 'both a mass organization . . . and governance structures that make leaders strictly accountable to the party rank and file represent definite obstacles' to effective adaptation to market requirements. He interprets the transformation of the British Labour Party from this point of view:

> In Britain's three-party system, the lack of a credible left-libertarian competitor frees the Labour Party from worrying about an electoral trade-off. Thus, the party should have had an easy time in adopting a centrist, market-liberalizing vote- and office-maximizing strategy. Instead, its organizational rules in the 1970s and early 1980s, endowing traditionalist or radical unions and militant socialist grass roots in a political-economic environment of decline with considerable power over the party leadership, prevented the electorally rational strategy from prevailing.
>
> After a sequence of bitter defeats, it took the party more than a decade to fully shed its reputation of the 'loony left' by replacing its leadership twice, revamping its program thoroughly, and changing its intra-organizational decision rules sufficiently to assure voters that the party is committed to a political-economic strategy of continued market liberalization without possibility of relapse into old socialist visions.[61]

The historical misrepresentations and political bias in this passage should not prevent us from recognising the essential truth at its core: catering to market forces and practising democracy are contradictory undertakings. In 1995 Wolfgang Streeck wondered, in relation to the EU, 'how democracy will react when the loss of its ability to protect society from the vagaries of the marketplace will be fully realised by its citizens'.[62] The answer had already been formulated frankly in the business literature: democracy was an 'unaffordable luxury'.[63] Both at the level of the state and at the level of party organisation, then, 'vote- and office-maximizing' politicians could be expected to try to insulate themselves from popular pressure and accountability. As chapter 3 shows, this was a marked feature of British politics in the 1980s and 1990s.

Notably absent from the 'new institutionalists'' account of the British case, on the other hand, is the fact that Thatcher was not reacting to pressures from forces operating in an already-existing global economy, but played a leading part in constructing a global economy. She was not driven to deregulate. Her decisive initial policy choices sprang from a primarily domestic agenda, to save British capital from the threat posed by the Labour left in the late 1970s and to reverse the social-democratic penetration of the state and public life that had resulted from the post-war settlement. Among other things she wanted to allow British capital to go abroad to benefit from higher returns overseas and to use the resulting domestic unemployment to weaken British trade unions. After a massive initial outflow of capital, and a drastic reduction of union power, a return flow of foreign capital developed, seeking an English-speaking workforce, relatively low wages, light regulation and access to the EU market; both Conservative and Labour governments have since regularly celebrated the UK's status as far the largest recipient of foreign direct investment in the EU. This story of ebb and flow illustrates the wider point: the global economy was a consequence as much as a cause of the neoliberal reconstruction of Britain.

The situation inherited by the Labour Party in 1997, on the other hand, was much more like the one the 'new institutionalists' imagine confronted Thatcher: the result of eighteen years of determined effort by Thatcher and Major to construct not just a liberal market economy, but a liberal market society and culture, based not on trust but on the most extreme possible exposure to market forces, with internal markets, profit centres, audits and 'bottom lines' penetrating the whole of life from hospitals to play-groups. How far the global economy that by then existed was responsible for preventing New Labour from reversing this state of affairs is one of the questions explored in the following chapters.

The long-run impact of the global economy on national politics

In tackling that question, however, we are soon reminded that the way global market forces influence the policy choices of governments is not necessarily as significant, in the end, as the way the new global accumulation system constantly shapes and reshapes social relations in all countries – their class structure, ideology and political organisation – and hence the balance of political forces in them. With national states no longer able to exercise much influence over the accumulation process, this reshaping is more dramatic and unconstrained than in the immediate post-war era, although not otherwise unfamiliar.

The restructuring of production, under the pressure of global competition, is increasingly expressed in a world-wide process of concentration through mergers and acquisitions on an unprecedented scale, as corporations jockey for position to become global oligopolists. In countries of the 'north', productivity gains are achieved with magnified social costs as companies shed all sentimentality in face of intensified cross-border competition. Abrupt announcements of thousands of 'job losses' become commonplace as manufacturers shift production to lower-cost sites, and retail chains and banks and other service industries seek profits from merging overheads, closing branches and transferring labour costs to their customers. Factor-price equalisation (a.k.a. the law of value), now operating on a global scale, drives wages towards world rather than national norms and restructures the workforce of even the richest countries in line with the new geographical options open to capital. The result has been a marked shift in the division of national income between capital and labour in the main industrialised countries and for less-skilled workers a decline in real wages, casualisation and higher unemployment. At the same time world demand for highly skilled labour has raised its price, while the increased returns to capital, and the reduction of taxes on them, have dramatically expanded the global cadre of millionaires (to nearly six million in 1998) and billionaires (358 in 1995).[64] The combination of these processes has already produced patterns of inequality (and disparities of power) not seen since the 1930s in some countries of the 'north' – signalled by new terms, such as 'the excluded', 'winners and losers', 'A and B teams', 'the two-thirds, one-third society', and the like; new levels of crime and preoccupation with crime; new patterns of regional differentiation within countries as well as between them; and new problems of migration, driven by economic desperation as much as by war and state collapse.[65]

To trace the impact of the forces just outlined on the social formation of even a single country is a major if not a novel task. In an industrial country the analysis must be set within the wider framework of speeded-up effects in the social relations of production: the decline of most 'northern' workers' ability to threaten production by withdrawing their labour; the dissolution of old class boundaries, and with them the basis on which political parties once rested in most countries of the 'north' – a dissolution linked to the rapid decline of manufacturing employment and the rise of service work; the increasing casualisation and growing 'feminisation' of wage and salaried work; the re-emergence of home-working; the expansion of consumption by those in work; the shift – especially notable in Britain – from rented accommodation to home ownership; the dissemination of shareholding, both individually and through pension funds; the growing dependence on self-provided pensions as the value of state-provided pensions declines; the individualisation of culture and the commodification and privatisation of daily life. And if the erosion of the foundations of the old industrial 'working class' has serious implications for social democracy, the new insecurity of 'middle-class' life has serious implications for traditional conservatism.

Political consciousness has also been profoundly affected by the 'mediatisation' of life both at work and at home, as well as of party politics. The former mass parties have been converted into elite organisations of a new type and party membership and electoral participation have declined. And almost everyone is affected by profound cultural changes caused by falling air travel costs, new forms of entertainment and the simultaneous multiplication of choice and homogenisation of tastes. The boundaries and institutions inherited from an earlier era of industrialism have been irreversibly weakened, from municipal pride and trade union solidarity to the authority of churches, teachers, judges, parents, politicians, males – indeed the very idea of authority has lost its former strength. National politics are also put increasingly in question by the dissolution of national borders, sometimes on the initiative of national states, (as in the EU), sometimes not (as with East and South-East Asia's 'Natural Economic Territories' or NETs).[66] And all such effects of global market forces need to be analysed in their interaction with particular features of the national social structure and culture inherited from the past, and the particular events, persons and institutions through which they are transmitted and experienced, and in terms of which they are interpreted.

Even a century that had become accustomed to change was aware at its close of a fresh unleashing of the forces famously described a century and a half earlier: 'Constant revolutionizing of production, uninterrupted disturbance of all social conditions, everlasting uncertainty and agitation. . . . All old-established national industries have been destroyed or are daily being destroyed. They are dislodged by new industries, whose introduction becomes a life and death question for all civilized nations. . . .'[67] National governments, however, were no longer able – even if they wished – to slow the process down, and much less able to cushion its effects.

3

British politics in a global economy

Between 1975 and 2000, while a new global economy was being constructed world-wide, a radical reconstruction also took place in the British political system.

It began with the political parties. In 1975, when Mrs Thatcher took control of the Conservative Party, it was still famous for its pragmatism, for having combined landed, commercial and industrial wealth behind national leaders who for more than a hundred years had successfully adjusted the interests of property to those of other classes and groups, and had been in office for fifty of the first seventy-five years of the century. By 2000 it had been transformed into a party of mainly English nationalism (with not a single MP among the seventy-two returned from Scotland), dogmatically neoliberal in its economics and authoritarian in social affairs, and with the fewest parliamentary seats in its modern history. The Labour Party underwent an even more radical transformation. In 1975 it was still the social-democratic political wing (however semi-detached) of the trade union movement, committed to a mixed economy and redistributive social policies. By 2000 it was an elite-controlled electoral machine, with an unprecedentedly large parliamentary majority, oriented to and increasingly funded by business and no longer even formally controlled by the unions.

The state was also radically reconstructed. In 1975 the civil service was still a coherent legal-rational hierarchy led by a small corps of patrician public servants dedicated to prudent socio-economic management and the gradual adaptation of policy to evolutionary social change. By 2000 it had been broken up into a set of small, central, policy-making ministries, led by civil servants promoted for their entrepreneurial style; and a huge range of national and local executive agencies, whether hived off from ministries, like the Prison Service, or the oddly named 'quasi-autonomous non-governmental organisations' ('quangos') such as the Office for Standards in Education ('Ofsted') or the regional health authorities, organised on business lines with chief executives on performance-related pay. In 1975, too, elected local government still enjoyed tax-raising powers, was landlord to about a quarter of the population, ran the schools and social services and public health and a large proportion of long-term residential and nursing care, as well as looking after local public transport, rubbish collection, road maintenance and other local services. By 2000 its tax-raising power had been effectively removed, as had responsibility for most housing, the operation of schools, and nearly all residential and nursing care. The Greater London Council and the big metropolitan councils of the midlands and north had been abolished.

In 1975 some 20 per cent of GDP was produced in the public sector. By 2000 the state had sold off virtually all its infrastructural and service operations, from the telephones to the railways. Those that remained, from the Post Office and the BBC to social services, had been internally reorganised as 'quasi-markets'. In 1975 the trade unions still enjoyed the legal immunities originally established in the Trade Disputes Act of 1906. By 2000 these were history, replaced by what Tony Blair approvingly called 'the most restrictive trade union laws in the western world'.[1] In 1975 civil liberties were among the most liberal in the world and the police were still divided into forty local forces, and subject to a degree of accountability to elected local authorities. By 2000 a series of Acts – the Public Order Act 1986, the Criminal Justice Act 1994, the Security Service Act 1996, the Police Act 1997 and the Terrorism Act 2000 – had considerably narrowed the scope for peaceful dissent and strengthened the powers of the police, who had also been made significantly more answerable to central government.

Momentarily, the incoming Labour government of 1997 took several initiatives that ran against the centralising, commercial thrust of all these changes: incorporating the European Convention on Human rights into British law; removing the political powers of the hereditary peers; devolving powers to Scotland and Wales; proposing electoral reform. By the end of 2000, however, these initiatives had halted. Although they were invariably described as the greatest constitutional reforms of the century, it is the ones that preceded them, almost all accomplished between 1980 and 1997, and which were not usually described in these terms, that in retrospect appear much more fundamental, and whose relationship to economic globalisation is perfectly clear. The national

political system was adjusted to cope with the demands that no longer
national economic forces would increasingly place on it. The main
direction of change was to make the state more serviceable to business,
and government less subject to pressure from voters.

The politicians involved were mostly keenly aware of this logic, even
if at times more narrowly political motives, or strong personal feelings,
predominated (e.g. Mrs Thatcher's abolition of the Greater London
Council in 1987). But as the global economy became consolidated and
global market forces grew progressively stronger, the nature of the link
between economic globalisation and domestic political change became
obvious to everyone.

British governments and economic globalisation, 1975–2000

The story begins with the reaction of British business to the upsurge of
left-wing activism and trade union militancy in the 1960s and early
1970s, in the context of the escalating balance of payments crises
produced by the declining competitiveness of the British economy from
the 1960s onwards. Edward Heath's famous 'U-turn' in 1972, imposing
wage controls amid rapidly accelerating inflation, led to a confrontation
with the still powerful National Union of Mineworkers in 1973 and the
Conservatives' defeat in February 1974. By 1975 the new Labour government under Wilson had negotiated a wage restraint deal with the
Trades Union Congress in return for various improvements in job
security, women's pay, and a plan to introduce a form of worker co-
determination – a British version of the German model. Business
confidence in the security of private property and 'management prerog-
atives' was severely shaken and business opinion swung strongly in
favour of abandoning the post-war 'deal' with organised labour in
favour of the neoliberal economic policies advocated by right-wing
think-tanks in the USA and Britain, and increasingly by the US and
British Treasuries, the IMF and the OECD.

In 1976 the Labour government, now led by James Callaghan, lacking
an overall majority in parliament and still faced with a rate of inflation
around 16 per cent and an unsustainable balance of payments deficit,
was forced to seek an IMF loan. The chief condition for the loan –
insisted on by the US Treasury – was that the government's budget
deficit must be eliminated and inflation attacked by cutting demand.

Large tax increases were politically impracticable, so government spending was sharply reduced and general demand cut by raising interest rates. From 1976 onwards Labour accordingly became 'monetarist'. Its leaders accepted that full employment could no longer be achieved by government spending but must be sought through private sector growth. For the necessary private investment to take place, prices must reflect real values, and this in turn required 'squeezing' inflation out of the system and permitting the free movement of capital. In 1978 Treasury officials began preparing to abolish capital controls.

The unions, on the other hand, were not convinced. The new economic strategy had not had time to produce significant results, and when in the autumn of 1978 Callaghan called for a fresh round of wage controls the low-paid public sector workers, who had borne the brunt of successive wage freezes throughout the 1960s and 1970s, went on strike. This was the famous 'winter of discontent'. An election was due in 1979. Margaret Thatcher, who had succeeded to the Conservative leadership in 1975 and begun transforming the party into an instrument of neoliberalism, won decisively. She immediately eliminated controls on cross-border capital movements and raised interest rates sharply; she also set in hand a series of legislative reforms that over the next four years removed the political power of the trade unions. The US had already abolished capital controls in 1974; in 1980 the incoming adminstration of Ronald Reagan raised interest rates to record levels, forcing other countries to follow suit in order to defend their currencies and capital supplies.[2] These policies, which caused a world-wide deflation and drove up unemployment, suited both Mrs Thatcher's and President Reagan's domestic political agendas, i.e. to break the power of organised labour, shift responsibility for social security back from the state to individuals and restore the pre-eminence of 'the market'. Large corporations everywhere, and especially banks and finance houses, were also lobbying hard for these changes, which shifted resources from productive capital to financial capital, setting in motion the world-wide expansion of capital funds that marked the 1980s.

The global economy was thus the creation of states, led – or pushed – by the US and the UK, but as it took shape and gathered weight the market forces developing in it had greater and greater impact on the economies of those states, including Britain's. This impact could, of course, be limited or cushioned in various ways by state policy, at least in the short run, but British policy under Thatcher was aimed at maximising it, not limiting it; and thanks to the peculiarities of the British electoral system and an unwritten constitution with virtually no checks and balances (for a Conservative government, at least), she was able to push through the dramatic changes described above over three successive parliaments. She and her chief lieutenants conceived of it as a crusade, to be carried as far and as fast as the electoral cycle permitted. While the central government's power was enhanced, at the expense of local democracy and civil liberties, the role of the state in the economy was sharply reduced. Publicly owned corporations were sold to private buyers, public services were 'outsourced' to private providers and the state's share of national income was reduced.[3] The tax burden was shifted from capital to labour: corporation tax was cut, taxes on higher incomes were cut, and indirect taxes were raised. Labour markets were made 'flexible' by weakening the regulations covering working conditions as well as by drastically curtailing trade union rights.

Mrs Thatcher's right-wing zeal eventually outran the masochism of even the British electorate, while her abrasive manners exhausted the patience of her colleagues; and under her successor John Major the Conservatives became increasingly mired in scandal and divisions over Europe. But although the Conservatives had lost their way, the market forces that Mrs Thatcher had let loose had grown extremely powerful. The British economy's traditional 'openness' remained very pronounced, especially when compared with the other large EU economies. Foreign direct investment in Britain was twice as important, in relation to GDP, as it was in France or Germany, and in 1997 accounted for close to 20 per cent of all domestic capital formation, compared with under 10 per cent in France and just over 2 per cent in Germany (see table 3.1). British companies also invested far more heavily abroad.[4] As British firms expanded overseas and foreign corporations steadily increased their domestic presence, the country's integration into the global economy became more and more palpable.

Tony Blair and his team of 'modernisers', coming to power in 1997 with a landslide majority, had long since concluded that winning and keeping political power depended on winning over former Conservative voters, and securing business approval. They announced their acceptance of virtually the entire legacy of the Thatcher and Major years – 'pro-business' trade union and employment law, privatisation, a 'mar-

Table 3.1.   The UK, France and Germany in the global economy

		UK	France	Germany
GDP at market prices (bn Ecus) 1998		1,253	1,297	1,922
GDP per capita (Purchasing Power Parities) 1998		20,613	19,956	21,797
Stocks of FDI as percentage of GDP 1997	inward	21.5	10.1	9.9
	outward	29.1	13.6	14.4
Flows of FDI as percentage of fixed capital formation 1997	inward	18.6	9.7	2.3
	outward	32.0	15.0	9.5
Cross-border mergers and acquisitions by seller in 1998 ($bn)		86.1	36.7	23.1

Sources: *Eurostat Yearbook* 2000 (Eurostat, 2000) and *World Investment Report* 1999 (UNCTAD, 1999).

ketised' public sector, a no longer universal welfare system, privatised housing, the neutering of local government. To protect themselves from the threat of capital flight – or, more precisely, to lower the 'risk premium' that the owners of capital could impose on the cost of borrowing – they undertook an intensive pre-election campaign to reassure the markets that they had no intention to reintroduce capital controls or raise taxes or do anything that would significantly threaten profits; on the contrary, they would actively seek to make Labour a 'party of business' and consult business at every turn.[5] They promised that a Labour government would make low inflation its priority, keep the public debt constant as a share of GDP over the business cycle, and only borrow for investment.

And once elected they followed this through by a series of measures that further strengthened market forces. They transferred the power to set interest rates to the Bank of England, with a mandate only to contain inflation, not to promote growth. They announced that they would stay within the tight spending limits set by the outgoing Conservative government for the next two years, and did so, at considerable cost to their popularity. They watered down their commitment to a minimum wage until the level adopted satisfied business opinion. They abandoned their manifesto commitment to a training levy on companies. They left essentially untouched the Conservatives' regulatory regime for the privatised industries.[6] They opposed proposals by other members of the EU to harmonise tax rates or in any way tighten the Union's regulatory regime; for instance they firmly resisted including in the Social Charter rights of representation for employees on company boards of management. They supported the OECD initiative for a Multilateral Agreement on Investment and the subsequent efforts to achieve the same result via the WTO. They backed the EU decision to permit the patenting of genes, insisting that 'provision of a secure and effective intellectual property regime' for biotechnology industries was 'central to the UK's approach'.[7]

Why did New Labour make such a wholesale commitment to Thatcher's legacy? Why did they not follow the 'Rhineland' or 'stakeholder' path urged on them by sympathetic political journalists like Will Hutton and advocated by various think-tanks and academics? The reasons are undoubtedly complex, but two stand out. One was the problem of 'credibility' with the financial markets. Once committed to the abandonment of 'heroic' macro-economic strategies, whether Keynesian or of any other kind, an incoming Labour government would depend on the willingness of private investors to invest, if economic growth was to be achieved – and without economic growth, it could not hope to win a further election. After twenty years of unremitting denigration by the Conservatives and the overwhelmingly right-wing press, Labour had a huge problem to solve in this respect. It had to get rid of its reputation or 'image' as a 'tax and spend' party beholden to the trade unions and convince the markets that it would make low inflation its priority and be generally 'business-friendly' rather than union-friendly. The intellectual convictions of Gordon Brown, as Shadow Chancellor and Chancellor, were also crucial. Having accepted 'post-classical endogenous growth theory', he believed that private sector growth was the only way of finding resources to alleviate poverty and start repairing the infrastructure. Brown's famous caution, or fatalism, about the constraints imposed by global market forces was transmitted to Blair, whose much-discussed Mais Lecture of May 1995 summed up their position: 'Low inflation is not simply a goal in itself. It is the essential prerequisite both of ensuring that business can invest and that supply-side measures can work to raise the capacity of the economy to grow.'[8] Anything else was seen as a risky diversion.*

The other obvious reason is that the Labour left had been so thoroughly marginalised that the party's collective mind was effectively closed to new alternatives. No one of any authority in the party now imagined a non-capitalist future, but even a 'stakeholder capitalist' alternative, which existed theoretically, was not on the agenda of a significant current of party opinion. In spite of the fact that Thatcher's neoliberal policies had not remedied the British economy's notorious weaknesses, the Labour Party had developed no alternative to fiscal and monetary prudence and business-approved supply-side measures, and otherwise seemed to rely entirely on the hope that maximum exposure to global market forces would eventually do the job.[9]

Market forces, social structure and ideology

While policies that reinforced market forces were thus constantly at work, affecting every field of public policy, they are certainly not the whole story. Global market forces also shape and reshape the social basis of politics and ideology – the way work is organised, income and wealth are distributed, status is assigned, and perceptions and beliefs and aspirations are shaped – and this too profoundly affects policy-making. An adequate account of these 'deep' changes in social relations would be a major research project, and one that is badly needed. Here we can only touch on a few of the more obvious and important of the changing political parameters.

---

* The chief academic advocate of the north European model of social-democratic market coordination has been the American political scientist Geoffrey Garrett. In a series of articles summed up in his book: *Partisan Politics in the Global Economy* (Cambridge University Press, 1998), Garrett argues that 'far-sighted capitalists' appreciate the competitive advantages to be gained from an 'encompassing' trade union movement able to deliver its members' cooperation in limiting wage demands and industrial unrest, and the state-backed training programmes and other advantages offered by this model, and will be happy in return to pay high wages and social security benefits. The question is whether it is possible for the government of a country that does not already have such institutions to construct them, especially if

Employment, incomes and wealth

In Britain the most immediately obvious effect of the restructuring of global production resulting from capital mobility was the continued decline of manufacturing, from 25 per cent of GDP in 1980 to 21 per cent in 1997.[10] Whole industries for which Britain had been famous, from coal-mining (which at the beginning of the twentieth century had employed a million people) to the manufacture of motorcycles, had all but disappeared, while labour-saving technology in other sectors had led to a continued decline in old-style manual work (down from about 50 per cent of all jobs in 1979 to 36 per cent in 1991), as well as facilitating the continued 'feminisation' of waged work – raising the proportion of women in the workforce from 37 per cent in 1981 to an expected 45 per cent in 2001. The shift to services meant, too, that by 2000 fewer than one worker in ten worked in a factory. On the other hand competitive pressures and the 'flexibilisation' of labour meant that casualisation had become commonplace again, half a century after it had been virtually eliminated; in 1999 about 40 per cent of men and 30 per cent of women were in temporary employment, mostly for lack of any alternative.[11] The decline of manual work, casualisation, the growth in low-level service jobs, high rates of unemployment in the 1980s and the curtailment of trade union rights all combined to produce a dramatic drop in union membership: by 1998 less than a third of all employees were in unions, a drop of 21 per cent in ten years. After the defeat of the 1984–85 mineworkers' strike, industrial

---

its capitalists are *short*-sighted – as British capitalists have famously been. Will Hutton's advocacy of a 'stakeholder' economy was effectively a proposal to start moving Britain in the direction advocated by Garrett. The idea was dropped, after being floated by Blair in a much-discussed speech in Singapore: 'Gordon Brown did not like stakeholding as an economic idea. He felt it was a hostage to fortune, exposing Labour to the risk of attack on grounds of social costs . . .' (Philip Gould, *The Unfinished Revolution: How the Modernisers Saved the Labour Party* [Abacus 1999], p. 255). For a careful discussion of Garrett's thesis in relation to New Labour see Mark Wickham-Jones, 'New Labour in the global economy: partisan politics and the social-democratic model', *British Journal of Politics and International Relations* 2/1, 2000, pp. 1–25. Wickham-Jones thinks a modified version of Garrett's thesis could work in Britain, but only on conditions that seem, on the face of it, rather unlikely ever to be fulfilled. For a detailed 'stakeholder' proposal see Colin Hay, *The Political Economy of New Labour: Labouring under False Pretences?* (Manchester University Press, 1999), chapter 6.

action declined to very low levels and worker resistance to privatisation, job losses and casualisation became generally spasmodic and weak. The lack of effective resistance to the changes in broadcasting and health services described in chapters 5 and 6, which had heavy costs for all the workers involved, is hard to explain unless the weakened position of the trade union movement is taken into account.*

As regards incomes, the chief effects of globalisation were, first, a big increase in total real household disposable income (an increase of 52 per cent over the years 1980 to 2000); but, second, its much more unequal distribution. In 1981 the poorest 10 per cent of households had average incomes of £110 per week, the richest 10 per cent £350; by 1997 the figures were £130 and £530 respectively, and 18 per cent of the population were living on 'low incomes', defined as less than 60 per cent of the median income. Within the EU only Portugal, Ireland and Greece had greater income inequality.

Wealth was even more unequally distributed. Share ownership had spread to 17 per cent of all adults, i.e. well beyond the ranks of the 'upper middle class', which had significant effects on people's attitudes to shareholding even if most of these shareholdings were on a very modest scale.† Yet if housing is excluded, by 1997–98 the richest 1 per

* Much has been made by some writers of the social effects of the so-called 'Japanisation' of the economy by inward investment during the last two decades of the twentieth century, but this has been greatly exaggerated (see, e.g., Joel Krieger, *British Politics in the Global Age: Can Social Democracy Survive?* [Polity, 1999]). The proportion of the workforce directly affected by the adoption of Japanese-influenced management practices is very small and their experience of it seems to be mainly one of no-strike agreements and acceptance of management control over all aspects of work, accepting job 'flexibility' and intensification of effort in the name of a more competitive way of organising production that actually depends heavily on low wages and low corporate taxation. In any case two-thirds of all inward investment is non-industrial and has had little apparent impact on productivity or work.
† Accurate data on the distribution of shareholding are essentially non-existent. According to *Social Trends 30*, 2000 edn (The Stationery Office, 2000), 17 per cent of adults owned shares in 1998. According to the London Stock Exchange's *Facts on File 1999*, 24 million people owned shares. The latter figure seems to have been calculated by including the number of members of building societies who had received shares in them when their societies 'de-mutualised' and became banks. It seems likely that a high proportion of these shareholdings would have soon been disposed of. Nonetheless a gradually growing minority of people undoubtedly owned a small number of shares. Looked at the other way round, individual British shareholders owned between

cent of the population owned 27 per cent of all marketable wealth, and the richest 50 per cent owned 94 per cent of it. At the other end of the scale a quarter of the population – including the long-term unemployed, pensioners dependent on state pensions and the great majority of single mothers and their children – lived increasingly different lives from those of the top 50 or 60 per cent, with their steadily rising annual incomes and their £101 billion of consumer credit; and because so many single parents were poverty-stricken, one child in three was growing up in poverty. Yet poverty was now seen as a 'minority' issue, rather than a shared problem of the working-class majority whom the labour movement and the Labour Party had represented in the past. That role was taken over by 'single-issue' groups – Shelter, Child Poverty Action Group, Age Concern, etc. – which both the media and the government could label as 'special interest groups' and largely disregard. The putative social solidarity once symbolised by universal flat-rate National Insurance contributions had largely disappeared.

Consumption patterns

The growth of incomes also had significant political effects through changes in consumption. Some improvements in living standards affected more or less everyone – for instance telephones, washing machines and deep-freezers, which had been absent from a quarter of all homes in 1981, were installed in virtually all of them by 1998–99. The significant divide was now access to a car, with 30 per cent of households still having no car and 70 per cent having one or more. By the end of the 1990s, too, 74 per cent of people were home-owners, an almost 50 per cent increase since 1979. In 1998–99 spending on leisure goods and services was for the first time the single largest item of average household expenditure (just ahead of food, housing and housing goods and services). Supermarkets had displaced small family shops (86 per cent of all consumer spending was with major chains) and shopping malls proliferated. Over half the population took part in the national lottery, spending an average of £200 a year on it. Holidays abroad had become normal. Spending on domestic service had also risen dramatically in the last decade, from £1.1 billion in 1981 to £4

---

them about a quarter of all shares, while foreign shareholders owned another quarter and institutions a half.

billion in 1998. Much of this was concentrated in households at the top
of the income ladder, and in London. But in most parts of the country
it had ceased to be unusual.[12]

Most people, in other words, were now home-owners, undertaking
considerable discretionary spending and spoiled for choice. The idea
that they should also, for example, buy school books for their children,
pay for their own dentistry, or buy individual health insurance – since
the schools and the dental service and the hospitals were so badly
underfunded – was no longer shocking or even surprising. Nor did
media coverage of the conspicuous consumption of the super-rich
(restaurant bills of £2,000, the ownership of multiple houses worth
millions of pounds and sports cars worth tens of thousands) or the
wretched state of the homeless any longer raise many eyebrows, let
alone stir much indignation. A telling indicator was the drop in ratings
for television documentaries on social problems. A leading documentary film-maker remarked, 'programmes were made about people sleep-
ing in the streets of London at a time when hardly anybody did. And
now thousands sleep on the streets and no one makes any programmes
about them.'[13] Consumerism, individualism and inequality had become
the norm.

Social class

It has become a commonplace that people no longer think in class
terms, but it is one that needs careful qualification. In 1999 people still
assigned each other to social classes, and a majority still thought of
themselves as working class, but the connotations of this had changed a
great deal. Being 'working class' probably meant that their income was
paid weekly rather than monthly and that they were not eligible for
various privileges reserved for management, such as private health
insurance or holidays longer than the legal minimum – unless they
happened to belong to a union that had won such concessions. There
was also still a recognisably distinct working-class culture, especially in
old industrial areas where the manual working class used to be concentrated, although even there it was under complex pressures of the kind
portrayed in films like *The Full Monty*. Elsewhere working-class culture
was increasingly diluted by opportunities to enjoy global tastes in music,
dress, food and travel, and its political implications had become problematic. Being 'working class' no longer meant being a manual worker

or a member of a trade union, living in rented housing or even voting predictably for the Labour Party. By April 2000 polls showed that Labour support among manual workers was barely higher than among managerial and professional workers, and only moderately higher than among 'intermediate and routine non-manual' (lower management and office staff) workers. Voting research seemed to support the view that even working-class voters had 'become more and more like discriminating consumers who evaluate competing products. As a result, voting decisions are now more heavily influenced by voters' assessments of the main parties' relative managerial competencies and by their evaluation of the rival frontbench teams' leadership abilities.'[14]

Politicians had in any case been acting on this assumption since at least the mid-1980s, responding to intensified lobbying by the so-called 'new social movements', and directing increased attention to issues such as gender, crime, sexual identity and the environment that could appeal to people across social class divisions – though with conspicuous lack of success, since most of these issues affected powerful vested interests. A good example was the Labour Party's 1997 election pledge to ban fox-hunting, which appealed to animal-lovers and exploited the general unpopularity of the moneyed hunting fraternity. This was promptly and effectively countered by the hunting lobby, which formed the Countryside Alliance (purporting to represent the whole rural population, united in resentment of neglect and discrimination by city-based politicians) and mobilised a highly successful mass 'march' in London in early 1998 that frightened the government into postponing the hunting question until 2001, and then promising a free vote on various options (including 'self-regulation' by the hunters – i.e. doing nothing), from all of which the government would remain formally detached.[15] Similar opposition was provoked by, for example, Labour's pre-election efforts to raise the proportion of women parliamentary candidates (outlawed by the courts at the instigation of disappointed male aspirants), by its measures in office to end discrimination against gays (leading to denunciation by the Catholic Church in Scotland as well as the right-wing press), by its plans to curb traffic congestion in cities (opposed by the motor industry and car owners), and so on.[16]

Party politics conceived on the model of a department store – offering a wide range of 'products' catering for a wide range of 'consumer' choices – were thus proving tricky, as well as expensive. The brashly over-confident and often mutually contradictory conclusions that the Labour leadership's electoral research advisor, Philip Gould, appeared to draw from his far from unambiguous findings about public opinion testified to how badly the once solid class foundations of party politics were missed.* But those class foundations were gone. Perceived class interests had once set limits to what market forces could expect either party to do in office. They no longer offered such a firm barrier; in every sphere, from town planning and food safety to university research and schools, a 'corporate takeover' had occurred that would have been unthinkable while those barriers remained.[17]

'Mediatic society'

By the end of the 1980s no one seriously involved in public life at almost any level could be unaware of the critical importance of the mass media, especially television. Every organisation, from central government departments and local authorities to political parties, companies, trade unions, universities, hospitals, churches and prisons, employed 'directors of communications' or 'public affairs', and 'press officers' or 'media liaison officers', who made corporate videos, maintained web-sites, 'strategised' over the production of 'logos', provided briefings, distributed 'information kits', gave press conferences and photo-opportunities, sought radio and television interviews, sponsored conferences, monitored news stories, kept databases and engaged in 'instant rebuttals'.[18] 'Spin' eventually became an object of universal resentment and scorn, but there was no avoiding it, because in the short term, at least, what appeared on the screen or in the press was what mattered. Policy announcements were 'trailed' days or even weeks in advance ('the Chancellor will announce that . . .') so that by the time they were officially made, adverse reactions had been anticipated and

---

* Gould was originally brought in by Peter Mandelson to advise the Labour leadership in the late 1980s. The bizarre mixture of unclear ideas and subjective interpretations, expressed in egregious ad-speak, of which his advice could consist was revealed through the leaking of two memoranda written by him following Blair's ill-fated speech to the Women's Institute in June 2000. Blair's reliance on such advice, revealed in another leaked memo, and his public defence of Gould, did nothing to enhance his reputation for clear and independent judgement. For the text of Gould's second memo, written in early May (which actually turned out to be a first draft, retrieved from Gould's garbage by 'Benji [Benjamin Pell] the Binman'), see *Guardian*, 20 July 2000.

helpful glosses added. Public meetings, in the sense of open access meetings between politicians and the public, with opportunities for questions and heckling – an old-fashioned test of competence and the common touch – had given way to carefully managed television appearances with handpicked interlocutors. (For example, before a speech by Blair to the Women's Institute in June 2000 the 'Strategic Communications Unit' in the Prime Minister's office had arranged for televised interviews with 'modern-looking' members of the WI to get their reactions to the speech – which were naturally expected to be favourable. As it happened, they weren't, and the interviews were abandoned).[19]

By the early 1980s the British spent, on average, nearly three and a half hours of every day watching television, and a further hour listening to radio. Most of what people watched was entertainment, and the 'production values' of sports and film gradually displaced those of reporting and argument. Celebrity – of film, music and sports stars, and television presenters – became very important. Party leaders sought photo-opportunities with stars, in effect getting them to endorse their political product (the Labour government even had plans, revealed after her death, to use Princess Diana as a sort of 'roving ambassador', and later toyed with the idea of promoting former 'Spice Girl' Geri Halliwell as a 'women's role model'). Politicians had to try to become celebrities too, changing their appearance and way of speaking; being 'telegenic' became a prime qualification for leadership. Neither parties nor trade unions any longer functioned as mass opinion leaders or sought to organise people's ideas and attitudes on a wide range of issues through continuous interaction with their memberships – a function largely abandoned to the mass-circulation newspapers with their often ultramontane right-wing bias. Two thirds of teenagers had little or no interest in politics and scant political knowledge.[20] One voter in five was functionally illiterate.* Knowledge of modern history was confined to a tiny minority who astonished audiences in radio and television quizzes. Images, music and other non-verbal signifiers increas-

---

* In 1997 one in five British adults could not locate the page for plumbers in the Yellow Pages phone book or calculate change; one in sixteen could not read a simple notice. One adult in three could not calculate the area of a room 21 feet by 14, even using a calculator. See *A Fresh Start: Improving Literacy and Numeracy for Adults* (Department for Education and Employment, 1999), pp. 1–4.

ingly displaced words. Party political TV broadcasts ceased to be reasoned appeals to either principle or pragmatism and became increasingly like commercials. The disjunction between policy-making – hopefully, based on analytic reasoning and facts – and the way voters were appealed to had become more marked than at any time since the introduction of universal suffrage.

The commercialisation of everyday life

One of Mrs Thatcher's chief aims was the creation of an 'enterprise culture'. Measures calculated to do this included giving local authority tenants the right to buy their homes at bargain prices; privatising the nationalised industries and offering everyone the chance to buy shares in them, also below market value; redirecting the school curriculum to equip people for work and business;[21] putting large new resources into policing social security benefits fraud while drastically cutting back on safety and health inspection and the policing of tax evasion, especially by businesses;[22] shifting the tax burden from the rich to the poor (to 'reward enterprise'); and tolerating the development of a 'black economy' (estimated in 2000 at between 5 and 8 per cent of GDP) among small businesses and self-employed manual workers.[23]

In 1999 survey research showed that these measures had failed to make a decisive impact on public attitudes. Eighty per cent said the gap between rich and poor was too wide and 53 per cent said the government should raise taxes on the better-off to spend more on the poor. Yet many did reveal a 'hardening of attitudes' towards welfare recipients and tended to believe that access to welfare benefits discouraged people from working.[24] The reality was that while Thatcher's reforms were seldom popular, they had become an accepted part of daily life – as Labour's 'modernisers' recognised when they decided to accept virtually all of them.

Most people now worked for private companies, and what remained of the public sector had been remodelled on 'business' lines, with 'profit centres', performance-related pay, annual 'market-testing', 'outsourcing', 'downsizing' and 'productivity savings' targets – and in sectors like hospitals and the arts, appeals to charities and companies for donations. Conversely, people now bought their phone services, water supplies, gas and electricity from other private companies. Buses, trains and train stations, airlines and airports were also now all privately owned and operated, as were more and more government offices and, imminently, hospitals and clinics. Prisoners were detained in private prisons. Fees now had to be paid for many public services that used to be free – for example, dentistry, eye care, university education, the use of government statistics, museums and research libraries, musical instrument teaching in schools. Official terminology had been changed to encourage the shift from a 'producer' to a 'consumer' culture: 'customer' replaced 'passenger', 'client' replaced 'patient'. People took the hint and (encouraged by lawyers) began suing the state; litigation against doctors, hospitals and the police, for example, increased dramatically.[25]

Cuts in public spending opened the way to other kinds of commercial penetration of the 'life-world'. Most major sports events had already become corporate ideological property (e.g. the 'Bank of Scotland Premier [football] League', the 'PPP Healthcare County [cricket] Championships'); the same was increasingly true of television shows, art exhibitions and conferences. By the late 1990s sponsorship had spread to schools and universities, train stations, the Labour Party, the National Health Service and even police cars.* Scientific research depended more and more on corporate funding, while public funding for large-scale social and economic research was increasingly oriented towards the search for 'economic competitiveness'.[26]

There was little serious resistance to all these changes. Within two decades the omnipresence of business and business culture had become as commonplace and apparently inevitable as the rain. In the London

---

* Police cars in Kensington in central London were sponsored by the country's most famous department store, Harrods, even though successive Home Secretaries, supported by the courts, had deemed Harrods' owner, Mr Al Fayed, unsuitable to be granted British citizenship. In 1998 delegates to the Labour Party's annual conference found their name tags advertising Somerfield, a supermarket chain; the 1998 conference to celebrate fifty years of the National Health Service was sponsored by the private medical insurance industry and the pharmaceutical industry; in 2000 the Lake District National Park Commission was reported to be considering inviting corporate sponsorship for the Park's best-known lakes and mountains. Other examples are cited by George Monbiot in his *Captive State: The Corporate Takeover of Britain* (Macmillan, 2000), pp. 1–4. It is interesting to speculate why the British, with their long history of inefficiency in market matters, were apt to go so far in such directions. In some cases government agencies, faced with annual cuts in their budgets that no 'productivity' increases could offset, turned to sponsorship and other forms of private sector links out of financial desperation; but the generally uncritical acceptance of sponsorship was nonetheless remarkable.

docklands district, the site of a vast private development boom in the late 1980s, people even speculated in housing 'futures'.* In the late 1980s and early 1990s the press and the Labour Party made constant attacks on top executives for awarding themselves enormous salaries, bonuses and stock options, calling them 'fat cats'. By the end of the century it was an issue only in exceptionally egregious cases. For example in July 2000 the £10 million bonus awarded to Chris Gent, the Chief Executive of Vodafone, for his takeover of Mannesmann was attacked by a significant minority of shareholders, but a bonus half that size might well have passed without controversy. An 'equal opportunities' case that was reported a month later seemed to epitomise the moral universe of the 'third way': a 'senior city analyst', who had resigned from a job in a merchant bank where she had been paid £120,000 a year, complained to an industrial tribunal that owing to gender discrimination she had been denied an annual bonus comparable to the £440,000 and £650,000 paid respectively to two male colleagues.[27]

Rich businessmen – Lord Young, Lord Sainsbury, Geoffrey Robinson – had prominent places in the Labour government; trade union leaders had none. Neoliberal doctrine may have been much less widely endorsed than in the USA but a general market-based ideology corresponded to everyday experience in Britain and had become well entrenched, steadily shifting the ground on which further debates would take place. Whereas in the 1970s the idea that the BBC should be funded by advertising, for example, had few supporters, by the end of the 1980s a majority of people thought, why not?[28]

Market forces in politics

In the 2000 edition of his standard study of pressure groups in Britain Wyn Grant concluded that 'business interests have tended to strengthen

* Whimster perceptively noted this as an example of the new individualised culture in its most alienated form: 'Career now has to be thought of as an asset, as a flow of future income, to be offset against the burdens of housing, private schooling and consumerism. Children, parents, education, housing and residential location in relation to collective services all enter into [the] uneasy calculation. . . . Trading in the future contracts of homes, as occurred in Docklands, is to treat one's life-world as a commodity' (Sam Whimster, 'Yuppies: a keyword of the 1980s', in Leslie Budd and Sam Whimster [eds], *Global Finance and Urban Living: A Study of Metropolitan Change* [Routledge, 1992], p. 329).

their privileged position in the 1980s and 1990s, especially at the EU level';[29] in the same year George Monbiot published a detailed analysis of 'the corporate takeover of Britain'. What lay behind the new dominance of business in the so-called 'policy communities' or 'networks' in every field of public policy was the importance all politicians attached to adapting policy to the interests of corporations.[30]

Moreover, as companies increased in size, chiefly through transnational mergers and acquisitions, they acquired increasing political leverage. In 1999 alone the total value of cross-border mergers and acquisitions was over $1 trillion, most of it within the OECD countries. The chief executives of some of these companies disposed of negotiating resources (not to mention personal fortunes) that dwarfed those of ministers. They might form pressure groups, such as the European Round Table or the Transatlantic Business Dialogue, and they might make temporary political alliances, like the British Media Industry Group in the 1980s; but what used to be called 'trade associations' were now typically significant only in fields where many small domestic producers predominated, such as farming or long-term health care. The chief executives and chairmen of large corporations relied on their own direct, carefully cultivated personal relationships with senior civil servants and ministers (or even the Prime Minister); their interest lay in being in at the formative stage of policy-making, before governments had taken public positions from which it could be electorally hard to retreat: for instance, 'when ICI was worried about a change in tax law which it thought would adversely affect its operations, meetings took place between the chairman of ICI and the then chancellor of the exchequer, the chief secretary of the treasury, and other ministers and senior officials of the Inland Revenue'.[31] Similarly at the level of the EU, 'weeks of patient lobbying may count very little when balanced against a conversation between the president of the [EU] Commission and the chief executive officer of a major company in the latter's corporate jet'.[32]

Occasionally this method fails and corporate chief executives threaten publicly to move their companies' operations abroad if their demands are not met. In October 1999, for example, Sir Richard Sykes, Chairman of Glaxo Wellcome (now GlaxoSmithKline), the world's largest pharmaceutical firm, threatened to move it overseas because the Minister of Health had accepted the advice of the newly-created National Institute for Clinical Excellence that Glaxo Wellcome's antiflu drug, Relenza, was not cost-effective. Chris Gent, the CEO of Vodafone, did the same in June 2000 when the government announced the closing of loopholes in the tax laws, threatening to upset the calculations on which his takeover of the rival German TNC Mannesmann had been based, involving elaborate plans to avoid tax in Britain.[33] More often they avoid this and accept the necessity of getting what they want in increments, like the Channel 3 independent television company Chief Executives Michael Green and Lord Hollick in their drive for a merger, described in chapter 5. Sometimes, as in the case of tobacco advertising, they find themselves fighting a rearguard action against a government responding to significant electoral pressure, though even in such cases they often enjoy a remarkable degree of tacit official support.* Much more often they are able to work round political opposition in collaboration with the government, as with the introduction of GM foods in 1999–2000. In this case widespread public concern and protests were effectively neutralised, permitting imports of genetically modified American maize and preventing the labelling of foods to indicate whether or not they contained GM ingredients. Monbiot shows how the US government, acting on behalf of US farmers and Monsanto, successfully pressured the British, Irish and French governments to cooperate – with little difficulty in the case of New Labour.[34]

The significance of all these changes in the 'substrate' of politics is hard to sum up usefully. Which is more significant, the growth in total incomes, or their increasingly unequal distribution? The rise in the proportion of women in the workforce, or the declining proportion of workers in trade unions? The dissolution of old patterns is clear: which of the emerging new patterns will prove the most politically significant is much less so.[35] Perhaps the more egregious forms of commercialisation of the life-world and the new-found political power and arrogance

---

* An unusually explicit account of the way officials colluded with the tobacco companies to resist curbs on advertising is provided by Melvyn D. Read, 'Policy networks and issue networks: the politics of smoking', in David Marsh and R. A. W. Rhodes (eds), *Policy Networks in British Government* (Oxford: Clarendon Press, 1993), pp. 124–48. What happened in this case would be described in the public choice literature as the 'capture' of a regulatory agency by the interests it was supposed to regulate, but what strikes one most forcibly is the willingness of the officials concerned to be captured.

of the heads of global corporations were 'morbid symptoms' of the transition.[36] Some more promising symptoms also appeared, however: especially the rise of new organisations reacting against the impact of global market forces on the environment, health, animal welfare and public services, to mention only a few. By the end of 2000, after the collapse of the WTO meeting at Seattle, governments were evidently becoming sensitive to demonstrations of popular opposition to the corporate agenda. None, however, seemed ready to stop supporting that agenda, and perhaps least of all New Labour.

Interlude: the 'Big Bang' and its fallout

While the shape of the new social order emerging from economic globalisation is hard to summarise, some singular events do demonstrate vividly both the interconnectedness of the external and internal phenomena involved and their political importance. One of the most dramatic of these is the 'Big Bang', which exploded in the City of London, the capital's financial core, in 1986, and which has been the subject of some notably original and fascinating research.[37]

The 'Big Bang' was a fundamental reform of the London Stock Exchange that made stockbrokers compete on prices – i.e. on the size of their commissions – and, as a result, opened up the Exchange to new financial institutions with sufficient capital resources to make money on the scale of their own dealings, not just from their commissions on trading for others.* It was precipitated by mounting competition from foreign financial centres, especially New York, as the speed and scale of global capital movements increased from the late 1970s onwards, and as Japanese capital increasingly dominated world markets.[38] The change was resisted by the members of the Exchange until they capitulated to what was in effect an ultimatum from the Thatcher government in 1983 to reform themselves or have reform imposed. As everyone had foreseen, the main reforms led rapidly to a cascade of further changes. Huge investments were made in new communications

---

* Until then traders enjoyed fixed commissions and membership of the Exchange was tightly restricted. Once access to membership of the Exchange was opened up and traders had to cut their commissions in order to compete they could only make substantial incomes by trading large quantities of shares on their own account.

technology; the traditional trading floor gave way to on-line trading in
a series of new systems (SETS, SEAQ, SEAT-PLUS); a new exchange –
the London International Financial Futures Exchange (LIFFE) – sprang
up alongside the equities and bond markets; options and derivatives
trading expanded dramatically; the cosy ascriptive ties between the
privately educated elite were replaced by more competitive, achieve-
ment-based links within a greatly expanded and increasingly multi-
national trading community – though still centred on the 'square mile'
of the City of London.

The relatively small scale – in global terms – of the old-established
British merchant banks made them easy targets for takeover by the
foreign banks that were now free to operate in Britain; the result was
that although by the end of the 1990s London's position as one of the
three leading financial centres in the world had been saved, virtually all
the major companies represented in it were now foreign-owned –
mainly by American, Japanese and German finance houses. Their needs
necessitated still further reforms, notably in the way the City was
regulated. The probity of the old regime had rested on a high degree
of social interaction and trust between the members of an elite
recruited from a small circle of private boarding-schools where they had
been educated together since the age of seven or eight. The influx of
large numbers of non-elite employees made the old supervision
arrangements inappropriate and ineffective. A series of scandals, the
most spectacular of which brought down the old London merchant
bank Barings in 1995, eventually led to the end of self-regulation and
the imposition of external regulation on both the exchanges and the
banks.[39]

So far the story is one of global market forces, whose power increasingly derived from the deregulatory initiatives of the British and American governments, driving a fresh round of domestic institutional
change in Britain – the basic pattern already described. But when we
consider both the preconditions for this change and its further effects
beyond the financial services sector the story becomes more complicated and even more interesting. The Conservative minister who in
effect obliged the Stock Exchange to accept the 'Big Bang' was Cecil
Parkinson, one of Mrs Thatcher's closest allies and an exponent of the
new, non-traditional, neoliberal Conservatism she represented. Thatcherites of his type, whose weight in the parliamentary party increased
with every election from 1979 onwards, represented a new, business-

based element in the Conservative parliamentary party that reflected the growing influence of market forces and was hostile to all the arrangements inherited from the post-war compromise – including the 'aristocratic' wing of the party (whom the tabloid press now dubbed 'Tory grandees') and its City of London friends who had been part of that compromise and enjoyed a privileged monopoly under it. It is doubtful if such a radical change would have been imposed so determinedly on the City by any previous Conservative government, but the Thatcherites, supported by a growing number of 'free marketeers' among officials of the Bank of England and the Office of Fair Trading, did not hesitate. The changed social and ideological context played an important role here.

The further consequences were far-reaching too. In saving the City the 'Big Bang' also restored the centrality of the financial service sector in British economic policy-making. Government policy had to continue to assure the financial markets that the value of the pound would be maintained by keeping interest rates high enough to control inflation, rather than keeping them low enough to encourage manufacturing investment. Schemes such as those suggested by Will Hutton for controlling 'short-termism' by taxing capital gains from short-term equity holdings, or laying special obligations on pension and insurance fund managers to invest long term in manufacturing production, were once again dismissed as jeopardising the goal of keeping London competitive as a financial centre.[40]

The 'Big Bang' also had striking social and ideological consequences. Thrift and Leyshon calculated that the 380,000 people working in the City in the late 1980s had between them at least £4.5 billion disposable after-tax income, boosted by the Conservatives' tax reductions on high incomes.[41] City earnings were two-thirds higher than the national average, thanks especially to the dramatically high earnings of the City's top earners: about 4,000 people were earning over £100,000 a year in 1986, accounting for about 50 per cent of all those in Britain with incomes of this level and for about 15 per cent of the country's estimated 20,000 millionaires at that time.[42] Even secretaries and support staff earned considerably more than their counterparts in the rest of the country. Many of the big earners were relative newcomers to the City; most lived in London or the 'home counties' surrounding it, and their spending not only reinforced the position of the south-east in the national economy, drawing further resources and talent into the region from the rest of the country, but also significantly destabilised the pre-existing social status system.

Thrift and Leyshon investigated one revealing effect of the new City wealth, namely its impact on the market for homes in the country. The newly rich City workers bought expensive cars and antiques, ate at expensive restaurants and sent their children to private schools, but none of these 'removed the taint of trade' as well as living in the country did. Since the emergence of capitalism in Britain every newly rich cohort has sought social status through landowning, and the new investment dealers, portfolio managers and foreign exchange dealers enriched by the 'Big Bang' were no exception. By the 1980s this form of 'cultural capital' had become modified (for the City's young rich at least) into a preference for country living rather than landowning as such, so the demand was felt in the rural housing market within commuting distance of London.

> ... one [1988] survey ... identified three different kinds of purchaser based on the degree of income or capital. The first of these consisted of younger purchasers looking for properties valued at under £250,000. They were taking the first step into the country house market via a mortgage. ... The second type of purchaser consisted of older executives with substantial incomes, often already established in the country house market but wanting to trade up. The majority of purchasers in this group were in the 35–45 age bracket with young or grown up children and were seeking a better life in the country – with riding, shooting, fishing, tennis, sailing and swimming nearby. They were also the highest paid group and were confident of borrowing £300,000 to £500,000. ... These people required properties in the £250,000 to £1 million price range. ... Finally there was a group of the very rich with sufficient capital to ensure that income was no longer a consideration. They rarely needed to borrow and were generally not concerned about the price of the house they bought.[43]

The effect was naturally to drive up the price of country houses in a wider and wider circle from the centre of London as less wealthy buyers were obliged to look farther afield. But the new rich in the City posed a wider challenge to the existing status order. City incomes led a sharp upward turn in the remuneration of business executives generally. Corporate law firms and management consultancies could afford to follow suit, but how were senior civil servants and MPs – or even ministers on comparatively modest pay scales – to keep up with young 'forex' dealers in their smart London apartments and country homes, their cellars stocked with vintage wines? The Conservative Minister of State Alan Clark was keenly aware that the new City money was rapidly changing what it meant to be rich, commenting ironically in his diary for 24 December 1987 that with only £700,000 in his 'Crazy-High-Interest' bank account, he was 'bust, virtually', and noting that 'the major domo at Aspers' . . . wouldn't take a tip. I'm out of touch with these things. I suppose my humble £20 note was beneath him.'[44] Less fortunate politicians had to find alternative sources of income if they wanted to be taken seriously by business executives typically earning twice or three times as much as an MP. The temptation to make politics pay by influence-peddling became too great for a growing number and led to the wave of corruption or 'sleaze' (especially the Aitken and Hamilton affairs) that engulfed the Conservatives in the 1990s and played a significant part in their electoral collapse in 1997.[45]

Otherwise it was necessary to find supplementary sources of income outside parliament, but this problem was made more difficult by the fact that politics had become increasingly a specialist career. You could make a fortune in business and still hope to get a Conservative seat at age forty, after making big donations to the party, but you would be unlikely to reach high office; for that you needed to get into parliament in your thirties.[46] Aspiring politicians of both parties increasingly started out as assistants to MPs or researchers in political 'think-tanks' or business or public relations 'consultancies', or as lobbyists of various kinds, hoping to be noticed by the leadership and helped to find parliamentary seats while still young. Yet an MP's salary would still not permit them to socialise with richer colleagues or the business elite. The options for supplementing it included less obviously corrupt forms of part-time 'consultancy' work, writing (for those with talent), and non-executive company directorships. All these forms of dependence on outside interests posed problems of political ethics and influence.*

* A symptomatic development noted by Peter Riddell has been 'the decision of many ministers to stand down from the Commons at the election after they leave office, rather than remaining for one or two more parliaments. . . . They believe that, after years as ministers earning much less than their contemporaries, they can get more money outside in new, or resumed, business careers' (Peter Riddell, *Honest Opportunism* [Indigo, 1996], p. 292). Also symptomatic, perhaps, is that Riddell takes it for granted in this passage that such ministers' 'contemporaries' are rich.

The 'Big Bang' was not responsible for all this, of course. It was only part of the rapidly growing inflow of foreign business from the mid-1980s onwards, above all to London but also to other parts of Britain, through foreign direct investment as well as mergers and acquisitions. The impact of the 'Big Bang' was nonetheless dramatic, like that of tourism in a third world country, exposing the natives to previously unimagined levels of luxury. It drove up non-financial corporate salary levels to keep pace and kick-started the transformation of London's housing and restaurant markets. Its effects also percolated through the ranks of the public services and converged with the Conservatives' drive to reshape them on business lines, as Whimster noted in his perceptive analysis of the 'yuppie' (of which the young City trader was the archetype):

> The egoism of the yuppie personality has come into its own as a response to increasing pressures ... the same assertiveness might also characterise the new public sector professional. There is no necessary reason to believe that public sector, 'caring' professionals, while disadvantaged for reasons of political ideology and under-funding, should conduct themselves with genteel altruism.'[47]

And indeed a new public sector social type, with the assertive, egoistic personality traits that Whimster describes, did emerge among the chief executives of the government's 'New Steps' agencies, hospital trusts and local authorities, university vice-chancellors, school head teachers and the like.

And so the links run on. But the point is not that the 'Big Bang' uniquely illustrates the impact of globalised market forces on politics in Britain. Important as the 'Big Bang' was, major shifts in all the dimensions touched on earlier had hardly less significant consequences. The point is to register the interconnectedness of these changes, and the way they mediated the basic shift in the balance of power between market forces and political forces that marked the new era.

Party politics

What happened to both the Conservatives and Labour during the last quarter of the twentieth century is only comprehensible in this context.

Parties, after all, reflect the society in which they exist (even more perhaps than the state, which Marx famously called the 'table of contents' of civil society); so it should be no surprise that parties, which played such a central role in the formation of the global economy, should be the first political institutions to feel its effects, and should undergo a mutation fully as radical as their transformation into mass organisations following the extension of the franchise.

The Conservatives, in spite of having a mass membership, were a 'party of notables' in which power rested formally and in practice with its MPs, and which had succeeded in governing the UK for most of the previous century and a half by successive adaptations of the interests of property to the demands of other classes.[48] After the franchise was extended in 1867 and 1884 the Conservatives needed a mass base for electoral purposes. This they succeeded in organising in the form of a network of local Conservative and Unionist Associations, or clubs, which took advantage of the deeply embedded caste-like features of the class structure, marked by patronage and deference, and which gave the membership no formal role in the making of party policy. But when Mrs Thatcher broke with the party's pragmatic tradition and declared herself a 'conviction politician' crusading for 'the free market and the strong state', the class alliance at the apex of this structure broke up. The 'Tory' elements in the party leadership were progressively displaced by free-market fundamentalist newcomers, the rural 'shires' lost their time-honoured precedence, and the divisions of interest within capital (finance vs manufacturing, importers vs exporters, small businesses vs TNCs, etc.), instead of being mediated through compromises struck within the party's inner circle, as in the past, were exacerbated by their new exposure to global competition.*

These divisions soon became focused on the issue of Britain's relationship with Europe. Formed to encourage closer political union through freer trade, in the era of globalisation the EC/EU acquired an ambiguous significance, with a potential to regulate capital in the interests of European citizens rather than only in the interests of

---

* Much was made at the time of the fact that the Conservatives' membership was rapidly declining from lack of new recruits; the average age of members was sixty-two and there seemed no early likelihood of large-scale renewal. With hindsight it is clear that since modern elections are fought largely through the media, large numbers of members are less important than large amounts of money.

capitalists. The Thatcherite wing of the party was therefore hostile, but as the EU by then accounted for 60 per cent of UK exports this conflicted with the party's ties to firms in the export sector. The EU's adoption of a single currency in 1999 aggravated the problem. Divisions over Europe played a large part in the party's 1997 election defeat, but when John Major finally resigned the leadership the 'Europhobes' in the parliamentary party replaced him with the little-known but anti-European William Hague. The more pragmatic 'Tory' wing of the parliamentary party shrank through resignations and retirement, and by 2000 Conservative MPs were predominantly neoliberal and neocon-servative ideologues who seemed unaware of the extent to which public opinion had moved away from the crusading neoliberalism of the Thatcher years, and looked liable to condemn the party to opposition indefinitely unless the Labour party self-destructed.

What is at issue here, however, is not the Conservatives' chances of rebuilding a successful political coalition on the basis of market funda-mentalism and 'authoritarian populism', but the changes that William Hague made to the Conservative Party's constitution soon after his election. These changes reduced the leader's formal dependence on the party elite by giving rank and file members a voice in future leadership elections – changes presented as a 'modernising' step, responding to the Labour modernisers' electoral success. Kinnock and Blair had marginalised the party's left-wing activists by taking formal power out of the hands of those who attended party meetings and giving it to the wider membership through postal votes (on topics chosen and worded by the leadership) – appealing to the principle of 'One Member One Vote', or OMOV. Hague confronted the opposite problem – his 'extremists' were Conservative MPs, but leaving power in their hands was equally dangerous. In the era of a global economy the leader must be free to pick his or her way through the complex field of policy choices, and trade off competing interests and pressures, dom-estic and international, without being answerable to any doctrinally united group. So Hague adopted the Labour modernisers' formula and rhetoric, declaring that he was democratising the party while in reality opening up the possibility of appealing to the wider membership over the heads of his parliamentary party.* Hague himself hardly personified

* Clearly formal autonomy from the parliamentary party does not imply real autonomy in circumstances where a majority of Conservative MPs lose confidence in the

the 'presidentialism' implicit in the new party rules, but the change had
been made and the party's long-term future could well depend on it.

The Labour Party, by contrast, was a mass party, originally formed by
and dependent on the trade union movement. Its leadership had always
tried to portray it as representing the national interest, as opposed to
the interests of the working class alone, seeking middle-class support
for measures to limit the impact of market forces on people's lives,
chiefly through mildly progressive taxation and the pursuit of full
employment along with state-provided social security, housing, education and health services. The 1976 crisis seemed to show that this
strategy was no longer viable. After four successive election defeats the
'modernisers' led by Blair were determined to accept Thatcher's legacy
virtually in its entirety, while most of the party's activists were desperate
enough to support almost anything that promised to end Conservative
rule – one 'old' Labour activist told the Labour MP Alan Simpson he
would vote for the healing power of cabbage if this was what it took. It
was very doubtful, however, if these same rank and file activists would
go on feeling this way if the leadership continued with Conservative
policies once they were in office. The modernisers therefore took great
pains to impress on the City that party policy was now determined by
the leader and a few close colleagues alone, and set about rewriting the
party constitution to disempower not only the rank and file members
and the trade unions but also, in effect, the parliamentary party. The
annual conference and the national executive were reconstructed to
exclude potential challenges from below on policy issues. Leadership
control was extended to the selection of candidates for election to
parliament, the Scottish Parliament, the Welsh Assembly and the European Parliament. Members of the Shadow Cabinet – and later, even
Cabinet Ministers – were required to clear all their speeches with the
leader's office.[49] 'New Labour' (as Blair and his team now called the
party) converged with the Conservative Party in its central organising
principle.

leader, but their informal power, already dramatically weakened in the course of the
previous half century, was also reduced by the loss of formal power. In 1995 Richard
Shepherd, an independent-minded Conservative MP, commented that attendance at
the Conservative backbenchers' 1922 Committee, which historically had exercised real
power in holding Conservative leaders to account, had dropped to a quarter of those
entitled to attend and discussed 'housekeeping', not policy (interview, 18 October
1995).

New Labour also faced new contradictions, mirroring those of the Conservatives. To distance itself not just formally but in reality from the trade unions the party needed alternative sources of funds. It turned to rich donors attracted by its new, 'market-friendly' but socially moderate policy stance, but this not only exposed the party to the suspicion of selling influence, as the embarassing Bernie Ecclestone affair showed, but also called for policies that further alienated the trade unions – for instance, retaining virtually all of the Conservatives' industrial relations legislation and introducing a legal minimum wage at a level far below what the unions had hoped for.* It also risked a serious loss of support among disillusioned 'old' Labour voters, and a loss of members who felt they were no longer part of the party's policy-making process and helping to carry forward the party's historic socialist project – a motivation that had worked very effectively, in spite of the very real limits to rank and file influence that existed under the old party constitution. And the degree of control that the leadership imposed over Labour's 'message', as it tried to square all these circles, had its own cost in the eventual reaction of journalists and the public against incessant 'spin'.†

---

* The background to the Ecclestone affair was that by 2000 20 per cent of the Labour Party's funds came from donations over £1,000 (and roughly 40 per cent from members and small donors, 30 per cent from trade unions, 10 per cent from fundraising events and sponsorship), whereas in the years 1988–92 the average share of donations in Labour's total funding had been less than 1 per cent (Martin Linton, *Money and Votes* [Institute of Public Policy Research, 1994]). The chairman of Formula One racing in Britain, Bernie Ecclestone, donated £1 million to the party before the 1997 election, a fact that came to light in November 1997 when the government exempted Formula One racing from its ban on tobacco advertising and sponsorship (a ban that anticipated a Europe-wide ban due to be implemented by the EU). Formula One racing employed 50,000 people in Britain and the threat that these jobs would go elsewhere was impressed on other European governments as well as the British. The party returned Mr Ecclestone's donation, protesting that its decision had not been influenced by it.
† Labour's modernisers saw their investment in 'spin' as an essential counterweight to the Conservatives' advantage in having the support of the outrageously partisan and unscrupulous tabloid newspapers – mostly owned by transnational media corporations – which were too powerful to be subjected to reasonable regulation. The issue gradually became a major problem for the Labour government, however, thanks to the frustration of journalists who felt manipulated by the party's obsession with 'presentation' and 'information management'. It came to a head in June 2000 after an ill-judged speech by Blair to the Women's Institute and the leaking of a series of internal memoranda revealing his preoccupation with image and appearance.

Again, what is at issue here is not the Labour Party's electoral prospects but what the new conception of party organisation, shared by both Labour and the Conservatives, implies for policy-making.[50] To put it plainly, politics are no longer about managing the economy to satisfy the demands of voters, they are increasingly about getting voters to endorse policies that meet the demands of capital. The party leader's task is to adjust policy to the pressures of market forces, and to use every available means to secure consent for this, as free as possible from all encumbrances of doctrine and constraints of faction. Necessary above all for this purpose are people skilled in image construction and information management and the conduct of attitude surveys and focus groups. Party politics have become, in Polito's apt formulation, a 'realm of hyper-politics, where politics is exclusively concerned with itself', 'a daily struggle to win the attention of a public which has its mind on other matters' and in which 'the *software* of politics becomes decisive, its ability to adjust itself . . . to the country's state of mind, to intercept and encourage its moods'.[51] The parties' leading functionaries fully accept this. Their view is clearly formulated in the *Handbook of Political Marketing*:

> Democracies around the world are relying on the same market-driven procedures to run their political systems that corporations use to ensure success in the commercial market-place. . . . In fact, it has become nearly impossible to win elections without the use of marketing. It is also becoming increasingly important for politicians in office to rely on marketing to successfully pass legislation.[52]

Peter Mandelson, Labour's election campaign manager in 1997, told the Institute of Directors in 1998 that

> it had been the job of New Labour's architects to translate their understanding of the customer into offerings he or she was willing to pay for. And then, and only then, to convey to potential customers the attributes of that offering through all the different components that make up a successful brand – product positioning, packaging, advertising and communications.[53]

Absent from this model is the idea that a party represents ideals, or even interests, on the basis of which voters may be appealed to and against which policies will be judged. Preferences are assumed to be given, though 'volatile', and the task of the party leadership is to discover what they are and then try to make the chosen response to the 'new reality' of globalised markets appear to be in conformity with them. The implications for the evolution of policy in any given field are that the agenda is set by market forces rather than the party in office.

Institutional and constitutional change

While the parties were undergoing this sea change the Thatcher governments of 1979–90 pushed through the institutional and consti-tutional changes touched on earlier, changes that were arguably more far-reaching and radical than any since the Tudors; and what the Conservatives began, Labour continued. The Conservatives not only sold off most of the public sector but also revolutionised the fiscal system, redistributing the tax burden from capital to income earners and from high incomes to low, and cutting back virtually all forms of social security.[54] In office after 1997 Labour continued with the privatis-ation of state-owned assets and state services and also pushed strongly ahead with the Private Finance Initiative, which channelled tax revenues into private hands by inviting the private sector (which now had a surplus of investible funds) to build hospitals and schools and offices and lease them back to the state, complete with privately employed support staff. It also went on cutting back the welfare system, reducing the allowances for single parents and the disabled, and adopting a 'welfare to work' approach to youth unemployment.

The Conservatives took away the most significant powers of elected local government (the provision of rented housing and the manage-ment of schools), and effectively ended local councils' freedom to raise local taxes and set their own budgets. After 1997 New Labour made no attempt to restore local democracy; on the contrary, it abolished the right of the public and press to attend all council meetings and legislated to create elected mayors with cabinets meeting in private and not accountable to their councils – reflecting the same philosophy that had guided the reconstruction of the party.[55]

The Conservatives set in hand a radical reform of the civil service, driving through a separation between policy-making, to be done by a small central elite, and implementation, to be carried out by independent executive agencies organised on business lines, with chief executives on short-term contracts and performance-related pay, 'profit centres' charging other branches of the state for their services, and annual budget cuts to encourage productivity 'savings'. They also imposed a quasi-market system of organisation on the National Health Service and the organisation of personal social services, and ensured that the nominally independent BBC followed suit. With the very partial exceptions of the BBC and the NHS, discussed in chapters 5 and 6, this policy, too, was retained by Labour after 1997. The Conservatives also expanded dramatically the number and scope of unelected 'quangos' in the administration of health, education, training and other services, until those organisations were responsible for a third of all public spending, almost as much as elected local government.[56] Since quangos were accountable only to ministers in London, and had very few duties to consult locally or even make their deliberations public, Labour had opposed this during the 1980s and 1990s, promising to 'roll back the quango state'; but once in office it left the system alone.[57]

The counterpart to the quasi-commercialisation of central and local government was the proliferation of *auditing*, i.e. the use of business-derived concepts of independent supervision to measure and evaluate performance by public agencies and public employees, from civil servants and school teachers to university lecturers and doctors: 'environmental audit, value for money audit, management audit, forensic audit, data audit, intellectual property audit, medical audit, teaching audit and technology audit emerged and, to varying degrees, acquired a degree of institutional stability and acceptance . . . very few people have been left untouched by these developments. . . .'[58] In place of a society of citizens with the democratic power to ensure the effective and proper use of collective resources, and relying on a large measure of trust in the public sector, there emerged a society of 'auditees', anxiously preparing for audits and inspections.[59] A punitive culture of 'league tables' developed (purporting to show the relative efficiency and inefficiency of universities or schools or hospitals). Inspection agencies were charged with 'naming and shaming' 'failing' individual teachers, schools, social work departments, and so on; private firms were invited to to take over and run 'failing' institutions.* Labour in office not only

---

* Why these divisive and largely counter-productive ideas and practices should have been adopted with such enthusiasm is a puzzle, and not just to foreigners. It began,

retained this approach but extended it to local councils, hospitals and prisons.[60]

In short, the Conservatives undertook a massive centralisation and *de-democratisation* of the state, which Labour pushed even further, in spite of previous promises to reverse it. In two respects Labour promises in opposition were kept in a form that inverted their original meaning. One was the promise to replace the unelected and largely hereditary House of Lords with an elected second chamber. In practice, in 1999 the voting rights of all but ninety-two hereditary peers were removed, a handful of new life peers were appointed, and the issue of election was then in effect postponed indefinitely.[61] As past experience should have led everyone to predict, once in power Labour preferred the quango model to that of elections – a preference reinforced by the outcome of the first trial of 'New' Labour's elected mayor principle, in May 2000, which resulted in the election by a large majority of London voters of Ken Livingstone, the one candidate the leadership had been determined to exclude.[62] The other promise made in opposition that was more or less reversed in practice was Labour's Freedom of Information Act, finally passed in 2000, whose list of exclusions appeared on balance to narrow public access to information rather than extend it. A third constitutional promise was to hold a referendum on whether the electoral system should be changed to make it 'fairer'. This promise was watered down, first by deferring a referendum until after the next

---

of course, with the Thatcherites' deep hostility to the public sector – which they saw, correctly, as a bastion of social-democratic ideas – and their almost religious belief in the values of small business. They did not like public servants of the traditional type and therefore would not trust them; in the absence of trust, they needed to be subjected to business-style auditing. Labour's modernisers had more mixed feelings, perhaps, but especially in the first two years after 1997, while public spending was held down to impress the financial markets, they wanted more output for fewer resources; and since relatively few teachers, social workers, and so on, were 'New Labour' enthusiasts, continuing the audit and penalty system may well have seemed the only way to get it. As Radice has pointed out in relation to higher education, however, it has produced a peculiarly British version of the Soviet mode of production, including rigid hierarchies, one-man management, quantitative targets, the concealment of resources, bullying, nepotism, cynicism, stress and demoralisation (Hugo Radice, 'From Warwick University Ltd to British Universities plc', *Red Pepper*, March 2001, pp. 18–21). The peculiarly paltry qualities needed by the bureaucracy of appraisers and evaluators to whom the 'audit' industry gives power are surely present in any culture, but it is sometimes hard not to feel they are more than normally abundant in Britain.

general election, and then by planning to limit the choice to one between the existing system and the Alternative Vote (which has no proportional consequences).

The only important exception to this story of continued centralisation and de-democratisation was the creation of a Scottish Parliament and a Welsh Assembly. Labour had supported this in opposition because the resurgence of Scottish and Welsh nationalism from the 1970s onwards was threatening the party's support in both countries, especially in Scotland, which sent a crucial bloc of Labour MPs to Westminster. Incautiously, perhaps, immediately after taking office Blair reaffirmed Labour's commitment to devolution, and the parliament and assembly, each elected on a mixed system of proportional representation, came into being in 1999. But Blair's hope that Labour could win majorities in both was disappointed. Labour had to form a coalition with the Liberal Democrats in Scotland, and formed a minority executive in Wales, where the London leadership also failed to impose its preferred choice of local party leader.[63] During the two bodies' first year of operation no major issue came to the fore that threatened to destabilise relations with London;[64] and the Scottish nationalists' decision to try to make use of devolution, rather than hold out for independence or nothing, did produce some of the internal dissension in the SNP on which Labour's strategists had counted. It was clear, however, that neither Scottish nor Welsh politics were as amenable to central management as before, and that in changed circumstances, such as a government with a much smaller majority at Westminster, or a major economic recession, this could pose serious difficulties.

But devolution was the exception that proved the rule: in every other respect, Labour and the Conservatives had converged in a reshaping of the framework of British politics whose core principles – centralisation and executive control – reflected the conditions in which politics now had to be conducted – the 'new reality' of the globalised economy. The divisions that had rent Labour in the 1970s and 1980s and the Conservatives in the 1990s were *effects* of the impact of global market forces on British society, whether in the form of rising inequality and the contraction of the welfare state that monetarism entailed (which divided the Labour Party), or in the form of the European Union and the Euro (which had split the Conservatives).

What party leaders and prime ministers now needed was freedom to temper policy to the requirements of markets over which they had less and less control, on the one hand, and the wishes of the electorate, on the other. By early 2000, for example, Blair had in effect decreed that the question of whether Britain should adopt the Euro was undiscussable, not only by the party's Annual Conference, or its pale avatar, the Policy Forum, but even by the cabinet – a decree that depended for its efficacy on the thorough-going de-democratisation of the party that he had consummated. Or to take an example from the Conservatives, in July of the same year Hague decided to reverse himself on a highly publicised guarantee he had given the previous year to cut taxes permanently when re-elected. The party's market researchers had evidently discovered that voters were now more averse to cuts in social services than to taxation, and knew that a recession must eventually be expected and that when it came, such cuts would be inevitable if taxes stayed low. In both cases we see a degree of freedom to determine policy unilaterally that even a Conservative leader might well have hesitated to exercise twenty years earlier, and which for a Labour leader would certainly have been out of the question.

Similar considerations apply to Labour's failure in office to reverse the de-democratisation of local government, the marketisation of the civil service, and so on. Many of the 'policy wonks' in the Prime Minister's office undoubtedly thought that they knew better what was good for the country than did elected local councillors, or than did the sort of people who were likely to win seats in an elected upper chamber (or, for that matter, than did many Labour MPs). This feeling was justified, in their minds, by their understanding of what they called 'the project', whose founding tenet was that economic globalisation was a 'new reality' to which all policy must be adapted, restricting government economic intervention to the pursuit of macro-economic stability and a range of supply-side measures.[65] To devotees of 'the project' the streamlining of the civil service on business lines, its orientation to the support of markets, and a focus on individual accountability for the fulfilment of market-friendly functions made sense. Debating resolutions proposed by party members at party conferences and calling for more egalitarian social policies did not. Nor did allowing elected local councils to raise taxes and spend money according to their sometimes less than 'market-friendly' ideas.

The social costs of market-driven politics

The centralising impulse corresponded to the fact that many people were paying a high price for economic globalisation. One of John Smith's first initiatives, when he replaced Neil Kinnock as Labour leader in 1992, was to set up a Commission on Social Justice. Reporting in 1994 (after Smith's death, and his replacement by Blair), the Commission showed that during the previous fifteen years economic and social inequality and poverty had risen dramatically. Britain's health statistics, for example – life expectancy, infant mortality, days lost from illness – were significantly poorer than those of countries with more equal incomes, and getting worse; 'sustainable economic welfare', after rising in step with GNP after 1950, had fallen again since 1974; crime rates, after falling from 1950 to 1955, had been rising ever since, with a notable acceleration from the early 1980s to the early 1990s. The Commission's report did not conclude that Thatcher's policies should be reversed; it conformed instead to the modernisers' agenda in proposing a series of remedial policies consistent with what it called an 'investors' Britain'.[66]

After 1997 the Labour government did implement some of the report's recommendations, at least in part, but the problems it had outlined continued to get worse. Income growth for the richest 10 per cent of households was 7.1 per cent from 1997 to 1999, while for the poorest 10 per cent it was 1.9 per cent. By May 1999 the percentage of households with less than half the average income had risen still further, from 16.9 per cent to 17.7 per cent. Pensioners accounted for most of the deterioration, but the number of children in poverty-stricken households had also risen (from 3.3 to 3.4 million) during New Labour's first two years in office.[67] An estimated 400,000 people were homeless.[68] And in 1998 crime levels, which had fallen back somewhat during the mid-1990s, had begun rising again.[69] Sentences had meanwhile become longer and the prison population, which had risen from 50,000 in 1991 to 71,000 in 1998, was still rising.[70] Also increasingly evident throughout the nineties was racism, which the Conservatives exploited (e.g. by encouraging opposition to 'bogus asylum seekers') and which Labour in office seemed afraid to oppose.[71]

The Labour government was undoubtedly concerned about these figures, but even if it had not been determined to placate the markets by staying for two years within the spending limits set by the Conservatives before the 1997 election, the supply-side policies to which it had largely confined itself had very limited power to make a serious impact on the causes of inequality, poverty, ill-health, crime and racism. These things are, evidently, predictable effects of market forces operating on a global plane with significantly reduced regulation by national governments. Unskilled and semi-skilled workers' wages are pushed down by competition from workers in lower-wage countries, to which capital otherwise threatens to migrate (or from which cheaper labour can be imported), while skilled workers can command a premium and very skilled workers and professionals can command substantial economic rents.[72] Even a policy of labour 'flexibility' – i.e. removing obstacles to the use of low-wage labour in 'precarious' (part-time, short-term, casual, non-unionised) jobs – does not prevent important segments of the workforce (especially older unskilled manual workers) being pushed permanently out of employment by the decline of old, labour-intensive industries. Others, like single mothers of preschool children, are unable to work, while old people who are dependent on state pensions, which were delinked by the Conservatives from the growth of GDP, automatically fall farther and farther behind the average.[73] A redistributive fiscal policy can of course make the after-tax incomes of rich and poor less unequal, and most of the worst poverty could be ended by a serious improvement in social security benefits. But going back to substantially redistributive policies was ruled out on electoral grounds (the Social Justice Commission was fully 'on message' when it declared that 'there can be no question of returning to the top tax rates of the 1970s').[74]

In view of all this it is not particularly surprising that crime rates increased, especially among young men growing up in poverty, attending poor schools (8 per cent acquired no qualifications) and facing a life of low-paid, precarious work or unemployment (the peak age for offending for men was eighteen, and 60 per cent of people in prison were functionally illiterate or innumerate or both).[75] While Blair had promised that Labour would be 'tough on crime and tough on the causes of crime', it was easier to be the former than the latter, and more in tune with his emphasis (shared with Thatcher) on making individuals responsible for their actions no matter what the circumstances. In office Labour retained – and extended – all the Conservatives' legislation on policing, prisons and public order. Britain had the

highest proportion of its population in prison of any EU country but
the government continued with a major prison-building programme
inherited from the Conservatives.* Nor was there any longer much
official talk about rehabilitation; the predominant if tacit idea was
'warehousing' society's 'troublemakers'. Substantial increases in spending on policing were also promised from 2000 onwards.[76] Some of
Labour's policies on 'law and order' were a response to the Conservatives' decision, in late 1999, to mount a new campaign calling for
tougher action on crime – backed by the tabloid press, constantly
highlighting crime and calling for more punitive measures to deal with
it. But they were also a logical response to the costs of the tendency
towards a 'market society' by a government that saw some of these costs
as inevitable.

Problems of 'third way' politics

By the end of 2000 some of the inherent problems of 'third way' politics
had become clear. 'New Labour' had promised a 'new Britain' based
on a long-term vision of 'left-of-centre' politics pursing what Blair liked
to call a 'radicalism of the centre'. Several things were wanting for this
vision to be realised, however.

For one thing, the focus-group-based electoralism that Blair and his
advisers copied from the Clinton Democrats had no centre, unless it
was themselves. Paying studious attention to the hopes and fears of the
'aspirant' skilled working class, who had deserted 'old' Labour for
Thatcher in the 1980s and been tempted back to 'new' Labour in 1997,
was not the same thing as constructing a robust coalition of social forces
– a 'historic bloc' – on which to pursue a politics of the centre, radical
or otherwise. New Labour's preoccupation with 'presentation' was part
of the problem. Philip Gould, the party's chief adviser on what voters
were thinking and how the party should present itself to them, records
how he and Blair's head of policy, David Miliband, spent 1995 and 1996
trying to find 'a new, election-winning politics based on principle:

---

* It must be admitted that Britain was ultra-liberal in this respect compared with the
USA and Russia. The numbers of prisoners per 100,000 population in 1999 were:
France 89; Italy 89; Germany 95; Scotland 119; England and Wales 125; USA 682;
Russia 729 (Home Office Prison Statistics division, personal communication).

"What is Blair's defining insight?", they asked. "How do we reconcile modernisation and community? Is it possible to conflate both concepts into one unifying idea?"[77] While the 'third way' theme that resulted graced many of Blair's subsequent speeches, material interests could not be so easily reconciled.

Among other things, by the end of 2000 the electorate was getting impatient with New Labour's continued adherence to so much neoliberal dogma, especially privatisation. The Conservatives' chaotic privatisation of the railway system – fragmented into over twenty-five separate regional operating companies, in an ill-conceived attempt to head off the accusation of creating a huge new monopoly like British Telecom – became the ultimate test of Labour's acceptance of market supremacy. As the 1997 election approached the New Labour leadership backed away from previous pledges to re-unify the railway system under government control, and, having won the election, contented themselves with setting up a Strategic Rail Authority (SRA) with the power to award and terminate rail operators' franchises – hoping it would prove capable of imposing order on the balkanised mess of track owners (Railtrack), train operators and their myriad sub-contractors. But in October 2000 a train crash at Hatfield, the third major fatal rail accident in three years, finally precipitated a crisis. Three thousand track inspections were ordered, months of speed limits on more than 200 sections of track were imposed, the national train schedule collapsed and the system descended into seemingly irretrievable confusion. The public scrutiny that followed showed that Railtrack had been told by consultants in 1999 that 20,000 miles of its track were in 'poor' or 'very poor' condition, and further revealed that its capital spending programmes were poorly planned and worse monitored and that safety had been widely compromised. The public was also reminded that since all the train operating companies were really local monopolies, there was no obvious incentive to efficiency. And yet Railtrack continued to pay substantial dividends to its shareholders, thanks to the annual subsidies, totalling nearly £2 billion a year and rising, which it received from the state via the rail operators.[78]

New Labour, however, was trapped. Thanks to buoyant revenues (including a recent windfall of £22 billion from auctioning the radio spectrum) the government could well have afforded to renationalise the railway system substantially. But doing this (as opposed to paying down the public debt, the chosen alternative) would have reopened a large question about New Labour's pro-market credentials. Worse, the government was pursuing two further transport privatisations of its own: the sale of half of the air traffic control agency, National Air Traffic Services (NATS), for £0.5 billion, and the award of thirty-year contracts to private consortia to renovate and maintain London Underground's infrastructure. Both plans had aroused widespread opposition, from air traffic controllers and others concerned with safety, and from Londoners and commuters whose confidence in privatised public transport was understandably at an all-time low.[79] Significantly, the decision to sell off half of NATS had initially flowed directly from the decision to stay within the Conservatives' spending plans for 1997–99, since those plans had notionally included such a sale; i.e. it was very much bound up with New Labour's search for City approval. By 2000, however, when legislative approval was finally required, that constraint had gone; but the Deputy Prime Minister, John Prescott, whose responsibility it was, was determined to prevail and the enabling legislation eventually passed. The government also pressed ahead with its Public–Private Partnership plans for London Underground, in spite of widespread opposition skillfully orchestrated by Ken Livingstone, the new Mayor, who would have to administer them.

Blair had repeatedly proclaimed that there were no sacred cows for New Labour, no ideological 'no-go' policy areas, but this turned out to be wrong: New Labour could not reverse itself on privatisation, however abysmal the consequences. Unsurprisingly, the Conservatives started to position themselves to take advantage of this.[80] After the next election, New Labour would have to shoulder the blame for a public transport disaster that was predicted to persist for ten years.

The problem went deeper than privatisation, however. Having distanced itself from the unions and the working class, and looking instead to the 'nation' as a whole (in the form of the middle-class voters of 'middle England'), New Labour could hope only for customer loyalty, i.e. conditional loyalty based on performance, not the more enduring kind of political loyalty that comes from shared beliefs and solidarity. Ever since taking office the New Labour ministers had presented themselves as the board of management of 'Britain plc', issuing glossy up-beat performance reports (modelled on company reports) at the end of each year in office. Not surprisingly, perhaps, the public expected the share price to go on rising and rising, and was dissatisfied when it didn't.[81]

Worse still, in spite of Labour's assiduous pursuit of business approval, business opinion seemed to remain unimpressed. Chairmen and chief executives of large companies, polled in September 2000, were scornful: only 20 per cent thought Blair had shown 'strong leadership' and 39 per cent declared that he had shown 'no good qualities' at all. As for Labour's Secretary of State for Trade and Industry, Stephen Byers, seen by the media as a model 'Blairite', a majority (57 per cent) of these big businessmen thought his interventions had been 'bad for British business'.[82] What these businessmen would have regarded as a good performance can only be guessed at, but in the new global economy it was evidently going to be hard for any government to earn credit from either voters or business, even for what might really be an objectively creditable performance on the global tightrope. Everyone wanted the much-vaunted benefits of globalisation without paying the price.

Conclusion

Yet the fact that the politics of the new political system created by Thatcher and her successors looked difficult did not mean that the system was fragile. On the contrary, no major political party dissented from it. Even a world-wide depression on the scale of the 1930s could not be expected to shake it. In the 1930s a century of collective struggle and organisation lay behind the popular reaction to the slump that eventually led to the triumph of social democracy and the Keynesian welfare state. By 2000 the collectivist tradition had been decisively defeated and the Labour Party, which had most successfully embodied it, had become a vehicle for a variant of economic neoliberalism with social-democratic overtones. However costly neoliberalism might prove to be, any collective alternative would have to be conceived afresh and striven for over a period that might be shorter than that which the first modern socialist project had required, but would certainly not be brief.

Meantime, in spite of politicians' rhetoric of 'national sovereignty', 'community', 'family values', and the like, not to mention the 'third way', they had in practice given up the idea that the fundamental task of political parties and politicians was to articulate and implement collective values and goals developed through democratic debate and organisation. Politics was now seen as the business of a full-time *professional elite* – a 'caste apart', in Peter Riddell's words[83] – absorbed from quite an early age in the world of power and influence; and its task was seen as consisting essentially of responding to *global market forces* as advantageously as possible and apportioning the resulting gains and losses – while trying to manage *public opinion* (constantly plumbed by polls and interpreted through focus groups) in accordance with the requirements of the *electoral cycle.*

To its practitioners this conception of politics seemed dictated by the 'new reality' of the global economy. But the fact that they were actually able to conduct politics in this way, which would have been unthinkable only twenty-five years earlier, was due to the far-reaching changes that global economic forces had produced in the structure and culture of British society. The workforce was no longer predominantly industrial or male. Class solidarities had been broken down by changes in the structure of work, the rise in disposable incomes, the 'minoritisation' of poverty, the weakening of the trade union movement and the abandonment of the Labour Party's historical role as the educator and defender of the working class. The commercialisation of everyday life made people willing to accept the impact of *market forces* as natural and even inevitable, and to accept that they themselves, rather than the state, were responsible for coping with the consequences. The profession of politics had become a game of a new kind and parties rewrote their constitutions so that their leaders could play it. The state apparatus was reshaped to serve the interests of business, and made more subject to central control and less accountable to voters. From now on society would increasingly be shaped in ways that served the needs of capital accumulation, rather than the other way round. To see what this entails, and how rapidly it transforms people's lives, we must shift the focus down further, to specific *markets* and the forces at work in them – the subject of the following chapters.

4

Markets, commodities and commodification

When we shift our attention to the direct impact of economic globalisation in particular sectors we have to look at the characteristics of the
markets for particular commodities. Real markets are not like the
'frictionless' markets with ghostly auctioneers assumed in economics
textbooks.[1] On the contrary, every real-life market is an elaborate set of
social institutions that allow a particular kind of commodity to be traded
with a degree of confidence and predictability, in spite of imperfect
information and other problems of the kind that neoclassical economics assumes out of existence.[2] So markets are highly political; what is
always at stake for every firm is survival, to be secured by any means,
not 'pure' competition alone. Even a slight acquaintance with the
burgeoning genre of 'corporate biographies' shows that politics have
played at least as large a part as marginal cost and revenue curves in
shaping the current landscape of most markets. To understand the
impact of global economic forces on national politics, therefore, the
operation of power and ideology has to be assessed not only at the level
of politics in general but also in specific markets – in bond markets,
food markets, futures markets, media markets, health care markets.

Real markets and politics

Real markets have three general characteristics that need to be kept in
mind. First, they are systems of rules and regulations, made and
enforced by both state and non-state agencies, including market actors
themselves, through trade associations, informal agreements and cus-
tom, or through market power itself (e.g. price maintenance by 'market

leaders'). The state, however, is key, in the sense that even non-state regulatory agencies operate by the state's explicit or tacit permission. What may be traded (quality and safety), when trading may occur (hours, days, holidays), where (hygiene, noise), by whom (entry qualifications), how much can be charged (price controls), what information must be made available to the state (statistical returns) or the public (product information) – everything is subject to regulation of one kind or another. This is where 'market politics' especially come in. A great deal of the attention of companies can focus on changing or bending these rules, and the scale of resources they can draw on for this purpose can be formidable. We have already noted the scale of SmithKline Beecham's investment in the campaign to secure the commercial patenting of genes in the EU.[3] The three enormous corporations that now dominate the US defence industry – Lockheed Martin, Boeing and Raytheon – spent $50 million on lobbying in 1997 alone, in addition to funding a variety of hawkish 'policy institutes' that promote military spending. Washington is said to be home to 22,000 lobbyists; Brussels, home of the EU Commission, already had 10,000 in 1992.[4] The vast majority of these represent corporations. It is consistent with most economists' attitude to markets that management texts like John Kay's best-seller *Why Firms Succeed* typically make no mention of lobbying.[5]

The second basic point to keep in mind about markets is that they are complex. For one thing they are typically linked to a wide range of other markets (for transport, intermediate inputs, insurance, advertising, etc.). Big corporations can reduce the transaction costs involved by absorbing many of these functions into their own structure of hierarchical control, but this too incurs costs, which is part (though as we have seen, only part) of the reason for the recent reaction in favour of 'outsourcing' and decentralised 'network firms'. Moreover, markets of a sort can also develop *within* firms, as Granovetter pointed out (using the example of Dalton's 1959 study of a large American chemical plant), while some apparently competitive markets are riddled with cooperative relations between buyers and sellers, from interlocking directorates to links with favoured suppliers.[6] These points about the complexity of markets can also be put more generally: markets are always 'embedded', directly or indirectly, in a vast range of other social relations, since the people who deal with each other in markets are also involved in these other relations and influenced by them. The more important these wider social relations are, the more changes in a market will raise larger political issues, as in the case of both television and health care.

The third basic point about capitalist markets is that they are inherently unstable, from the nature of competition itself. Firms are always concerned to enlarge their sales, as the price of not being driven out of business by others. They can try to increase their share of an existing market by competition, both price and non-price (quality, design, service, etc.), or they can try to expand the market (e.g. by advertising), or bypass it by developing new products to displace the existing ones (e.g. compact discs, GM crops). Moreover, market success confers greater power not just within the market but outside it too (the firm disposes of more resources), ultimately giving rise to some global firms that can easily dominate a particular national market (as for example Murdoch's News Corporation dominates the UK national newspaper market, and Berlusconi's Fininvest dominates the Italian television market). Failure to recognise the inherently unstable nature of markets was a basic flaw in the social-democratic concept of the 'mixed economy' – the idea that a public sphere of economic activity could co-exist stably with a private sphere. Firms under pressure to survive constantly look for ways of expanding the market, or displacing it, not just of enlarging their share, whereas firms in the public sector were not placed under any similar imperative; on the contrary, they were mostly forbidden to behave like private firms in this respect.

One strategy for firms under pressure is to expand markets by occupying hitherto non-market spheres, i.e. by the conversion into commodities of services or goods produced at home, or the 'privatisation' of state-provided services. The more acute competition becomes, the more incentive there is to pursue this option. So non-regulated markets are developed alongside the regulated ones: eurodollar markets alongside state-controlled dollar markets, for example, or private radio stations aimed at local consumers but broadcasting from adjacent jurisdictions where domestic bans on them are inoperative. Industry-wide lobbying is mounted to change the law, typically by getting approval for an entering wedge, represented as a special case (such as the 'walk-in' private medical clinics that were established in British train stations) that can then – typically through 'cream-skimming' (in this example, treating only low-cost cases) or using it as a 'loss-leader' – be represented as a 'success story' and serve as an argument for a wider opening-up to market forces. Here the whole range of market politics comes into play, involving both inter-firm cooperation (to get a field opened to private accumulation, or strategic alliances to carve up a market) and competition (to be first into it), and using political influence, cash, market power and social connections to get the rules changed or to have the breaking of them ignored.

Depending on the nature of the non-market spheres in question – what their product or service is, how long they have existed, what scale of investment they represent, how important they are in people's lives, how popular they are, and so on – their conversion into fields of capital accumulation can present some problems, even if the regulatory boundaries that insulate them from the market can be penetrated. At least four conditions must be met. (1) The things they produce, or (more typically) the services they provide, must be capable of being commodified and must actually be commodified, i.e. broken down and 'reconfigured' as discrete units of output that can be produced and packaged in a more or less standardised way. (2) The public must be persuaded to want these products or services as commodities, i.e. to think they have a use-value that justifies the price they have to pay. This requires not only advertising outlays, but also, in the end, that a non-commodified alternative (i.e. one more or less free at the point of use) must cease to be available. (3) The existing labour force of producers or service providers must be redefined and re-motivated to become wage-workers producing commodities to generate a surplus for shareholders. Again, this is likely to mean that it must become impossible for many of them to find work for the same pay on the basis of their former motivation. (4) The change to for-profit provision involves substantial investment and some risk, which private capital typically tries to get the state to absorb. For example, where non-commodity provision of services financed out of state revenues involves, in effect, substantial income transfers (in the health care case, again, transfers from rich to poor, young to old, healthy to sick, etc.), the effective demand for the same services sold as commodities will be much lower. In such cases, companies entering the field will require the fees charged to individuals to be supplemented by substantial payments out of state tax revenues, in the shape of direct subsidies (as with privatised railways in Britain), tax expenditure (tax exemptions) or some other form of payment by the state.

How much difficulty each of these requirements presents will vary from case to case. First, some non-market services like policing and public health are 'public goods', i.e. 'non-rivalrous' and 'non-excludable', and so by definition not commodifiable, because there is no way to charge for people's use of them.[7] Opening such services up to market forces involves getting people to devalue these public goods and place a higher value on what are presented as equivalent non-public goods (e.g. to overlook the shared benefits of policing and to wish only for individually purchased security services), and this may not always be easy. Second, other publicly provided services that are not 'public goods', such as education or health-care services, may still not be easy to commodify: for instance, basic computer training may be broken up into 'modules', each with a price, and studied on interactive computer programs, but it is less certain that the training of consultant neurologists or professors of physics can be. Third, even if non-profit services can be commodified – e.g. by substituting self-instruction computer programs for colleges with teachers – there may be an inadequate demand for them so long as there is a choice. Even if state-run college fees are as high as or higher than the price of the programs, people may well prefer being taught in a college, so it may be necessary also to get fees raised and/or colleges closed. Fourth, it may also be difficult to convert a labour force (e.g. hospital staff) trained, organised and motivated to provide a service seen as a public service into one that will generate surplus value for shareholders. Unionisation, professional values and social values may all prove hard to subordinate to the drive for profits. Fifth, even if there is potential demand, it may not be effective: i.e. the cost of the commodity may be beyond the reach of most individuals, as in the cases of both education and comprehensive health care. The case of health care is particularly interesting, because the per capita cost falls through the widest pooling of risk, putting private provision for limited numbers at an inherent disadvantage – unless 'cream-skimming' is allowed. Sixth, even if the costs are relatively affordable, there is still a risk that people will not be willing to pay enough for what they have been getting free at the point of use.

But firms will always try to overcome these obstacles by devaluing public goods; eroding the boundaries protecting the non-market areas; reducing the resistance of non-market sector workforces and creating alternative, market-based incentive structures for them; getting resources shifted from the non-market to the market sector through tax cuts and getting state spending redirected to private service providers. A comprehensive strategy of this kind calls for inter-firm collaboration in a long-term strategy to influence opinion leaders, public opinion, political parties and the civil service – precisely what we have witnessed in the era of 'deregulation'. Many companies have substantial resources to contribute to all these tasks, although rivalry between them also limits collaboration (producing what City analysts call 'co-opetition').

Gordon White's four-fold typology of the dimensions of market politics is a valuable starting-point for analysing market politics of this kind.[8] First, there is the state's role in markets, through state-owned enterprises, or more generally, through regulation, both in ways specific to particular markets and through the sheer 'saturation' of all aspects of all kinds of production, distribution and exchange by state-determined rules and practices, from industry standards and working conditions to public holidays. Second, there is the power disposed of by associations of firms, vis-à-vis both governments (lobbying, threats of non-cooperation, etc.) and other firms (group pressure). Third, some firms (most obviously monopolists or oligopolists) possess 'structural power' – a classic example being the US military budget, which reflects the campaign fund contributions of the three major US arms manufacturers. Fourth, power relations are involved in the social 'embeddedness' of every market. This cuts both ways, of course: on the one hand, companies benefit from their directors' access to government ministers, and from politicians' desire to see jobs kept in their constituencies; on the other hand, companies are constrained by the dependence of sales on national tastes, by public concerns about health and safety and the environment, and so on.

White's typology is particularly relevant to the question of capturing non-market spheres. The state's rules – both the boundary rules and many others – are placed under pressure, first by business associations and networks – what White calls 'the politics of market organisation' – seeking to influence government policy through their weight in party finances, through the state's dependence on them for information and investment, through substantial spending on lobbying and propaganda, and through the contacts established by senior directors and CEOs of large firms with senior politicians and civil servants. At the level of 'market structure' powerful firms can afford highly qualified strategic planning teams to design ways of enlarging their market share or whole markets, and teams of lawyers to find ways to avoid restrictive rules (including tax liabilities), take advantage of subsidies, and so on. And by permeating popular culture generally (especially through advertising) with individualist and consumption-oriented values, private capital can gradually erode public support for the collective, non-market provision of services.

In the light of this discussion, we can hypothesise that the penetration of non-market spheres by market forces, and their conversion into fields of capital accumulation, will be easier (a) the more difficult the boundary rules are to draw – for instance where technology is rapidly changing the nature of the service involved and the labour processes associated with it, as is clearly true of the media and to only a slightly lesser extent, health care; (b) the stronger the effective (i.e. money-backed) demand is for a commodified product – e.g. a strong demand for subscription channel televised sport programmes as opposed to virtually no demand for self-paid heart transplants; (c) the weaker the public service ethos is, and the less professional values are in conflict with commodified service provision in the field in question (e.g. nurses are more resistant than television crews to working in for-profit organisations); (d) the less 'lumpy' are the resources needed to provide the service in commodified form (e.g. the low cost of establishing a private nursing agency or a radio station compared with the high cost of establishing a private acute hospital or a satellite television service);[9] (e) the less collectivist, and the more individualist and consumerist, is the ambient general culture. But however difficult the penetration of any non-market sphere may appear, there will always be an incentive to try.

The private lives of commodities

Crucial to understanding the social and political consequences of 'marketising' hitherto non-market activities are the transformations commodities undergo as a result of competition. What makes something, or some service, a commodity is that it is produced for sale, which means producing it in such a way as to make it saleable. It has to be given a price that someone is willing to pay, and under capitalism the price must yield a surplus over the cost of production or it will not be produced. When we speak of 'commodification', however, we normally have in mind not the one-off sale of a single item, but the conversion of a whole class of goods or services into commodities and a resulting stream of sales. An interesting example was the proposal – which amazingly enough was briefly experimented with in the 1980s –

to provide oxygen booths in the centre of Mexico City where people could buy a few lungfuls of clean air (an increasingly scarce public good). A more familiar example is the proliferation of restaurants and fast-food outlets (an appropriately industrial term) selling goods and services that used to be produced in a non-market sphere.*

Some commodities, like raw materials, remain largely unchanged over time, although even raw materials undergo some changes as new methods of production modify the outputs of mineral extraction, agriculture and fishing. Most commodities, however, and especially consumer goods and services, change constantly. This process is sometimes obscured by the tendency of textbooks to refer to 'widgets' rather than actual commodities like personal computers or banking services. But once a good or service is being produced under capitalist market conditions, very strong tendencies come into play to change its character; it becomes subject to a 'product cycle', i.e. a process of development, maturity and eventual replacement by a new product. One kind of change is driven by the search for lower production costs, including the redesign of products to make them cheaper to produce. Fewer different parts, cheaper materials, the substitution of machinery for labour and, above all, standardisation of the product make possible economies of scale, on the model of the famous domestic 'white goods' (cookers, refrigerators, washing machines). But the search for ways to enlarge market share, or to break into or out of a given market, also leads to non-price competition, through the introduction of improved model designs (as with cars), or substitute products (computers replacing electric typewriters, DVDs replacing video cassette recorders replacing cinema seat sales), or products fostering and catering to new desires or needs (personal computers and cell phones).

The debate over 'flexible specialisation' is pertinent here. The distinctive social relations found in Japan and some other parts of the world, such as Emilia Romagna in Italy, when combined with computer-based information technology and computer-assisted design, gave rise to the possibility of combining mass production techniques with rela-

---

* Of course eating out and 'fast food' have been a feature of cities immemorially. But when restaurants and food services account for 8 per cent of all employment and 4 per cent of GDP, as they do in the USA today, we are looking at a classic process of commodification with huge social implications, including for family life (nearly half of all spending on food in the USA is spent on eating outside the home).

tively small batch sizes.[10] This allowed goods to be much more closely adapted to particular 'niches' in consumer markets without losing the advantages of mass production. Globalisation meant that these techniques had to be imitated everywhere, especially as rising personal incomes in the OECD countries led to increased competition based on quality and quick adaptation to changing consumer tastes, and 'e-commerce' speeded up the process still further, and allowed it to be extended to new sectors. A dramatic shortening of the product cycle resulted in many fields: in automobiles, for instance, it fell from ten to four years between 1966 and 1978, while the number of combinations of final specifications offered to the purchaser of a Toyota Crown car increased three hundred-fold.[11] On the other hand, a basic standardisation remained. Toyota now offered a choice of four different engines for most of its models, but they were basically the same four engines; it was the capacity to vary the mix without slowing production that was key. The logic of standardisation remained powerful. As Theodore Levitt remarks,

> There is no conceivable way in which flexible factory automation can achieve the scale economies of a modernized plant dedicated to mass production of standardized lines. The new digitalized equipment and process technologies are available to all. Manufacturers with minimal customization and narrow product line breadth will have costs far below those with more customization and wider lines.[12]

We do not need to concern ourselves with the debate about how far these new techniques of management and production define the era of globalisation, as some authors have maintained, rather than just being a significant development that has accompanied it in some sectors and some countries.[13] What matters for our purpose is the fact that both strategies, of customised production aimed at niche markets and mass production aimed at maximising scale economies, may be adopted by different firms in a given market at different times. Standardisation can pay off handsomely for producers at times when they face little competition – such as Sony with its 'first mover' 'killer application' of miniaturised audio technology, the Walkman; on the other hand, producing for relatively narrow market 'niches' may be an attractive option for small producers in highly competitive markets. All that is certain is that whatever strategy is adopted, it will lead to change in the commodity produced, a change accelerated by advertising and marketing. For example, markets for satellite television broadcasts, mobile phones and private insurance policies for specific 'health-care products' were all created by very heavy investments in publicity. Once they existed, these new product markets had profound impacts on the markets for terrestrial broadcasts, fixed-line telephony and public health-care provision. The services in question, including the non-market services with which the commodified services competed, underwent continual change under the pressure of this competition.

Services as commodities

The specific characteristics of every good or service affect what happens when it is made into a commodity. But we are particularly interested in the commodification of non-market goods and services, and almost all of the non-market activities undertaken by states are services; so it is helpful first to consider services as a whole, before looking at television broadcasting and health care – the subjects of chapters 5 and 6.

Some services, like catering, cleaning and garbage collection, seem relatively easy to commodify in as much as they are quite impersonal and can be organised into a clear hierarchy of skill levels, from management through skilled supervision to low-skilled labour; and within limits, productivity can be raised in them through labour-saving capital investments such as garbage trucks and vacuum cleaners, the redesign of 'upstream' products (e.g. the shape of offices and hospital wards, food packaging), or more efficient communications (e.g. mobile phones). Some other services, like dentistry, medical care and higher education, seem at first to present greater difficulties because of the skill levels required. Once commodified, however, these services too are liable to constant transformation under the logic of capitalist competition, as we shall see. All service delivery processes can be rationalised on industrial principles – 'Taylorism' – so that the less skilled parts of the service are performed by less skilled and cheaper workers (dental hygienists, nurse practitioners, graduate student teaching assistants) and machinery is introduced that raises the productivity of skilled workers (remote-controlled surgery) or allows less skilled workers to do what formerly required skilled workers (computer-linked check-out machines in supermarkets, interactive self-instruction training videos).

Telecommunications also allow 'digitisable' personal services to be broken down into separable parts, those that are not inherent in the face-to-face transaction itself being assigned to remote locations where the optimum mix of skills and wage levels is to be found (airline ticketing and accounts in Ireland, medical records in India, etc).[14]

A significant aspect of the change that takes place in services when they are commodified is the transfer of some of the work to the recipient, as with on-line banking and airline ticketing, supermarkets and garbage recycling. This is accomplished by a mixture of incentives, such as greater choice (supermarkets), or appeals to community altruism (recycling), or just taking away the old service (bank branches, doctors' home visits). But all these changes still leave some paid labour, however 'Taylorised', at the core of the commodity; the ideal, from the point of view of capital, is to replace this altogether with sales of a material commodity with which scale economies can be obtained. Then instead of receiving a service, people buy an object: maidservants are replaced by vacuum cleaners and refrigerators, bank clerks by computers, dentistry by fluoride toothpaste, laundry services by paper tissues.

There are undoubtedly some limits to this process, as Baumol and Bowen pointed out in 1966 in their book *Performing Arts: The Economic Dilemma.* Performance arts like live theatre and concerts, they argued, were inherently unsusceptible to productivity increases, and therefore bound to become steadily more expensive relative to other commodities the production of which is subject to constant productivity improvements. In live performances

> the performers' labors themselves constitute the end product which the audience purchases . . . the activities are themselves the consumers' good. Whereas the amount of labor necessary to produce a typical manufactured product has constantly declined since the beginning of the industrial revolution, it requires about as many minutes for Richard II to tell his 'sad stories of the death of kings' as it did on the stage of the Globe Theatre. Human ingenuity has devised ways to reduce the labor necessary to produce an automobile, but no one has yet succeeded in decreasing the human effort expended at a live performance of a 45 minute Schubert quartet much below a total of three man-hours.[15]

The analysis of 'Baumol's cost disease' (as this has perhaps significantly come to be known – why not 'cost theorem'?) was extended by Baumol to other services, including health care, in articles published in 1972 and 1993.[16] While recognising that other factors also influence costs in these sectors, Baumol argued that

> the services that have been infected by the cost disease are precisely those in which the human touch is crucial, and are thus resistant to labor productivity growth ... Some of them entail production processes that are inconsistent with standardization. Before one can undertake to cure a patient or repair a broken piece of machinery it is necessary to determine, case by case, just what is wrong, and then the treatment must be tailored to the individual case. ... A second reason why it has been difficult to reduce the labor content of these services is the fact that in many of them quality is, or is at least believed to be, inescapably correlated with the amount of human labor devoted to their production. Teachers who cut down the time they spend on their classes or who increase class size, doctors who speed up the examination of their patients, or a police force that spends less time on the beat are all held to be shortchanging those whom they serve.[17]

It is interesting to reflect on the assumptions involved in this influential line of thought. In his earlier papers Baumol assumed that these services were irreducibly resistant to productivity increases, although people would go on being prepared to pay for them. A telling example from his 1972 article is the following: after remarking on our reluctance to give up the personal attention of a doctor in favour of some standardised treatment, he says that 'it is not difficult to think of other activities for which standardization is virtually impossible, including such disparate services as painting, the teaching of children with special problems, and the repairing of watches'.[18] But thirty years later house painting has become the 'do-it-yourself' industry *par excellence*, teachers of children with special problems are increasingly available only to children with rich parents or those lucky enough to attend specially resourced schools, while watches have joined the growing number of products that are designed to be thrown away when they go wrong, rather than repaired.* In other words, the logic of commodity produc-

---

* Of course Baumol may have meant painting pictures, not houses, although this would more naturally be conceived of as artisanal production of material goods rather than a service. It is interesting to reflect on how the ability to reproduce paintings has transformed the market for them too, as foreseen by Walter Benjamin in 1936 ('The

tion has worked to transform two of these services into material commodities (paint and paint rollers and throw-away watches) and to
transfer the labour costs (in the case of painting) to the consumer. It
has also made the third (teaching children with special needs) more
and more expensive relative to other expenditures, to the point where
it is increasingly either rationed, or priced, for most people, out of
reach.[19]

What is significant here is not only that so much has changed in the
lifetime of a single generation, but also that so many of capital's
solutions to the problems presented by services are represented in these
examples. Other examples abound in Baumol's work. In his 1972
article, for instance, he considered the relative costs of producing a
haircut and a fountain pen. Assuming that productivity rises at 1 per
cent per annum in haircutting, but at 3 per cent in the manufacture of
fountain pens, he reasoned that a haircut that initially cost the same as
a pen would end up after a century costing over seven times more.[20] In
reality, after less than thirty years fountain pens have disappeared,
except as luxury items for conspicuous consumption, and haircuts cost
from twenty to a hundred times as much as a ball-point. Haircutting
has also been increasingly divided into 'standard' haircuts for the mass
market and 'styling' by hairdressers with higher skills, taking more time
and charging much higher prices, while a market-driven change of
fashion even created a demand for do-it-yourself head-shavers for young
men.

These examples are not recalled in order to criticise Baumol; the
continuing evolution of market forces has vindicated his general analysis, though not his initial liberal optimism about markets and culture.*
Nor is he the only one to have underrated the constant resourcefulness

---

work of art in the age of mechanical reproduction', in *Illuminations*, [Fontana, 1992],
pp. 211–44). Part of the appeal of installation art for artists today has to do with the
fact that it tends to defy reproduction.

* In his early writings Baumol constantly reiterated his belief that the performing arts
would continue to flourish in spite of their ever-rising costs. In his later writings this
optimism gives way to the fear that even such foundations of civilisation as education
and universal medical care will be cut back or abandoned as 'unaffordable', and that
we will find ourselves in an economy 'where wealth accumulates and men decay' –
even though, as he points out, the real cost of even these services is falling (however
slowly) and productivity gains in other sectors make us constantly better able to afford
them ('Health care, education and the cost disease', in Ruth Towse [ed.], *Baumol's
Cost Disease: The Arts and Other Victims* [Edward Elgar, 1997], p. 520).

that capital displays in its efforts to resolve the problems it confronts –
including its ability to wean consumers from services onto consuming
material goods and providing the labour component themselves. Following Daniel Bell, many people have supposed that whatever other
service fields might be subjected to Taylorisation and the substitution
of goods for services, a few – especially education and health care –
could not. Gershuny, however, pointed out in 1978 that there was no
obvious foundation for this belief. In higher education, he noted,
interactive self-teaching was already possible, and with some 'minor'
developments in video and image storage technology it could soon
become general practice once the necessary broadband infrastructure
was in place. And while medicine was not so far advanced, nonetheless,
'if there were no powerful lobbies interested in preventing it, over how
distant a horizon would be the diagnostic and prescribing machine?
Twenty years? . . . Fifty years?'[21] Part of the interest of chapter 6 will be
the extent to which both Taylorisation of the medical workforce and
the substitution of goods for medical services has begun to take place
even in what is still, in Britain, a mainly non-commodified service field.

In a joint article published in 1984, Baumol and his wife Hilda also
considered television, specifically excluding the possibility that the
advent of the mass media might change the situation for the performing arts. In their view, even if transmission and other broadcasting costs
fell (thanks to technical advances), and the audio- or video-taping of
performances enabled them to be disseminated by tape sales or broadcasts to hugely increased audiences, the fact that productivity could not
be much increased in programme production – 'writing, set design and
construction, and performance (acting, playing the music, etc.)' –
meant that programming costs must constantly rise relative to other
costs, so that total costs must eventually increase.[22] Accepting this
analysis, Garnham and his colleagues commented in 1988 that 'unless
fifth generation computers and robots can wholly take over TV production, the incidence of Baumol's disease can only be postponed'.[23]

But is it really so obvious that television is any more immune to the
substitution of goods for services than are medicine or education? Not
only has television equipment – cameras and editing equipment,
especially – become dramatically cheaper, it has also become smaller
and lighter and more versatile and needs fewer scarce skills to operate
– to the point where it is already possible for one person to produce,
direct, film and edit a programme more or less unaided. Moreover,

'virtual sets' are already used instead of real ones, and the replacement of actors by virtual actors ('vactors' or 'synthespians') is imminent. Robotic directors may not yet be with us, but technological advances have helped delay the onset of Baumol's disease, even if the programmes produced sometimes seem to call for robots to watch them.

Jonathan Burston has shown that these processes are already far advanced in the world of 'megamusicals', where TNCs have been formed to mobilise Hollywood-scale investments and Hollywood production techniques to launch musical shows that are then reproduced and staged as franchised clones of the original in half a dozen rich-country cultural centres simultaneously. In these productions visual effects increasingly dwarf the actors' performances, which are in any case specified in immense detail in the franchise contract, rigorously enforced from the TNCs' headquarters in London or New York. The attraction of virtual actors for this kind of commodified theatre is obvious. Burston cites one of the leading developers of 'synthespian' technology as saying, 'You don't have to pay a [virtual] actor. There will be no drug addictions or delays. [Virtual] actors will be on the set every day.'[24] (And, Burston suggests, 'one may also assume that union complications will likewise be a thing of the past.') If live musical audiences can be trained to accept virtual actors, television audiences surely can be too.

We may not be quite there yet, but as with health care, part of the interest of the story of television recounted in chapter 5 lies in how far television already shows the pattern of commodified 'service sectors': i.e. 'industrialising' the labour process to reduce labour costs, substituting capital for labour, substituting material goods for a service and getting consumers to undertake the labour – and, finally, consigning any residue to small 'high-end' markets, or leaving them to (increasingly beleaguered) state provision.

The specificity of commodities: television

We have already begun considering television, so it is convenient to go on and consider its specific characteristics more closely. It is also convenient because, complex as it is, it is perhaps simpler than health care.[25]

Television programmes differ from live performances or original works of art precisely by being reproducible and, hence, natural candidates for production as 'cultural commodities'. As a sub-set of commodified services, cultural commodities have several distinctive features.[26] First, it is clearly very hard to tell in advance whether a cultural commmodity will be successful. In the record industry in the late 1980s 'only one single in nine and one LP in sixteen ma[de] a profit', a situation unchanged in the age of the CD, and most films fail to cover their costs.[27] Successful producers of musical recordings, films and television programmes therefore have to produce 'repertoires' of them, large enough to include sufficient 'hits' to make a profit after paying for the flops. This requires large-scale production. Second, the 'first copy' costs of production – producing the film, television programme, musical recording, etc. – are very high, whereas the marginal costs of both reproduction – making copies of tapes, CDs and videos – and distribution are very low (in the case of television broadcasts, virtually zero). This, too, implies large-scale, vertically-integrated operators, controlling distribution and thus able to spread the initial costs over the largest possible number of sales. Third, some cultural products, including television programmes, have little value – in the same market – as soon as they have been consumed (i.e. watched or heard) once. The resulting need for the great majority of broadcast programmes to be new also places heavy demands on the producers, which only those with large market shares may be able to meet. Each of these features of cultural commodities thus tends to foster monopolies, and the tendency is aggravated by the advantages gained by 'first movers' with successful new technologies, such as BSkyB's subscriber management system and its decryption technology, discussed in chapter 5, which gave it *de facto* control over what seemed, for a time at least, likely to be a crucial 'gateway' in British television.

'Free-to-air' television broadcasts have a further characteristic. Like policing and municipal sanitation they are 'public goods'; my watching a programme doesn't prevent anyone else seeing it, and anyone can tune in. To make any money from free-to-air broadcasts, therefore, a commercial broadcaster needs advertising and sponsorship revenues. The alternative is to be able to exclude viewers (via subscription cable services or encrypted broadcasting) unless they pay a fee to get a bundle of channels ('pay-TV') or individual programmes ('pay-per-view').[28] Both alternatives drive broadcasters towards the largest possible scale of operation. To attract mass advertisers, audience shares generally need to be large (the opportunities presented by 'niche' channels being relatively limited); subscription channels also depend for profitability on large numbers. In both cases this means having attractive channel content, which is scarce. Once again, large-scale operators have an advantage in being best able to afford it. The mammoth mergers of TNCs in the communications and media industries in 1999–2000 reflect this need for market power and economies of scale. The general effect of these features of television as a cultural commodity is that market-based television will tend towards monopoly unless this is offset by technology changes or regulation; which means, in effect, that television markets have an even stronger tendency than most markets to become unable to do what markets are supposed to do, i.e. allocate resources efficiently in response to consumer demand.

This raises the general question of 'market failure'. The expression needs to be approached with caution, since it can refer to at least three different sorts of problem. One is caused by the imperfections (from the point of view of neoclassical economics) in actually existing markets, which prevent them from doing what they are theoretically supposed to do – imperfections that are always present in reality, such as imperfect information (BSkyB's potential monopoly of the national 'EPG' [Electronic Programme Guide] in Britain is a case in point). A second kind of 'market failure' arises from the nature of particular commodities. Television programmes provide an example of this in that they are 'information goods': we can't know the value of a programme until we have seen it, so the demand for valuable programmes can't be indicated by the price mechanism (how many people would have paid in advance to see some programmes that they subsequently judged exceptionally good?). A third kind of 'market failure' refers to the inability of the most perfect market imaginable to achieve goals that are not those of individuals but collective goals. Here markets don't fail on their own terms, they are simply unsuitable for this purpose. Welfare economics treats these unmet goals as 'negative externalities' of markets – i.e. social needs or values that market behaviour doesn't serve, or actively negates. Alternatively, it sometimes postulates a peculiar kind of good that people theoretically want but aren't in practice willing to pay for. These are called 'merit goods' – educational television programmes and physical exercise are two examples; goods of which markets will not produce enough because people won't pay enough for them.[29] These different kinds of market failure can of course co-exist and sometimes reinforce each other.

Many, perhaps most, of what are seen as 'market failures' are of the third kind. In the case of broadcasting they include things like the fact that including a great deal of violence in programming to attract audiences may foster violence, or the tolerance of violence, or make people fear violence. In the same way, competition for ratings and concentration of ownership tend to narrow the diversity of what is broadcast (both subject matter and its treatment); concentration also tends to discourage journalism and current affairs programming critical of corporations or the government; market-driven programming, especially in the age of globalised markets, seldom does a good job of providing educational programmes or representing and developing national culture or fostering an inclusive sense of national identity. More generally, normal market operations can produce perverse results even from the point of view of individual consumers. For instance, if competition between television channels drives up the cost of scarce programme content, while audience fragmentation between more and more 'niche' channels means that costs per programme hour rise, in the end no channel will be offering quality programming. Graham and Davies sum this up as follows: 'If consumers fragment and prove unwilling to pay the higher prices that good programmes will then require ... then broadcasters will not have the incentive to invest in producing such programmes. Conversely, if broadcasters are not providing such programmes, even well informed and far sighted consumers cannot buy them ... Putting it bluntly, we will be "dumbed down". ... '[30]

Other commodity markets present other forms of 'failure', as well as some quite similar to those encountered with this particular 'cultural commodity'. The point is that in each case various social values and goals are disregarded, or actively negated, including some – range of choice among them – that markets are supposed to be best at serving. One more example from the debates about television in Britain makes this point clearly, while also bringing out an important fact about even such an apparently straightforward commodity as television, namely that how it is paid for significantly affects its character. Koboldt, Hogg and Robinson propose a matrix for analysing the relationship between different ways of paying for television and the social values television potentially serves. Seven possible methods of funding are considered: (a) pay-per-view; (b) subscription; (c) rights sales; (d) sponsorship; (e) advertising; (f) licence fee; and (g) grant-in-aid (direct funding by the government). These are then compared in terms of how far each (1) allows viewers to signal their preferences; (2) allows access to all viewers; (3) gives broadcasters a stable income; (4) fulfils social policy objectives; and (5) produces 'merit goods'.[31] The authors conclude that only publicly funded television is likely to serve the last two goals. This is noteworthy, but what is more interesting for present purposes is that the first five different forms of commercial funding really involve *five different markets* for *three different commodities*. Pay-per-view, rights sales and sponsorship are ways of selling *individual programmes*, but to three different kinds of customer. Pay-per-view means sales to individuals in the home country, rights sales are mainly to broadcasters in other countries, and sponsorship means selling programmes to corporations operating in domestic markets. These three different kinds of customer have different preferences – they attach different use-values to the same commodity. Subscription refers to *packages* or *'bundles' of channels*, with more or less specialised contents, sold to individual viewers. Advertising revenue comes from sales to companies selling to consumers in home markets, not of programmes, but of various categories of viewers, or *viewer 'demographics'*, whom the advertisers want to reach and who can be attracted by particular kinds of programming and scheduling.

Whatever approach is used, programme makers will bring professional values to bear to produce the best programmes they can with the resources available, but what kinds of programme are made, to what standards, with what aesthetic, cost, political and other considerations in mind, and when they are scheduled, will depend on the markets – for single programmes, bundles of programmes, or viewer demographics – the programme commissioners are serving. What we can be sure of is only this: if any of the five for-profit methods of payment serves any of the five purposes (1) through (5) above, this is not the primary motivation of any of them.* What drives commercial television, like any other product or service, must be sought in the nature of the specific commodity markets in which it operates. The programmes that result are really by-products of this.

---

* This applies just as much to pay-per-view as to the other methods of payment; otherwise BSkyB would shift entirely to it rather than reserve it for the occasional boxing match for which demand is such that the payments net of administration outweigh the cost of purchasing the exclusive television rights.

The specificity of commodities: health care

Health care, considered as an actual or potential commmodity, or set of commodities, is very different from television, in many ways besides not being primarily 'cultural'. For one thing, whereas watching television is still felt to be a form of discretionary consumption, like going to the cinema, health care is felt by virtually everyone to be a necessity, at least in countries with extensive health-care services; even the very old, who are most dependent on television, share this view. Health care also consumes much more of the national income, about 5.6 per cent in Britain in 1999, perhaps ten times as much as television, and is easily the single largest field of employment, with nearly one million workers, compared with about 50,000 directly employed in broadcasting, film and television combined in 1999. Partly because of its sheer omnipresence, but also because in Britain it is the second largest item of public expenditure (accounting for 14 per cent of the total), health care is always politically sensitive. Because the National Health Service has had a near-monopoly of health care and provides it at one of the lowest costs per capita of any OECD country, health care only became a major focus of attention for economists in Britain with the advent of market-oriented governments in the 1980s.[32] In the USA, by contrast, where 58 per cent of health-care funding is private and most health-care provision has always been profit-driven, the scale of the markets involved – accounting for fifteen per cent of the GDP of the world's largest national economy – has attracted a correspondingly huge specialist economic literature over the past thirty-five years, overwhelmingly concerned with keeping down costs (as opposed to maximising 'health gain').

To a remarkable extent, however, the findings of even this literature are inconclusive, partly because data are lacking, partly because of the cost and technical difficulty of doing research in this field,[33] but also because 'health care' really covers a large range of different commodities and markets. Most text books focus on the market behaviour of patients, doctors and hospitals, and on acute rather than long-term care, but even within these limits there are many complications. Even in the USA most hospitals remain non-profit institutions (either publicly owned or owned by non-profit agencies) and not all doctors are self-employed small businesspeople (some are salaried by non-profit hospitals and a growing minority have become effectively salaried employees of Health Maintenance Organisations or HMOs). The behaviour of hospitals and doctors is also influenced by the movements of many other markets linked to and interacting with the markets for their services, including the markets for laboratory tests, drugs, long-term care, ambulatory care, home care and 'alternative medicine', to name only a few. All this makes it difficult to draw firm conclusions from empirical data gathered on the behaviour of hospitals or doctors alone.*

Moreover, within the private sector there are many different forms of financing, as insurance companies seek ways to control health-care costs in the interests of keeping premiums down and profits up, and these have different effects on the behaviour of doctors, hospitals and patients. Most of the insured population in the US are members of managed care plans, mainly for-profit HMOs, which act as intermediaries between patients and the doctors and hospitals who provide them with health services. Some HMOs employ doctors and own hospitals, but more often they make contracts with independent hospitals and doctors, specifying the services they can provide, offering them financial incentives to limit the costs incurred, and monitoring and vetting their clinical decisions to keep costs down.

The point here, however, is not to sketch even the outlines of the US health-care system, but only to emphasise what a complicated mixture of markets 'health care' can comprise, leading to great difficulty in drawing firm conclusions about cause and effect within them.† Some of the complexity is due to American history; market-based health care would undoubtedly take different forms if introduced elsewhere, to the extent that it did not deliberately follow the American model. But much of it is due to the specific peculiarities of health care when it becomes a commodified service: principally (a) risk, (b) asymmetric information

---

* In 1995 the distribution of total health-care spending in the US was estimated as follows: hospitals 35 per cent, doctors 20 per cent, drugs and nursing homes each 8 per cent, dental care and administration each 5 per cent, home health care 3 per cent, and 'other' 16 per cent (David A. Kindig, *Purchasing Population Health: Paying for Results* [University of Michigan Press, 1997], p. 27, citing K. Levitt et al., 'National health expenditures', *Health Care Financing Review* 18/1, 1996, pp. 175–214). Most administrative costs are clearly not disaggregated in these data.

† I do not mean to imply that television markets are not also linked to many other markets. The scale of health-care markets, however, and the range of services involved, makes this aspect both more salient and harder to comprehend in any overall analysis.

between doctors and patients, and (c) 'principal/agent' problems arising from (b).[34] Under (a), risk, health care is a commodity whose consumption we mostly cannot plan for and which may be catastrophically expensive if we are unlucky enough to fall seriously ill, so rather than find ourselves unable to pay for it we buy insurance to cover the risk. This gives rise to 'moral hazard' (in this case, a hazard for the insurer): once people are insured, doctors and hospitals have no incentive to keep their charges down and may overcharge or provide more health care services than patients need, while patients have no incentive not to demand more than they need. Under (b), asymmetric information, doctors know more than patients about what they need, but are both advisers to patients and suppliers of that care, giving rise to (c), the question of how to ensure that they do not recommend and provide more care than patients need, in order to increase or maintain their incomes. It was to create cost-reducing incentives for all concerned, and to oversee the patient/doctor (principal/agent) relationship, that 'managed care' organisations came into existence in the USA.[35]

Donaldson and Gerard maintain that health care as a commodity is unique in combining risk and uncertainty, asymmetric information between suppliers and consumers, and major 'externality' problems (e.g. those arising from the transmissibility of diseases, among many others).[36] They argue that 'all of these characteristics occurring in one commodity would render market failure so complete as to result in government intervention being the optimal solution for its financing, though not necessarily for its provision';[37] but while this logic has largely governed health-care policy in West European countries, US legislators, faced with intense lobbying and 'public relations' campaigns by the private health-care industry, have consistently rejected it (apart from allowing tax-relief on private health insurance premiums). Yet the facts show quite unambiguously that markets in health care, at least in the USA, do indeed fail by comparison with non-market provision. The richest country in the world spends 15 per cent of its GDP on health care – almost three times as much per capita as Britain, for example – but its mortality and morbidity statistics are close to the OECD average, and some of the most basic ones – infant mortality, for instance – are significantly worse than Britain's.[38]

Some of the reasons are clear enough. First, the transaction costs of the US health-care markets – the costs of advertising competing HMOs, collecting premiums, recording and billing for every item of expenditure on every patient, paying the bills, etc., etc. – are huge; some estimates put them as high as 25 per cent of total health-care costs, compared with an estimated 6 per cent in Britain before the market-oriented changes of the 1990s.[39] Second, about 15 per cent of Americans have no health insurance, for various reasons, chiefly because they are unemployed, or have jobs with no health-care benefits; and the uninsured include a relatively high proportion of people with low incomes, which are strongly associated with poor health.[40] Third, population health is affected negatively by socio-economic factors such as high inequality and poor educational levels[41] – features of life that are being aggravated everywhere by globalisation. Fourth, there is serious duplication of resources in the US health-care markets that 'managed care' has so far failed to reduce significantly; for example, short-term hospital bed occupancy rates were still 57 per cent in 1997, compared with over 80 per cent in the UK.[42] Fifth, there is heavy spending on litigation arising from the for-profit nature of the US system, and there are huge losses from fraud.[43]

But the effects of the 'market failure' that Donaldson and Gerard predict, while less easy to establish conclusively, are also at work, as the proliferation of devices for trying to counteract them attests. There are 'co-payments' (fees) by patients for the (otherwise insurance-covered) services they receive, to discourage 'excessive' use of them (in spite of the apparently complete lack of evidence that Americans are so addicted to medical treatment that they demand more than they need, this is a major theme of cost-containment theory and practice); and there are the 'managed care' organisations that regulate and limit the services their subscribers receive. Both devices work in the sense that they reduce patients' use of medical services, but they do not seem to reduce overall costs, because doctors tend to maintain their earnings by giving more treatments to patients when they do see them. Moreover, although 'managed care' patients go to hospital less, they cost more in other ways: 'PPO enrollees [preferred provider organisations, i.e. insurers offering lower premiums for accepting treatment by designated lower-cost doctors and hospitals] incurred increased expenditures as a result of expanded outpatient use and ineffective utilisation management which swamped the effects of reductions in inpatient use and discounted fees'.[44]

To counter 'moral hazard' (from doctors overbilling or 'overtreating'), HMOs set fixed fees for treatments, or put doctors on salary, and in either case often link their earnings to the financial performance of the HMO, so as to remove any incentive to overtreat. All non-emergency hospital admissions must also be authorised by the HMO, and second opinions must be obtained before surgery is undertaken; further patients' progress in hospital is reviewed by HMO doctors concurrently with the admitting doctors – all of which helps to explain why in one way or another the costs remain high, even though HMO patients tend to get a 'less hospital-intensive style of care' than those in non-market systems. To counter moral hazard from hospitals, HMOs and PPOs have shifted from reimbursing them for the costs of services to patients to paying them in advance on the basis of an analysis of the 'case-mix' that their insured members can be expected to present; and hospitals have to compete for these organisations' business by reducing their prices. But hospitals also respond in a variety of ways to maintain their profitability. One is to reclassify Medicare (government-insured elderly) patients into higher-paying 'DRGs' (Diagnosis-Related Groups), either inadvertently or deliberately ('opportunism'). Other responses include charging more for patients still on conventional reimbursement insurance schemes, 'patient-shifting' to modes of care not included in the pre-payment schemes, 'cream-skimming' (specialising in the less complicated, and so less costly, cases), doing more expensive laboratory tests, and discharging patients earlier – in some cases before they have been 'stabilised'.[45] Some evidence exists on the health effects of some of these responses to 'moral hazard': '. . . introducing cost-sharing does result in reduced utilisation of health care relative to free care at the point of delivery. Further, there is evidence to show that most of this reduction in utilisation is by people in lower-income groups and, more specifically, children. The evidence additionally suggests that it is effective treatments for which demand is reduced as well as trivial or placebo care.'[46] The effects are felt by the elderly too. In one study of Medicare patients with broken hips it was found that

> Although the mean length of hospitalisation fell (from 16.6 to 10.3 days) after the introduction of PPS [Prospective Payments System – fixed-sum advance payments based on diagnosis-related groups], the number of physiotherapy sessions also decreased (from 9.7 to 4.9) and the proportion of patients discharged to nursing home care increased (from 21 per cent to 48 per cent). More revealing about effects on patient well-being is

that, after six months, 39 per cent of patients remained in nursing homes under PPS as opposed to 13 per cent pre-PPS.[47]

Another response by some hospitals, described by Eastaugh, is particularly interesting. They want to be sure that the doctors who admit patients to the hospital and treat them there (and who, being self-employed, bill patients or their insurers for their own services independently) are in tune with their economic strategy.

> In 1991 a few hospitals began to make medical-staff membership decisions [i.e. which doctors had the right to admit patients] on the basis of cost profiles [i.e. what their patients were costing the hospital] and forecast sales quotas as to how much volume the individual would 'harvest'. If the sales-quota concept seems a bit aggressive, more radical approaches may come in the future. At the extreme, some hospitals may one day require that independent contractors (called physicians) pay the hospital a security deposit or rent in order to admit patients (e.g., the way some car mechanics pay their garage). If the physician is cost-effective from the hospital's viewpoint, the deposit or rent is returned to the physician. However, if the 'body mechanic' wastes resources of the firm (the garage or hospital) that he or she controls but does not own, then the professional (mechanic or doctor) must make good the cost overrun . . .[48]

Even without such a further development, these hospitals' approach to appointing medical staff was intended to affect the health care offered in them – who gets admitted, for what conditions, what treatments they receive, how long they stay, and so on. By this point the main conclusion of the previous section comes back to mind – that every commodity is shaped and reshaped by the markets in which it is produced and traded; it becomes not so much a product as a by-product.*

---

* American health economists contemplate this with varying degrees of comfort: Sorkin, for instance, notes that 'HMOs have financial incentives to reduce all but the most necessary care', without commenting on the significance of reducing all necessary care that falls short of being 'the most necessary' (Alan L. Sorkin, *Health Economics: An Introduction*, 3rd edn [Lexington Books, 1992], p. 214. Their position usually is that all health care has opportunity costs and has no absolute claim on resources, and that the market-based nature of the US system is a fact of life that Americans have shown they prefer. Health economists in countries that have not yet surrendered collective provision are more sceptical, although they are apt to seem to hanker for market provision, in spite of its manifold failures, because of the primacy of markets in their theoretical formation.

Two final points need to be made before leaving this brief discussion of the peculiarities of health care as a commodity. One is that it is important not to imagine that professional medical ethics act as a major brake or limitation on the operation of the market forces in commodified health care. They are certainly a factor, as are the laws of fraud; there are things doctors would lose their licence for doing, and others that many of them will not do because of their professional values, and HMOs have to take this into account. But markets are markets. Most HMOs are owned by 'investors', not doctors, and most doctors are self-employed small businessmen and -women with employees, overheads and overdrafts, in competition with other doctors. What ultimately drives the way they practise medicine, like the way producers make commercial television programmes, is the logic of accumulation, rather than maximising the health of their patients, let alone that of the population.

The other point concerns the health-care industry's response to cost inflation. We shall return to this in chapter 6 but it is convenient to note here that Baumol's 'cost disease' seems to have been at most very indirectly the cause of the rise in medical expenditures that sparked the American obsession with making the health-care market more competitive. From the 1960s the chief driver was the tendency of the American market to overproduce doctors, attracted by the famously high incomes of the post-war years. Doctors compensated for their declining market shares by 'intensifying' their treatment of patients (i.e. performing more, or more expensive, procedures), and over the whole period 1960–91 this played a larger part than medical-care cost inflation in raising total health-care expenditure, while down to 1975 doctors' incomes increased barely ahead of general inflation, and then fell behind it.[49] But although the reasons may not be those that Baumol envisaged, the American reaction to cost inflation is particularly interesting in that the market-based US system offers so many opportunities for 'industrial solutions' of the classic type: substitution of cheaper labour for more expensive, substitution of capital for labour in production, substitution of material products for services and the transfer of labour costs to consumers, and the consignment of the highest quality of personal care to a restricted 'high-end' market for rich consumers. How far similar developments are in evidence in the British health-care system as it too is subjected to increased pressure from market forces is, as has already been suggested, an important issue at stake in chapter 6.

*

The aim of this chapter has been to try to build a conceptual bridge between the national and the sectoral levels of analysis, making four main points. First, real markets are deeply political, and national-level politics penetrate, through the ominpresence of the state, into all of them, so that national politics and the state are always targets – especially of constant effort to secure favourable regulatory changes, including getting access to hitherto non-market sectors. Second, there are some key prerequisites for the successful conversion of such sectors into profitable markets: converting goods or services into saleable commodities, creating an effective demand for them, converting the workforce into one oriented to profits, and the underwriting of risk by the state. Third, market competition constantly transforms commodities, and in particular tends to transform services by substituting the sale of material goods for the sale of services and transferring the residual labour to the consumer – a change with far-reaching social implications. Finally, every commodity has particular characteristics that give rise to particular consequences in the course of commodification: in the case of television, a tendency to monopoly, loss of diversity and 'dumbing down'; and in the case of health care, inequality of provision, high costs and corruption.

5

Public service television

President Reagan's Chairman of the Federal Communications Commission, Mark Fowler, famously declared that television is a toaster with pictures, and Michael Green, the Chief Executive of Carlton Television in London, asserted that there is no difference between a television programme and a cigarette lighter.[1] Both men were making it admirably clear that in their opinion television is, at bottom, a commodity. Against this stands a different conception that has seen first radio and then television as a 'public service', serving the polity, not the economy.

In Western Europe, in the early days of broadcasting, the idea that it should be a public service predominated. Broadcasting was too important to be left to the broadcasters; on the other hand it was too important to democracy to be entrusted to whoever happened to hold state power. Out of this tension arose the idea, often very imperfectly realised, of broadcasting serving neither private interests nor the government of the day but the democratic process itself, by combining entertainment with the information, education and debate that people need for effective participation in political life. Indeed one can easily envisage a democratic constitution containing clauses providing for broadcasting understood in this way, in the same way that other clauses provide for elections.[2] But although broadcasting as a public service has been given public funding and varying degrees of autonomy, it has rarely, if ever, been constitutionally protected. It has had to co-exist with broadcasting as an industry operating in a market, and what this chapter shows is how the former idea gives way to the latter once a significant bridgehead in broadcasting is opened up to market forces, and how the product is transformed as commodification proceeds.

Yet the fact that broadcasting can become purely a business, governed by the profit motive alone, doesn't mean that it ceases to be central to the political sphere. The significance of this needs emphasising. Not only is the public dimension of politics transacted largely *through* radio and – even more – television, but the whole of modern life is conditioned and shaped by the fact that we spend so many of our waking hours – on average some twenty-five hours a week in Britain in 1998 – listening to and watching 'flows' of sounds and images that have been carefully constructed to serve the purposes of the broadcaster, whatever they happen to be ('the dark art of scheduling').[3] Loss of programme 'diversity', 'quality' and objectivity, and other well-known deficiencies of broadcasting aimed primarily at making money, are therefore serious problems for politics. Yet speaking of 'deficiencies' doesn't quite do justice to what is at stake, which is that television has come not just to represent, but to *embody* the life of modern society, as Guy Debord said in his famous manifesto of 1967:

> The whole life of those societies in which modern conditions of production prevail presents itself as an immense accumulation of *spectacles*. All that once was directly lived has become mere representation. . . . The spectacle is not a collection of images; rather, it is a special relationship between people that is mediated by images. . . . Understood in its totality, the spectacle is both the outcome and the goal of the dominant mode of production . . .[4]

Or as Jay Blumler has written, 'the modern publicity process [is like] the near-irresistible force of a magnet, obliging those that enter its field to conform to its pull', and shaping not just party politics but the way everyone thinks and lives.[5]

Some people think that the advent of digitised communications means that the era of the *mass* media in broadcasting is closing, to be succeeded by one in which individuals will personalise what they want to watch on their television sets – or their computers or their WAP (Wireless Application Protocol, i.e. internet-linked, video-capable) mobile phones, or some even newer device – and intermingle this with other on-screen activities – communicating with each other, studying for exams, consulting their doctors, playing games, shopping, banking and planning their summer holidays.*

---

* And taking part in politics: 'In the more simplistic formulations of the role of the media democracy is like a political supermarket in which customers wander from counter to counter, assessing the relative attractions of the policies on offer before

But it is not necessary to speculate about what this may mean for public service broadcasting, notwithstanding the large speculative investments being made in 'new media' technologies at the end of the 1990s. At that time listeners and viewers had not shown a marked tendency to give up their viewing habits. Total viewing hours had declined over the previous fifteen years, but only very slightly (from 3.8 hours per day in 1985 to 3.6 in 1998), and the appeal of the established channels remained remarkably constant.[6] Even in the USA, where audience fragmentation and the penetration of new media technologies were most advanced, at the end of the 1990s most people still watched at most half a dozen channels out of the 40 or 100 available to them and the six major television networks still accounted for over 60 per cent of all viewing.[7] In Britain, even in multi-channel homes (i.e. homes with cable or satellite television, offering up to forty channels), the five public-service-regulated terrestrial channels still accounted for almost two-thirds of all viewing at the end of 1999.[8] In short, public-service-regulated television (and radio, though it will not be discussed here) was still a major feature of the media scene in Britain. Nevertheless, public service broadcasting is giving way to market-driven broadcasting. What this chapter seeks to analyse is the logic that is driving this change, and the mechanisms through which it works.

Public service broadcasting in Britain

How public service broadcasting is defined and institutionalised varies from country to country. In Britain, public service television reached its peak in the 1960s and 1970s.[9] The BBC, with two channels (BBC1 and 2), was required to provide free 'programmes of information, education and entertainment'. This mission – covering BBC radio too – was enshrined in its Royal Charter and spelled out in more detail in an 'Agreement' with the Treasury. The BBC provides programmes of comprehensive, authoritative and impartial news coverage, and high-quality programmes in a wide range of genres, on the basis of which

---

taking their well-informed selection to the electoral checkout' (Peter Golding, 'political communication and citizenship: the media and democracy in an inegalitarian social order', in Marjorie Ferguson (ed.), *Public Communication: The New Imperatives* [Sage, 1990], p. 84).

the Treasury gives it the proceeds of the annual licence fee paid by all
television set owners.

Then, beginning in 1955, a number of for-profit Independent Television (ITV) companies were authorised to start broadcasting, with
separate regional franchises but sharing a single channel (Channel 3)
and offering a single national schedule for most of the hours broadcast.
They had the exclusive right to broadcast and sell advertising airtime,
in return for which they paid the government a levy on their profits.
Although the ITV companies were commercial operations and enjoyed
a monopoly, they could not be taken over while they held their
franchises, and were very much part of the public service broadcasting
regime. Their franchises spelled out public service requirements like
those in the BBC's Agreement, but were even more specific about the
kinds and amounts of public service programming they had to transmit,
the impartiality they must show in news and current affairs, and so on.

The BBC's performance was overseen by its government-appointed
Board of Governors and reviewed – loosely and retrospectively – by a
parliamentary select committee.[10] The commercial companies were
closely monitored by an Independent Broadcasting Authority (IBA),
which owned the transmitters and vetted schedules and programmes in
advance to ensure they complied with its rules. The IBA also limited
the amount of advertising that could be shown per hour and per day,
and tried to ensure that advertisers had no influence on programme
content. As a consequence, the public service ethos was strongly inter-
nalised over the years by all the professional broadcasters, including
those in ITV, most of whom had initially been trained in the BBC.

Moreover, up to the early 1990s both the BBC and ITV had buoyant
revenues. The BBC's licence fee income rose as people switched from
black and white to colour television, with its more expensive licence,
and the ITV companies' revenues expanded as advertising increased in
line with economic growth. In this situation the commercial broadcasters were happy to spend large sums on programming; thanks to the
fact that they faced no commercial competition, were not quoted on
the stock market and were protected by the IBA from takeovers during
the life of their franchises, they could meet their public service obligations and still be extremely profitable. Lord Thomson of Scottish
Television indiscreetly remarked that an ITV licence was 'a licence to
print money'.[11]

What is more, with only two mass channels (BBC1 and ITV), a really popular programme on either of them might be watched by more than half the entire adult population. The chance to occupy this unprecedented public space attracted the country's most creative talents: as the veteran producer Tony Garnett recalled thirty years later, 'it was the most exciting place to be. There were just two channels, but the whole nation, it seems, was watching and talking about it the next day.'* Alongside popular entertainment a wide range of serious programmes also flourished: 'investigative' television journalism, single dramas, documentaries on foreign affairs and domestic political, economic and social issues, and critical discussions of government policy, plus fairly rich offerings of programmes for children and programmes on the regions, religion and the arts. The glory days of public service broadcasting can be romanticised but this was when British television, employing less than 40,000 people, provided a unique forum for 'the main formative conversations' of British society and acquired its world-wide reputation for excellence.[12]

After Margaret Thatcher came to power in 1979 the golden age of public service broadcasting came to end, along with the rest of the post-war settlement; a gradually accelerating shift began from broadcasting seen as a public service to broadcasting seen as an 'an industrial area from which profits could be extracted over an extended period'.[13]

The transition to market-driven broadcasting

The transition to broadcasting as an industry has followed a roughly cyclical pattern. Commercial interests anxious to expand into broadcasting have lobbied the leadership of the main political parties and prepared the case for a change. After some delay, often involving a public inquiry, legislation has been passed, embodying at least part of the commercial sector's demands and creating a new set of opportunities and incentives for corporate media interests to exploit – a new 'micro-structure of accumulation' – leading to a process of restructuring

---

* Tony Garnett, lecture presented to a conference at Reading University, 3–5 April 1998. A contemporary from the BBC also recalled that 'this was a time when you (I mean I) could transmit a documentary about a reasonably serious subject – an examination of the true facts behind the legend of Dick Turpin – at 7.30 pm on BBC1 and get an audience of 25m for it' (Nigel Williams, 'You just can't get the quality any more', *Guardian*, 19 August 2000).

Figure 5.1.   Public service television: a chronology

1926	BBC established with a Royal Charter
1955	ITV (Channel 3) begins broadcasting
1964	BBC's second channel (BBC2) begins broadcasting
1980	Broadcasting Act establishes Channel 4, makes ITV companies go public
1982	Channel 4 begins broadcasting as a 'publishing' broadcaster
1983	First cable franchises awarded for subscription television
1986	Peacock Committee reports: BBC required to take quota of 25 per cent of programming from independent producers Financial squeeze on BBC begins
1987	Alasdair Milne dismissed as BBC Director-General
1989	Sky TV begins subscription satellite broadcasts
1990	BSB begins subscription satellite broadcasts Broadcasting Act extends 25 per cent independent production quota to ITV Channel 4 takes over sale of its own advertising Sky–BSB merger gives BSkyB a satellite broadcasting monopoly ITC replaces IBA as commercial TV regulator
1991	New ITV licences auctioned
1992	John Birt becomes BBC Director-General
1993	BBC 'internal market' introduced ('Producer Choice')
1997	Channel 5 begins broadcasting Broadcasting Act relaxes cross-media ownership rules and provides for digital terrestrial TV
1998	Digital broadcasting begins
1999	Davies Panel on BBC financing recommends digital licence fee supplement NTL and Telewest establish cable company duopoly Greg Dyke becomes BBC Director-General
2000	Government rejects digital licence fee supplement Granada and Carlton establish ITV duopoly Dyke outlines new seven-channel BBC TV plan White Paper on Communications proposes a single regulator

from which a new set of pressures for change has arisen, beginning the cycle again.[14] At each stage the corporate interests involved have been better established and their lobbying resources have increased; the climate of resistance left over from the hey-day of public service broadcasting has been weaker; the regulators have been less confident about enforcing the rules; and the interval before the next reform has shortened. The process has been greatly assisted, of course, by the wider changes simultaneously being driven through by successive governments; at each stage the public has been less likely than before to see television as a collective good, and increasingly likely to see it as a commodity to be individually consumed.

After a second channel (BBC2) was awarded to the BBC in 1962, going on air two years later, the advertising industry set its sights on the fourth channel, which was then presumed to be the last available. Channel 4 was finally licensed in 1980, after protracted debates, and started broadcasting in late 1982. By then Mrs Thatcher had been in office for three years, but she had not yet developed a market-oriented policy for broadcasting as a whole, other than to encourage the rapid development of local commercial radio. As a result Channel 4 was not only made subject to new and distinctive public service obligations, particularly to serve minority interests and undertake innovative programming, but was established as a subsidiary of the IBA, not as a privately owned company. Moreover the Broadcasting Act of 1980, which established Channel 4, made the existing ITV companies responsible for selling its advertising, so that their monopoly of airtime sales remained intact; on the other hand it meant that there was now more airtime to sell, which tended to reduce its average price.

But the 1980 Act took a crucial step towards full commodification when it required all the ITV companies to become public companies within eight years of the start of their franchises. This meant that they would become liable to takeover, and far more sensitive to shareholder pressure; making money would no longer be so compatible with meeting their public service obligations (since meeting these obligations typically costs more or attracts fewer viewers, or both). This was dramatically illustrated when Gerry Robinson, a former supermarket chain executive appointed as Chief Executive of Granada Television in 1984 to 'sort out' the company for its shareholders, dismissed its much-admired Director of Programmes, David Plowright, for resisting the programming budget cuts that he was demanding.

This shift in the ITV sector coincided with another significant change, caused by the fact that Channel 4 was to be a 'publishing broadcaster'; it was to commission all its new programming from outside, a 'substantial proportion' from independent producers rather than the existing ITV companies.[15] The government's aim was to create a new, competitive market for independent production companies, in accordance with its strongly-held small business creed. A sharp increase in the number of independent production and facilities companies resulted, set up and staffed mainly by people leaving the BBC and the ITV companies. By 1991 Channel 4 was buying most of its commissioned programmes from a total of 668 (mainly very small) independent companies (the 'indies'); and these in turn depended on a network of small facilities companies and freelance journalists, scriptwriters, cameramen, designers, etc., not to mention actors and presenters, all obliged to hold down their prices in order to survive.[16]

To widen their market the 'indies' quickly formed a pressure group (the Independent Programme Producers Association, or IPPA) to get the government to require both the BBC and the ITV companies to take a significant part of their programming from them as well. The government needed no persuading, and from 1987 required the BBC to take 25 per cent of its non-news and current affairs programming from the newly-formed independent sector. In the next Broadcasting Act, passed in 1990, this requirement was extended to all the terrestrial broadcasting companies as well as the BBC, creating a new market of competing, and mostly very weak and dependent, programme suppliers.

Because the BBC was required to outsource first it took the lead in cutting staff, but the ITV companies, under government pressure and anticipating the 1990 legislation, followed suit. Between 1987 and 1996 the BBC shed about a third of its staff, or 6,000 jobs, of which perhaps 5,000 were in television; in the ten years from 1986 to 1995 the ITV companies shed 44 per cent of their staff, or 7,000 jobs.[17] Despite the drastic scale of the job losses, organised resistance was short-lived, as a result of the Thatcher government's earlier measures to restrict union rights. By the end of the 1990s it was estimated that 60 per cent of all broadcasting employment had been casualised, and while the pay of 'star' presenters and entertainers rose dramatically, real wages in broadcasting had fallen sharply, especially at the bottom of the scale in the independent sector, where new entrants were quite often expected to work for nothing 'to gain experience'.[18]

Meanwhile in 1985 Mrs Thatcher had appointed a committee to report on the financing of the BBC. The composition of the committee (especially the choice of Alan Peacock, a leading neoliberal economist, as chairman) and its remit – to consider the effects of using advertising and sponsorship to fund the BBC – made the government's intentions clear. It was therefore no surprise when the committee reported in 1986 that 'British broadcasting should move towards a sophisticated market system based on consumer sovereignty.'[19] On the other hand the committee recognised that if the BBC were to take advertisements, as Mrs Thatcher wanted – urged on by her business friends, because increasing the time available, and competition between the BBC and ITV, would cut the cost of advertising airtime – there would be a 'ratings war', driving both the BBC and ITV to neglect their public service obligations in favour of maximising viewer numbers. The committee argued that once a wide choice of channels existed, and ways had been developed to charge people for what they watched, the market could be relied on to provide all the things that, in the words of the report, 'some of us' want to watch but are only able to see now because the broadcasters are obliged to show them. (In other words, the committee's conception of public service obligations was that they were really about catering to *minority* tastes for things like educational or current affairs programmes, not about providing critical political information for everybody, and a forum for collective debate.) Until that point was reached, however, the committee recommended that the existing system should continue, but be made more efficient, so as to hasten the advent of the more 'mature' broadcasting market that was needed. The BBC should move from depending on the licence fee to offering a subscription service – i.e. people would have to pay to receive its programmes. Because the need to attract subscribers would also tempt the BBC to maximise audiences at the expense of its public service mandate, a Public Service Broadcasting Council should be established to distribute public funds – not just to the BBC but to any broadcaster – to make public service programmes the Council deemed worthy and broadcast them free of charge.

The political implications of ending the free reception of BBC broadcasts alarmed the government and the idea was rejected, together with the idea of a Public Service Broadcasting Council. Instead it was the committee's recommendations for injecting efficiency into ITV that eventually became the centre-piece of the 1990 Broadcasting Act –

paradoxically, since ITV was outside the committee's remit. The ITV companies had a monopoly of the sale of advertising, which the committee pointed out was against free-market principles. The government agreed with this, and so, as well as being required (as the BBC already was) to outsource 25 per cent of all their new programming, the ITV companies were now to bid for their franchises before they fell due for renewal in 1992. Instead of paying a levy on their profits they would in future pay the Treasury whatever annual sum they had bid to win their franchise.[20] The IBA was also abolished (a separate Radio Authority was created to regulate radio) and replaced by an Independent Television Commission, which would award the television franchises to the highest bidders, subject only to the programming specified in their bids meeting a so-called 'quality threshold'. At the same time, unlike the IBA, the ITC would not itself be a broadcaster. The IBA's transmitters were privatised, and while the ITC took over the IBA's responsibility for regulating ITV programmes it would do so only retroactively rather than approving them in advance as the IBA had done. The ITC could impose fines and in an extreme case take away the licence – although this was really a power too strong to be used against a major ITV licensee, as everyone concerned realised.

In the short run the Peacock Report had two main effects. Since the committee had rejected the idea of making the BBC depend on advertising, and the government had rejected the idea of making it depend on subscriptions, the government instead initiated a campaign of public and private pressure to make the BBC cut its costs and conform to the government's values. The BBC was put under an explicit financial 'squeeze': the licence fee was set to rise below the rate of inflation and over the years 1986–91 real licence fee income fell by almost 1 per cent a year.[21] The Board of Governors was also made into an instrument of government pressure, by filling it with Conservative businessmen and encouraging them to assume a much more direct role in management. Political programmes unwelcome to the Conservatives were attacked and in some cases withdrawn by the Governors. In January 1987 Thatcher's choice as Chairman, Marmaduke Hussey, unceremoniously dismissed the Director-General, Alasdair Milne. Milne's successors were naturally more alert to the changed political situation and set about cost-cutting and seeking commercial revenue from publications, videos and programme sales abroad. In spite of this, when the licence fee level had to be set again in 1991, the government continued the squeeze.[22]

In that year the Governors also appointed John Birt as Director-General. Birt, a former ITV programme director, took up his post in January 1993 and set about reorganising the corporation as an 'internal market', similar to the one that was then being implemented in the National Health Service by the Conservative government of John Major, as described in chapter 6. Called 'Producer Choice', the BBC plan involved dividing the corporation into some 480 separate accounting units, each of which was required to pay for itself by charging the others for its services in competition with outside sources of supply, which producers were free to choose if they thought they were better value for money.[23] For the rest of the 1990s saving money replaced creativity as the corporation's watchword.

As for the ITV companies, having to bid against newcomers when the time came to renew their licences made them concentrate much more single-mindedly on cutting costs and improving their ratings. Moreover, there were several new competitive threats on the horizon. One was the development of cable services offering subscribers a variety of channels for films, sports, music, entertainment and a range of special-interest programming. Throughout the 1980s this progressed very slowly, essentially because subscribers in the first areas to be passed by cable did not find the channels offered them very interesting. In the early 1990s, however, the rules were changed to allow non-Europeans – i.e. Americans – to own cable franchises, and to offer telephone services as well; by then, too, more and better channels were on offer. Cable subscriptions began to take off and started offering serious competition for viewers.[24]

Successive projects were also put in hand during the 1980s to inaugurate direct broadcasting by satellite (DBS). At first these failed, essentially because the signals from an affordable medium-powered satellite were thought to require a large, expensive and unsightly reception 'dish', and because the government imposed a costly 'buy British' policy on the consortium set up to pioneer DBS.[25] Eventually this requirement was abandoned and the first licence for three DBS channels was awarded in late 1986 to a company called British Satellite Broadcasting (BSB), which ordered two satellites from the US Hughes corporation. The proliferation of broadcast channels envisaged by the Peacock Report was getting under way.

But before BSB could begin broadcasting it had to overcome serious technical problems, particularly with its special 'squarial' receivers, and to get enough of them into the shops at an affordable price.[26] The launch was repeatedly postponed; BSB's five channels finally went on air only in April 1990. The delay was fateful because it gave Rupert Murdoch over a year's head start when in December 1988 he launched his Sky service with four channels, aimed at British viewers but using the Luxemburg-owned Astra satellite, which meant it did not require an ITC licence. Moreover, although the Astra satellite was only medium-powered, the latest technical advances meant that the conventional round 'dish' needed to pick up its signals was now much smaller and much cheaper than previously envisaged. So by the time BSB began broadcasting, Sky had a huge 'first mover' advantage. Although Murdoch's corporate empire came close to foundering in the competition that ensued, BSB had been launched on the assumption that it would have a satellite broadcasting monopoly; instead it was losing several million pounds a week and soon faced collapse. It therefore agreed to a merger – in effect a takeover by Sky – in November 1990, after only nine months of operation.[27] Now the combined company, BSkyB, had a monopoly, and by 1994 had nearly 3 million subscribers and had turned in its first annual profit of £94 million.[28] It was also supplying most of the programming that was carried by the cable companies, thanks to having made exclusive long-term contracts with (mainly US) 'content' suppliers. The terms on which it allowed the cable companies to carry this programming were onerous, but the channels were at least popular enough. By 1998 over half of all British homes were passed by cable and the 'penetration rate' (i.e. the proportion of those passed that subscribed to a cable service) was rising steadily, thanks also to the growing attractions of cheaper phone and internet-access services. This in itself did not worry BSkyB; it just meant that more subscribers would be receiving Sky channels via cable than by satellite. BSkyB would still get a large share of the revenue.

While the profits of BSkyB grew dramatically its revenues came overwhelmingly from subscriptions; as late as 1998 advertising accounted for only 14 per cent of its income. Nonetheless the combined share of total net television advertising revenues taken by satellite and cable combined had risen from 6 per cent in 1994 to 13 per cent in 1998.[29] Meantime the 1990 Broadcasting Act had also removed the ITV companies' right to sell advertising for Channel 4, and by 1998 Channel 4 was earning 18 per cent of total net television advertising revenues.[30] On top of this, a fifth terrestrial channel had been allocated to a private company, Channel 5. Channel 5 started broadcasting in 1997 and by the end of the decade had nearly 5 per cent of all viewing and 5 per cent of net advertising revenues.[31] Competition was intensifying.

Faced with all these new competitors, not to mention the unknown potential of the internet and other applications of digitisation, the ITV companies looked to their defences. Some protection against takeover by foreign predators was given by the Broadcasting Acts, which excluded non-European ownership, but European companies like Havas and Bertelsmann were amply strong enough to pose a threat.[32] Consequently the ITV companies wanted to grow, and pressed the government for a relaxation of the anti-monopoly rules that prevented a company from owning more than one television franchise and barred the 'cross-media' ownership of newspapers, television and radio. The first of these rules was relaxed in 1993 and a wave of takeovers quickly reduced the number of major ITV companies to three, owning all but five of the UK's sixteen regional licences between them: Granada, United News and Media, and Carlton.[33] The cross-media ownership rule was relaxed in the 1996 Broadcasting Act, which permitted national newspaper owners to own up to 20 per cent of a television franchise provided their paper had no more than 20 per cent of the total national newspaper market.[34]

The next phase in the cycle of re-regulation that we have been retracing came with the appointment in 1998, by the new Labour government, of a 'Review Panel on the Future Funding of the BBC' chaired by Gavyn Davies, a senior City economist and long-time Labour Party adviser. The Panel's main task was to recommend how the BBC should be funded until 2006, when its Charter was due to be renewed in what would clearly be a very different broadcasting environment. The immediate issue was how much money the BBC needed to enter the digital era, and how it should be provided. The Panel recommended a transitional 'digital supplement' payable by all owners of digital receivers from 2000 to 2006, or alternatively an increase in the normal licence fee, in either case allowing the BBC's real income to rise roughly in line with the growth of GDP, which it forecast at an average annual rate of 2.5 per cent.[35] In return, the BBC's spending should be supervised by outside accountants and the National Audit Office, and the corporation should privatise both its Resources (production facilities) division and its commercial arm, BBC Worldwide.

The entire commercial television sector – the ITV companies, BskyB,

Channels 4 and 5 and the cable companies – united in opposition to the digital supplement, on the grounds that it would delay the uptake of digital receivers and damage their investments in digital broadcasting. They were also, though not openly, opposed to any significant increase in the BBC's income. After considerable delay, in early 2000 the government predictably took the line of least resistance, accepting the recommendations on financial supervision, rejecting those on privatisation, rejecting the digital supplement and setting the licence fee increase at 1 per cent above the general price index, i.e. at less than half as much as the Panel had recommended – and a small fraction of what the BBC had asked for. The BBC was told to find any additional funding from further savings. The financial squeeze was to continue.

By now the broadcasting market was becoming relatively densely occupied, even without the addition of newcomers attracted by the potential of new applications of digital technology. Digitisation was going to cost all the existing broadcasters, and the viewing public, a lot of money. As far as conventional broadcasting was concerned, while there were some advantages to viewers, in the form of better picture and sound quality, these were not comparable to the gain in quality that had come with the shift from black and white to colour. As for interactivity in broadcasting, its attractions remained problematic (early experiments with 'near video on demand', for instance, proved unsuccessful everywhere they were tried). The chief financial gainers from the switch to digital broadcasting would be the government, which would be able to sell to other users the radio spectrum that the switchover would release (valued at £8 billion in 1999, but probably worth a great deal more in light of the £22 billion raised in 2000 by the auction of spectrum for third-generation cellphones); and so a compulsory close-down of all analogue broadcasting was envisaged for some time between 2006 and 2010. The 1996 Broadcasting Act had provisionally regulated the use of spectrum for terrestrial digital services, allocating frequencies to the BBC free of charge and selling others to consortia of commercial users. By the end of 1999 all the terrestrial broadcasters were offering their existing channels via digital as well as analogue transmissions, while BSkyB and a few cable companies were transmitting digitally a mixture of their existing channels and new interactive ones. A complex structure of competition (or 'co-opetition') was developing as all broadcasters tried to position themselves to survive in the uncertain new media arena.

Table 5.1.   UK television in 2000

	BBC 1	BBC 2	ITV	C4/S4C	C5	Cable	BSkyB
Estimated workforce	10,000	8,000	1,000	250	4,000[a]	4,000
Subscribers (m.)[b]						5.32	4.95
Viewing share (%)[c]	26.5	10.4	29.7	9.8	5.0	17.6	

C4 = Channel 4; S4C = Welsh Channel 4; C5 = Channel 5
[a] Cable companies plus all non-terrestrial channels other than Sky
[b] *Source*: Company websites, November 2000
[c] BARB data, October 2000

The television market, 1999–2000

We can sum up the broadcasting market and its chief players at the turn of the century as follows.

The BBC

The BBC with its two channels had about 37 per cent of all viewing, compared with ITV's 30 per cent (see table 5.1), and a total net income of £2,090 million – of which some three-quarters was available for television – which no future government was likely to increase significantly. It was obliged to compete across the board, offering longer broadcasting hours and broadcasting on all delivery 'platforms' (terrestrial and satellite, analogue and digital, and the internet), in order to keep its visibility and its share of total viewing as high as possible; otherwise, everyone knew, the compulsory licence fee would become increasingly hard to defend. It had the big advantage of having two terrestrial channels, so that it did not face the task of having to satisfy 'high' and 'low' tastes on a single channel, as ITV did; and it could promote its own programmes, and its new digital and internet services, on both of them.[36] Moreover in spite of downsizing, and the demoralisation and inefficiencies Producer Choice had caused within the corporation, it remained far the biggest broadcasting employer, with large resources of talent – including strategic business talent. The popularity of its programmes remained high in spite of constant press attacks on the organisation itself.

On the other hand it was facing unprecedented competition, in an increasingly unsympathetic ideological climate. Greg Dyke, the new Director-General, summed it up in his 2000 MacTaggart lecture: 'Our competitors today are bigger, richer and more ruthless than at any time in the BBC's history. They are increasingly part of a global media industry which has access to vast capital funds. This is competition on a scale the BBC has never seen before.'[37] And even if the corporation had not been starved of funding, its public service remit would have prevented it from maintaining its ratings by devoting ever-larger sums to sports and film (or soft-porn) programming in competition with the largely unregulated BSkyB and cable companies, and the less severely regulated ITV companies. But the BBC's most acute long-run disadvantage was that it was financed by the compulsory licence fee – in effect a regressive tax that the BBC's competitors used every opportunity to highlight and criticise. As the spread of pay-TV channels became commonplace, public willingness to pay the licence fee was undoubtedly declining and politicians were more and more resistant to increasing it.[38]

The ITV companies (Channel 3)

In 1998 – when their national audience share was still over 32 per cent – the ITV companies had total net revenues of £1.8 billion (plus sponsorship income of some £40–50 million). Under the 1990 Broadcasting Act they co-owned the ITV Network Centre, which effectively ran a single national commercial channel (Channel 3) with modest regional variations. But during the 1990s, as competition from Channels 4 and 5 and cable and satellite intensified, the ITV companies' advertising revenues stagnated; advertisers complained about both the small size and the demographic mix of ITV audiences (not enough younger, upper-income viewers), and shareholders complained about the level of profits.[39] The Network Centre pledged to raise ITV's peak-time audience share to 38 per cent in 1998, 39 per cent in 1999 and 40 per cent in 2000;[40] and although ITV's overall ratings continued to decline, this 'flagship' target was only narrowly missed in 1999, at 38.8 per cent, thanks to some ruthlessly 'down-market' evening scheduling.[41]

In this situation the ITV companies needed other sources of strength. Since 1994 they had consolidated as far as the rules allowed, but in November 1999 Carlton and United News and Media proposed to merge, anticipating a further change in the rules that was widely expected in a new Broadcasting Act to be passed in 2001.[42] After a complex contest, however, United News and Media was forced to give way to the more powerful Granada, and a further relaxation of the ownership rules was expected to lead to the eventual emergence of a single ITV company in 2002 or soon after, with the lion's share of terrestrial television advertising revenues. Such a company would be able to promote its subscription digital services nationally on Channel 3 and drive a harder bargain with advertisers. Its market power would be roughly equal to the BBC's. Its relations with the political parties would be strong, through social relations and financial contributions. Its associational power – its ability to exercise political leadership in the commercial sector – would also be considerable, and its populist orientation, essential to its advertising income, would give it popular support.

The ITV companies' main target continued to be the BBC. They opposed a digital supplement being added to the licence fee, as recommended by the Davies Panel, but they did not want to see the BBC forced to take advertising, as this would cut into their own revenues. To the extent that they really wanted the BBC to survive at all as a mainstream broadcaster they wanted to see it steered away from competing with them for ratings (i.e. shares of total viewing hours) and told to measure its success in terms of its 'reach' instead (i.e. the proportion of the potential audience watching a BBC programme at some point during each week):* in the words of Richard Eyre, the Chief Executive of the ITV Network Centre, 'The appropriate mix of programmes will flow from the BBC if it is tasked quite simply to achieve the maximum possible weekly reach.'[43] The implication was that the

---

* '**Audience share** is simply the proportion of total viewing or listening accounted for by a particular television channel or radio station. The BBC's share of adult viewing and listening in 1998 was 42%. **Audience reach** measures the proportion of the potential audience who have spent some (non-negligible amount of) time viewing or listening to a particular service during a given period. In 1998 the BBC achieved a weekly reach of 93% of adults, this being driven mainly by TV viewing which in itself had 92% reach' (*The Future Funding of the BBC* [the Davies Report] [Department for Culture, Media and Sport, 1999], p. 43).

BBC should concentrate on doing only, or at least mainly, what commercial broadcasters found unprofitable. If that meant that people stopped being willing to pay the licence fee, few commercial broadcasters would be surprised or upset.

Channel 4

By the end of 2000 Channel 4 had nearly 10 per cent of total viewing, while net advertising revenue for the last published year, 1998, was £537 million. Its public service mandate required it particularly to cater to minorities, but also to undertake innovative programming. Its audiences were small but relatively up-market, which attracted advertisers of expensive goods, financial services, and so on; and as a publicly-owned company it did not have to pay dividends to shareholders. Its healthy finances made it liable to be privatised by a cash-hungry government – in 2000 the Treasury was said to be pressing for it, while the Department for Culture, Media and Sport resisted.[44] Meantime it was a significant but not a major market player, and was under no other threat. Its chief market significance was its key role in sustaining the independent production sector. Unlike the BBC and ITV, Channel 4 did not usually ask its programme suppliers, the 'indies', to contribute financing for the programmes it commissioned; for the smaller independent producers this kind of contract was crucial. In return, however, Channel 4 acquired all the secondary rights to the programmes – overseas broadcast rights, format sales, and so on. By contrast the ITV Network Centre was only allowed to buy the rights to two airings of a programme, leaving the rights to subsequent sales in the hands of the producer. This meant it paid less. Consequently independent producers for ITV, like most of those producing for the BBC, usually needed to find some of the financing themselves. The number of independents working for Channel 4 was therefore much larger – 465 in 1998, compared with between thirty and sixty working for all the other broadcasters combined.[45]

The independent production companies

In 2000 579 independent production companies were members of PACT (the Producers Alliance for Cinema and Television, the successor to the IPPA), which estimated its members' total income from British television broadcasters in 1999 at £792 million.[46] Roughly two-thirds of these companies were 'small', defined in a 1995 survey as having an annual turnover less than £0.5 million and a core staff of two.[47] Although the proliferation of channels meant that the market for programme hours had expanded rapidly, the new broadcasters were looking for very low-cost material. In 1999 two-fifths of the estimated total of nearly 10,500 programme hours produced for broadcasters by PACT members were for cable and satellite, but earned an average of only £12,000 per hour – compared with an average of £114,500 per hour paid by the terrestrial broadcasters.[48] A few larger producers, including those who had joined some of the ITV companies in their 1991 licence bids, had steady work and significant earnings from long-run deals with particular licence-holders, but all the rest had to take more or less whatever terms they were offered.[49] Most of the sector was really an informal labour pool. Its total size was very hard to determine, but at an estimated 5,000 people in the mid-1990s it accounted for perhaps a fifth of all those working for television at that time.[50] It included people involved in all aspects of programme production, acting sometimes as contractors with broad-casters and sometimes as freelance employees working for others. The low overheads involved, and the employment of untrained, often vol-unteer, labour on a project-by-project basis, permitted so-called 'life-style' independents – i.e. people who liked the life even if they lived precariously and made little money – to survive; and their existence forced in-house producers in the BBC and ITV companies to cut costs and break union power in order to compete with them – exactly as Mrs Thatcher had hoped. In the 1990s PACT had less political leverage than it had under Thatcher, now that it was no longer needed as a stick to beat the BBC and the unions with, since both had been brought to heel. But it continued to press for new regulations to raise the 25 per cent quota and give its members greater power vis-à-vis the BBC and the commercial broadcasters. It sought to overcome its members' acute market weakness by calling for state intervention to, in effect, divert fresh revenue streams in its members' direction.[51]

Channel 5

The last available space on the spectrum for a terrestrial analogue broadcaster was awarded in 1996 to Channel 5, a new company partly owned by the ITV company United News and Media. A major reason for its establishment was that advertisers demanded an alternative to the ITV monopoly.[52] It also expanded the market for the 'indies' since it was a publisher-broadcaster like Channel 4, not a production company. Its public service obligations were also lighter than those of the ITV companies, and were at first leniently enforced, enabling it to rely heavily on films, light entertainment and sport; Dawn Airey, Channel 5's programme director and later its Chief Executive, agreed it was about 'films, fucking and football'.[53] Although Channel 5 started very modestly in 1997, after three years it was already prospering financially. By the end of 1999 it had a programming budget of £110 million and advertising revenues of £128 million – more than double the previous year; and a year later it announced an increase in its programming budget to £180 million, signalling a move away from its initial reliance on imports and soft porn – i.e. a move to more direct competition with ITV. By comparison, the ITV Network Centre had a programming budget of about £600 million and advertising revenues of £1.8 billion, but its overall audience share was declining and its advertising revenues were static.[54] Tunstall's comment is apt:

> Channel Five, in the more competitive late 1990s, was given fewer 'public service' obligations than any other conventional British channel, including ITV. It was therefore certain – despite predictable lamentations from the ITC regulator – to draw ITV into a more aggressive defence of its leading audience share and also to draw Channel Four into a more aggressive defence of its 10 plus per cent audience share.[55]

Cable

By 1998 half of all homes in Britain had access to cable services, and one in three of these – a sixth of all households – subscribed to them, for television channels and/or telephone and internet services. A total of £8 billion had been spent on laying cables, and an estimated £4 billion more was needed to complete the programme. The Broadcasting Acts set no limits to concentration and by the end of 1999 a dramatic process of takeovers had led to all but six of the country's 136 operational franchises being owned by just two companies, NTL and Telewest, both of them American. Neither were significant players in programme production; both were paying high fees to BSkyB to be able to carry the most popular channels, for which Sky had acquired the rights until early in the next decade; both were losing money.[56] But the attractions of cheaper telephone services, and the ITC's 1998 decision to limit 'bundling' (whereby channel suppliers like BSkyB made subscribers take an expensive bundle of channels, including some they did not want, to get those they did want), were beginning to improve the 'penetration' rate. The companies were looking to make their money from three sources: telephone and internet connections, demand for which was expanding faster than they had expected; interactive television programmes and services, taking advantage of the hundreds of channels that broadband cable or ADSL (assymmetrical digital subscriber line) technology could provide; and, ultimately, the new markets for television that would be opened up if the BBC were forced out of its leading position in mainstream broadcasting. They joined the commercial alliance opposed to the BBC and laid plans for corporate mergers with 'content' providers like Flextech (another US company, which supplied channels for pay-television).

The American-owned cable companies were not prominent on the public stage, or close to leading politicians, as to some extent all the terrestrial broadcasters were, and especially BSkyB's top executives. They still lacked significant market power, and were not yet 'embedded' in British society. But they had the potential advantage of offering consumers greater interactivity than did the satellite channels, their parent companies had deep pockets, and they intended to get a return on their investment. In the next phase of development they were likely to represent a significant new American presence in the British broadcasting market.

Satellite: BSkyB

One of the many interesting things about BSkyB is that the households that subscribed to it spent less time watching Sky channels (10.8 per cent of their viewing) than watching BBC1 (19.8 per cent), not to mention ITV (37.2 per cent); and most of that 10.8 per cent was accounted for by just four channels – Sky1 (entertainment) and Sky Sports 1, 2 and 3.[57] Sky was obliged to carry all the terrestrial broadcasters' channels, and these remained the main ones people watched; what people were getting for their subscriptions was mainly access to film-only services and live sports programmes that the public service broadcasters were not allowed or could no longer afford to provide. By the end of 1998 the number of dish owners seemed to have reached a – perhaps temporary – plateau, at a little over four million, and the 'churn' of subscribers (new subscribers offset by de-subscribers) had increased. But Sky's success in developing long-term contracts with the suppliers of channels meant that it could license cable companies to carry them and still be very profitable: its profit in 1998 was £271 million on revenues of £1.4 billion. Murdoch's aim from 1997 onwards was to put 'Sky in every home', with new 'mainstream' programming, and become a serious rival to ITV in the digital era while remaining a pay-TV service.[58] In 1999 BSkyB was devoting new resources to 'in-house' programme production, as well as commissioning more from the independent sector. It planned to switch its satellite services entirely to digital in 2002.

BSkyB had three big competitive advantages. First, it was substantially unregulated by the ITC, and so had no public service obligations other than to carry the terrestrial broadcasters' channels. Second, thanks to the acumen and ruthlessness of Murdoch and Sam Chisholm, BSkyB's first chief executive, the company was the 'first mover' not just in satellite broadcasting but also in encryption technology (the set-top box), subscription management and pricing, and the acquisition and packaging of content – notably sports and films, but also a string of other (mainly American) channels. Third, its principal shareholder, Murdoch, also owned newspapers with a third of the British market. Murdoch's *Sun* and *News of the World*, and the *Times* and *Sunday Times*, could be used to support Sky and attack its opponents. They constantly heaped obloquy on the BBC, easing up only when the BBC agreed to collaborate with BSkyB (e.g. by joining it in its successful bid for the exclusive rights to live Premier League football matches in 1992).[59] Murdoch's press power also weighed heavily with politicians. Tony Blair's decision to court him before the 1997 election, in order to avert the vicious attacks that the *Sun* had made on previous Labour leaders, testified to the power he was thought to wield. The desire to keep Murdoch's papers 'on-side' for the next election, expected in 2001, seemed likely to have been a factor in a number of the government's policy decisions in 1999–2000, including the rejection of the Davies Report's recommendation of a digital supplement to the BBC's licence fee, which Murdoch bitterly opposed.*

---

* The fraught concordat between Murdoch and Blair was the subject of constant

The new media

The digitisation of communications is a good example of competition driving technological innovation, rather than the other way round, as so much rhetoric implies. Like many other innovations, the way digitisation finally affects broadcasting will depend on how competing corporate interests seize upon it and try to take advantage of it. The way electricity eventually came to be produced and distributed in the USA is an instructive earlier example. Nothing in the technology of electricity generation or distribution decreed that industrial and commercial users should not generate their own. That they all ended up buying it from a few major generating companies was the result of intense market politics. Granovetter and McGuire conclude: '. . . it is up for grabs, early on, exactly which product will fall inside and outside an industry's boundaries, and even what will be defined as a product. To understand the outcome, one must analyse socio-economic and institutional links among self-designated competitors. . . .'[60]

This applies very well to what has been happening in digital communications. The new technology can be used to break established monopolies as well as just to cut costs in existing organisations. Both motives were very much in evidence in broadcasting at the end of the 1990s. 'Multi-media' (digitised sound, images, moving pictures, graphics, etc., used interchangeably) and 'multi-skilling' were prime means of cutting labour costs, eliminating old functions and reducing the labour time involved in performing those that remained; any company or organisation that failed to adopt the new technologies would soon find itself uncompetitive. But even more radical changes were implicit in the digital recording and transmission of data, and the associated developments of new 'platforms' to carry them: communications satellites, the internet, broadband cable, and clever new ways to use old-fashioned local telephone lines (ADSL). A variety of new delivery systems for broadcast content had become practicable; the limit to the

---

media comment. Murdoch did not always get his way; for instance, in 1999–2000 he tried unsuccessfully to get Blair to make the BBC abandon its free round-the-clock television news service, News 24, which cable companies were choosing to carry in preference to Sky News. But the Prime Minister frequently acknowledged Murdoch's power, for instance by going out of his way to reply in person to a wide-ranging attack on him and his government published in a *Sun* editorial on 1 May 2000, the third anniversary of the 1997 election.

number of broadcast channels was no longer spectrum scarcity but only the number of ways broadcasters could devise to make a channel profitable. Reception and recording devices were another potential field for profitable innovation. Two-way or interactive communication could also be extended from the telephone to the television set, and anything a television set could do, the personal computer and a WAP mobile phone with a video screen should be able to do too.

All this created a seemingly golden opportunity for new players to break into – or break up – what had been 'broadcasting', as defined by the previous round of technological innovation – i.e. broadcast colour TV, dominated by a handful of more or less closely regulated monopolists or oligopolists. Even though past experience shows that the end result of the introduction of such disturbing innovations is almost always the restoration of monopoly, 'first movers' in the new media might well hope to be among the winners, and the threat to established industry players was real enough.[61]

The BBC, for example, was vulnerable not just because of the new channels and audience fragmentation, intensified competition for ratings, constant private sector rubbishing of the public service ideal and the general climate of commercialisation. There were also the heavy costs of occupying the new 'platforms' that digitisation and cable and satellite technologies had made available, costs that had to be met at a time when licence fee revenue was stagnating and governments were unwilling to increase it.*

The ITV companies, for their part, were increasingly vulnerable to inroads on their advertising revenues by cable and satellite pay-TV broadcasters as their subscription bases expanded, as well as by Channels 4 and 5. But like the BBC they were also vulnerable to competition for viewers from new interactive services (if any could be invented that had significant audience appeal), and from WAP mobile phones carrying specially designed 24-hour televised news services. Another impending threat came from new services that allowed viewers to construct

---

* There was the further potential problem that the licence fee was for owning a television set – not a WAP mobile phone or a personal computer. The constant complaint of the BBC's competitors was that it enjoyed the proceeds of a tax on television sets paid by people who seldom or never watched BBC programmes; soon it would also be called an unfair tax on television sets as opposed to computers and phones (see, e.g., Tim Congdon 'Does "new media" make the licence fee redundant?', *Prospect*, April 2000, p. 17).

their own personalised schedules of programmes by 'time-shifting' – i.e. selecting and recording them, for later viewing, from any mixture of channels – as opposed to relying on the choice of programmes that happen to be on screen at the time of viewing. BSkyB was perhaps the best placed of all the broadcasters to withstand all this, with its dominance of pay-TV and its strong lead in content ownership; yet the two cable companies could eventually erode these advantages, thanks to the greater interactivity they could potentially offer.

Other sectors of the communications industry were also threatened. The telecommunications companies – British Telecom and its smaller rivals – now faced competition from cable companies offering entertainment as well as telephone services, and from internet servers offering a wide range of 'e-services'. Newspapers were threatened with declining readerships in a world saturated with 24-hour radio and television news services (now also available on mobile phones as well as their radios and television sets), and with the loss of classified advertising to the internet – all of which could force them to raise their prices and initiate a vicious circle of declining readerships and declining advertising revenues.[62]

Restructuring

The result was a convulsive process of restructuring in which the global nature of the broadcasting economy was brought more clearly into view. It began with the major US telecommunications companies and spread outwards to the 'media' industry (i.e. film, music, newspapers and magazines as well as broadcasting) and the internet and information technology industries, and from the USA to other countries, until few were untouched. The telecommunications companies became major owners of cable television channels, film archives, suppliers of 'near video on demand' and internet services. Cable companies became owners of internet servers and media companies. Software companies bought stakes in all three.[63]

Those strong enough to expand by taking over competitors did so. In October 1999 MCI Worldcom, the second-largest long-distance phone company in the USA, took over Sprint, the third largest, for $108 billion, creating a virtual duopoly with AT&T.[64] In November 1999 the largest British mobile phone company, Vodafone, made an ultimately successful bid to take over Mannesmann, the largest German mobile phone company, for $149 billion. Others sought protection by moving into competing fields, by mergers or strategic alliances. In January 2000 America Online (AOL), the world's largest internet server, took over Time Warner Inc., one of the largest cable companies in the USA, and a major media producer and publisher, for $160 billion. Microsoft invested a more modest $5 billion in AT&T and allied itself with Excite@Home, a cable network company, among many other diversifications. The *Washington Post* allied itself with the television network NBC and NBC bought the internet company CNet for a mere $64 million;[65] Disney Corporation bought the internet company Infoseek for $70 million. AOL bought Gateway, a computer manufacturer. Hollywood studios invested in companies making and distributing films on the internet.

Similar diversification and blurring of boundaries occurred in Britain. The *Financial Times* bought a share in a leading American financial website and invested $70 million in developing its online news service into a 'full-fledged internet portal'.[66] The *Daily Mail* made heavy investments in on-line advertising and in digital teletext services. Specialist magazine publishers started trying to capture the markets they already 'owned' in the print media by extending their operations to similarly specialist internet sites, interactive television channels and e-commerce ventures.[67] British Telecom created a new division to develop its internet business, to deal with the competition it would face from 2001 when its local phone lines had to be made available to competitors, and when it would also be permitted (after a seventeen-year ban) to compete with the cable companies in supplying entertainment. Microsoft bought shares in NTL and Telewest, the two dominant cable companies.

Among British broadcasters, the biggest move was Rupert Murdoch's attempt in 1999 to merge BSkyB with Vivendi, which controlled Canal Plus, France's biggest pay-TV company. This was blocked by the Monopolies Commission, but Vivendi raised its share in BSkyB to 25 per cent and Murdoch went on to acquire a 24 per cent shareholding in Premiere, the pay-TV arm of the German Kirch group. He also had plans to buy some of Deutsche Telekom's cable operations, and took a 10 per cent shareholding in Manchester City football club (to improve Sky's chances of holding on to its Premier League rights after 2002).[68] Murdoch's News Corporation was also investing heavily in the internet and in July 2000 bought a controlling interest in Open, an interactive television-based shopping, banking, news, email and education service. Similarly both the remaining cable companies, NTL and Telewest, planned to make their channels available to mobile phone subscribers.

As a publicly-owned broadcaster, the BBC could not buy into or merge with private companies, even if it had been free to borrow for the purpose; and inaugurating digital services was already consuming 10 per cent of its licence fee revenues. Its main strategic response had so far been to invest in websites, based on a prediction that by 2005 more people would be receiving BBC programmes world-wide via the internet than through television or radio. In 1999 its free website was already the most visited in Western Europe, and the corporation hoped to extend this lead into a news website 'delivering rolling bulletins in text, graphics, audio and video over the internet for delivery to a host of devices, including mobile phones, laptops and palmtops, PCs, and conventional television sets, once they can be used on the net'.[69] The BBC saw its advantage as lying in its possession of creative and technical resources that allowed it to design programmes for each kind of receiver and customer, rather than merely 're-versioning' traditional broadcast programmes.

In late 1999, however, Greg Dyke's appointment as Director-General to succeed Birt set the BBC on a new course. 'Producer Choice' was swept away, administrative jobs were cut to release funds for programming, and all the corporation's channels, terrestrial and digital, were to be recast. Whether these measures were all well judged remained to be seen, but Dyke clearly intended to fight hard to restore the BBC's competitive edge in the new era.

By contrast, the ITV companies' preoccupation with concentration seemed to many observers to have distracted them from doing more than start 'simulcasting' their existing programmes digitally through Ondigital (a terrestrial digital 'multiplex' jointly owned by Granada and Carlton), though there was no doubt that a single consolidated ITV company would have the resources to do more.[70] (It also distracted them from anticipating the BBC's renewed competitive vigour under Dyke, as we will see shortly.) Granada and Carlton also jointly invested in a US internet search engine (Ask Jeeves), and Granada developed an information and entertainment website, G-Wizz. ITN (Independent Television News) launched a purpose-made service for mobile phone users.

In all this, while the trend to the internet was clearly visible, it was

Table 5.2. Pay-TV and internet connection forecasts

	Percentage of households in the UK subscribing to				
	Cable	Satellite	Terrestrial digital	Total pay-TV	Households on-line (m.)
1999	14	16	2	30	1.5
2003	17	19	7	43	12

Source: KPMG, 1999.

equally clear that no one could really tell what digitisation would finally entail. Some industry observers believed that television would retain its family-centred popularity, others that a new generation, used to computers, would abandon television for the personal computer and internet-delivered programmes and services. Some were convinced that scarce content would be the critical determinant, favouring companies rich enough to buy ever more costly talent, sports rights and film archives. Others thought that consumers would confound the media industry by preferring to use the internet like a glorified telephone system, or for games, not as a substitute for radio listening and television watching.[71] Piers Morgan, the editor of the *Mirror*, thought that newspapers would never lose their appeal.[72] Still others had faith that the taste for high-quality television programmes and channels with mixed programming would also survive; but it was far from obvious that any broadcasters would survive with the resources or the incentive to offer such things at a price most people could afford – let alone the relative wealth of high-quality programming that was available to everyone for the price of the licence fee before broadcasting was opened up to market forces.

Tables 5.2 and 5.3 show the best guesses of the management consultants KPMG about the growth of pay-TV and the distribution of television revenues by 2003. Even if they were out by a margin of 15 or 20 per cent, they implied two fairly obvious conclusions.[73] One was that with less than 20 per cent of total television revenues the BBC would not be able to maintain a dominant position across all the main television platforms and genres for very long. The other was that when over forty per cent of households subscribed to pay-TV with up to 200 or more channels, and half of all households were able to receive

Table 5.3. Television revenue forecasts (£bn)

	Licence fees	NAR[a]	Sponsorship	Subscriptions	PPV[b]	Transactions[c]	Total TV revenue
1998	1.6	2.8	0.04	1.6	0.2	–	6.2
	(26%)	(45%)	(1%)	(26%)	(3%)	-	(100%)
2003	1.6	3.3	0.09	3.6	0.3	0.76	9.7
	(17%)	(34%)	(1%)	(37%)	(3%)	(8%)	(100%)

[a] Net Advertising Revenue
[b] Pay Per View
[c] Based on 10 per cent commission paid to broadcasters on transactions carried out through interactive services.
Source: KPMG, 1999.

television services via the internet, serious enforcement of ITC licence-holders' public service obligations was going to become more and more problematic, if not impossible. Even if the public service channels' audience shares diminished more slowly than their share of television revenues, the advent of the new media did seem to represent a decisive turning-point. Before we look ahead at the likely implications for what is broadcast, however, we need to look back briefly at the mechanisms that brought television to this juncture.

How television became a field of capital accumulation

The emergence of giant media companies and the complex and fast-moving markets in which they worked seemed, by the end of the 1990s, to have come about almost naturally and inevitably, but this was clearly far from true. The reconstitution of broadcasting as a field of accumulation, rather than a set of primarily political institutions, had been a complex political as well as economic process. Chapter 4 suggested four prerequisites of such a change: the conversion of services into commodities; the creation of a demand for those commodities; the conversion of the labour force into one willing to produce profits; and the intervention of the state to lower the risk of investment. It is instructive to view what has happened to broadcasting from this angle.

The conversion of publicly-provided services into commodities

The conversion of a publicly provided services into commodities capable of being priced and sold in a market was relatively easy in the case of broadcasting, in that a model for doing this was already available in the USA. Because both the BBC and the ITV companies had their own in-house production, it fell to Channel 4 to pioneer the practice in the UK. Channel 4 decided what it could afford for a programme of a given genre; the independent producer had to work out a budget, and the final contract normally covered the agreed production costs plus a production fee. When John Birt introduced Producer Choice in the BBC the process took a new step forward: now the contribution of every element in the BBC's organisation had in theory to be reflected in the cost of every programme, and a producer who found he or she could get it made more cheaply outside – or could get post-production work or anything else done more cheaply outside – had to go outside. Initially there were 480 separate 'cost units', involving phenomenal transaction costs and innumerable absurdities; they were reduced to 200 in 1993, but a basic handicap remained. Outsiders competing for BBC business had numerous advantages. The smaller ones had much lower overheads, while the larger ones, following normal business practice, could price their bids on the basis of marginal rather than average costs, or could deliberately subsidise them to force an entry into the market, so their bids tended to be cheaper. The only way BBC 'units' could compete was by cutting and casualising staff. As we have seen, the ITV companies followed suit, on an even more radical scale.

A natural result was that not only did the absolute cost of programmes acquire a new prominence in the thinking of all broadcasters, but also their cost relative to their ratings potential. This was the significance of Paul Jackson's celebrated remark, as Carlton's Director of Programmes in 1992, that 'If *World in Action* [ITV's flagship investigative journalism programme] were in 1993 to uncover three more serious miscarriages of justice while delivering an audience of three, four or five million, I would cut it. It isn't part of the ITV system to get people out of prison.'[74] Investigative journalism is one of the most expensive television genres (after drama);[75] and in 1998 *World in Action* disappeared.[76] The point here is not to evaluate this change, but just to note that for Jackson it was the cost/price ratio of a programme, rather than the 'use-value' of its contents, that mattered – the price in this case being the price that an advertiser could be expected to pay for an audience of three to five million.

Commercial broadcasters justify this by saying that it is no use broadcasting something people will not watch, and also that high-quality programmes are needed to keep big audiences. But the cost/price ratio is never far from their minds. They are also aware that very small audiences can sometimes be profitable, either because they are 'niche markets', attractive to niche market advertisers (in the much more populous USA 'some networks with perhaps only a 0.2 or 0.3 per cent audience share will be making big profits'),[77] or because minority-interest (or plain dull) programmes can be 'bundled' with more appealing ones and still earn their keep if they are cheap enough. Horsman describes how 'from 1993 on, Sky put the price of its channels up each year, each time adding services to the basic package as a way of convincing subscribers they were getting value for money', and quotes Frank Barlow, the Chairman of BskyB, as saying: 'It is marvellous. What you do is give people more of what they don't want, but it allows you to put the price up. It's so clever.'[78] The attitude towards programme content that goes with this approach was well illustrated by the reaction of a senior BSkyB executive when the House of Lords banned the sale of exclusive television rights to some major national sporting events, including the Grand National steeplechase: 'A seven-minute race isn't much good to us. We need to fill 12,000 hours.'[79]

Pay-TV was of course a significant step in the commodification process because it was viewers, not advertisers, whose money was now being sought. 'Pay-per-view' would take it a step further, charging fees for individual live events such as boxing matches and eventually perhaps many sports. For every taste and price range, 'programming material' can then be produced that will maximise returns, while production methods are constantly reorganised to minimise costs and raise productivity. TV soap operas are one of the more notable products of broadcasting commodification, achieving 'large, or very large, audiences at a remarkably low cost per audience-hour, and at a surprisingly low cost per year. The successful soap achieves this happy financial result with a specialized production system designed for a continuous through-put of drama.'[80] A team is responsible for continually developing the story line, multiple teams of scriptwriters are responsible for turning this into screenplays, another team is in charge of casting, and so on. Serious drama is not the aim, nor the result; as Collins, Garnham and Locksley observe, 'it hardly makes sense to ask who is the author of *Dallas* or *Coronation Street*.[81] What successful soaps achieve are profitable sales of audience demographics.

Clearly not everything that people want to see on television lends itself to industrialised production the way soaps do, though, given the complex team nature of all television production, the scope for this should never be underestimated, and production costs in all genres have been reduced by technological changes as well as by paying fewer producers and smaller crews lower wages for longer hours. In fact as with musicals, discussed in chapter 4, it probably makes most sense to see commodification as applying to the total flow, which Raymond Williams identified as the essence of television output, not just to each individual component in it. Where there are few production economies of scale to be had, for instance in 'one-off' dramas (with their new scriptwriters, new sets and new casts for each programme), the genre can be drastically cut back, as single dramas were at the BBC, or dropped altogether, as they were from ITV schedules after 1990.[82] Otherwise the laws of competition drive production methods in one direction only, succinctly described by Gillian Ursell, writing in 1997:

In traditional producer-broadcaster regimes, programme budgets of £600,000 for one hour of drama production are not unknown. Such a budget supports a large production team; location shots; costumes; luxurious shooting and cutting ratios; relatively indulgent reliance on post-production for editing and graphics. It supports frequent scene changes, frequent cutaways and complex lighting requirements. It supports the use of film as against video. Nowadays that kind of expenditure can only be justified if the audience is going to be massive, preferably international. But the producer-broadcasters are under very serious pressure from the satellite and cable companies. These newcomers are commissioning at rates which can be as low as £2,000 per hour. To survive on very low budgets (i.e. £2,000–£10,000 per hour), the programme producer must: 1. try and negotiate a deal to make a very large volume of the same programme, for example 26 or 52 episodes; 2. use a very small production team; around five people, all of whom are multi-skilled and multi-functional; 3. adopt very simple production techniques: fixed locations, simple lighting, no cutaways, no graphics, video not film, longer sequences, very tight shooting and cutting ratios, and so on. Inevitably this has consequences for the type of product that is made.[83]

This degree of quality degradation could be avoided, perhaps, by innovative conceptions of industrial organisation. What was needed now, one independent producer thought, was

> the ability to make an interesting and engaging piece of television for £25,000 for an hour, instead of £25,000 for a half hour, which is still a bit of a struggle. There's a very limited number of people who can do that. There are ways of doing it, taking people who are very experienced and getting them to manage groups of relatively inexperienced but talented people at that critical stage of their careers when they're willing to do all that. But these are different types of organisational models than they've had in broadcasting. Whether they've got the flexibility to do that – to say, 'what we need here is a cadre of twenty people, probably in their early 20s, they're director/cameramen, we've got the format, just go out and shoot it to the format, come back and edit it, they've got two weeks to do it, it will cost us £10,000 a programme . . .' But we can't do that unless we've set up a factory to make it. Whether [broadcasters] have the imagination and the skill to set up those factories, I don't know.[84]

In short, the transformation of the product under the normal pressures generated by commodification was under way.

Creating demand for television programmes as commodities

In the market-oriented public discourse of the 1980s and 1990s it would be a mistake to underestimate the appeal of anything new; anyone who doubts this must explain, among other things, the astonishing take-up, by the allegedly conservative British, of mobile phones (owned by more than half the total population – adults and children). Even so the take-off of BSkyB, the key driver of commodification of British television since the late 1980s, was dramatic. By 1992, after barely three years, BSkyB had two million subscribers paying £17 per month for six channels, and only a small minority of these subscribers were on high incomes. Clearly there was a demand for more of what Sky offered, especially films. But as Sam Chisholm, BSkyB's Chief Executive, well understood, what was needed to make the company profitable was to have a 'USP' – a 'unique selling proposition' – something competitors would find it even harder to compete with than Sky's encrypted films. This need was met by acquiring exclusive rights to televise live Premier

League football matches. ITV had scooped live television coverage of top football away from the BBC through an exclusive deal with the First Division Clubs in 1988. Now Sky, with no obligation to commit resources to expensive public service programming, took live coverage of the new top-level Premier League away from both the BBC and ITV. The BBC's straitened circumstances and ITV's stagnant advertising revenues throughout the 1990s, coupled with Murdoch's growing ability to bankroll Sky from other divisions of News Corporation when needed, meant that more and more sports events ceased to be available on the established free-to-air channels. And not just sports: towards the end of the decade, as competition intensified from the unregulated cable and satellite channels and the lightly regulated Channel 5, the price of other programme material tended to rise too. The cost of a five-year contract to broadcast live Premier League matches was £304 million in 1992, and £670 million in 1996; in 2000 the cost was about £1 billion for just three years.[85] The salaries of successful sports commentators, presenters, and scriptwriters rose commensurately, with top television presenters commanding £1 million a year. By the end of the 1990s 'talent inflation' was said to be running at 17 per cent a year, and at 40 per cent for popular quiz and chat shows.[86]

The government's long-running financial squeeze meant that the BBC could not compete in all these markets; besides losing most live top sporting events it lost a series of well-known broadcasters to the commercial companies. In 2000 it even lost (to ITV) the rights to broadcast recorded highlights from Premier League matches (the famous *Match of the Day* programme). Between 1993 and 1998 the BBC's revenues only rose in real terms from £1.8 billion to £2 billion while total commercial television revenues rose from £2.6 billion to £4.6 billion.[87] By the end of the 1990s the BBC was also, as we have seen, spending 10 per cent of its licence fee income to establish a bridgehead in digital broadcasting and the internet. All the BBC's programming suffered, encouraging viewers to switch to other channels.[88] The only consolation for the BBC was that ITV's revenues were also stagnant, because the growth in commercial revenues went to BSkyB and cable and Channel 5; but unlike the BBC, the ITV companies were operating no radio stations and only one television channel, and also unlike the BBC they could borrow, or raise capital through share issues, to buy their way back into the game.

The BBC might be unable to compete in the market for the most expensive sports and media stars, but it could still compete effectively in relatively high-cost genres such as drama, journalism and the arts. So long as such programmes achieved high ratings the commercial broadcasters had to follow suit to some extent, recouping the cost through differential pricing where possible. BSkyB and the cable companies could offer subscribers a range of channel 'packages', priced according to cost and demand; in this way, as with other services (from hairdressing to market-based health care, as we saw in chapter 4), to the extent that high-quality television programming resists industrialised production it can be priced accordingly and sold to the more limited numbers of people who can afford it.[89]

The conversion of the workforce

The conversion of a workforce from one providing a public service to one producing a surplus for shareholders is seldom straightforward. In health care, for example, difficulties have been encountered (as chapter 6 shows), and comparable difficulties could be expected in other fields. In the case of broadcasting, however, it proved relatively easy, as the earlier discussion of the formation of the independent production sector has already indicated. Inside the BBC and the ITV companies the technical staff had been strongly unionised. With the drastic cuts in ITV staff levels between 1988 and 1993, and the slower but protracted downsizing at the BBC, continuing until the late 1990s, together with the Thatcher government's general assault on union rights, the broadcasting unions' power was broken; the last major union confrontations with management took place in the ITV sector between 1985 and 1988 and ended in complete defeat, with the employers unilaterally terminating the industry's national agreement.[90] As for the professional staff involved in television, they had mostly been unionised but had not depended heavily on their union for their job security or pay; on the other hand, neither did they see themselves as a profession. Television producers, for example, had not formed a professional body to regulate entry, training or ethics; as Tunstall points out, unlike lawyers they had no clients, and unlike doctors, no patients; and as they achieved seniority they tended to leave production and become managers.[91] Their outlook was closer to that of actors and scriptwriters, who have always typically been freelance. From the start of commercial broadcasting many BBC producers and presenters transferred readily to the ITV companies, and continued to do so in the period of much harsher competition from the mid-1980s onwards.

For all these reasons there was little effective resistance to much longer work-days, including evening and weekend working with little or no overtime, or to the demand for multiple skills and casualisation. Thanks to the expansion of the number of channels, wages for the most highly skilled producers, cameramen, etc., did not fall, but Ursell's research in the north of England suggests that there, at least, most freelancers' incomes fell sharply between 1993 and 1999, and that intense self-exploitation throughout the industry resulted:

> One northern independent producer (ex-BBC staff) in late 1998 accepted a commission to make a 43-part series. His budget for this was the same as the same commissioner granted him in 1995 for a 6-part series of similar content and duration. In another example, a northern producer who, in the early 1980s, had enjoyed repeat orders and generous budgets from Channel 4, in 1999 was surviving on low budget, mass production of travel material for a satellite station. He shot his own material and edited it at home on his own non-linear editing suite. The workloads, against tight deadlines, were stress-inducing. His coping strategy, as also that of the ex-BBC producer, was to seek free labour from students and other media wannabees.[92]

As Ursell notes, this explains the high proportion of people with very low incomes at the bottom of the industry, as well as the high 'churn rate' of more experienced people in the independent sector. But somewhat similar conditions now existed in the BBC. Barnett and Curry note that there 'contracts grew shorter and shorter, to the point where they might be just weeks long (and some departments deliberately left gaps between contract periods to ensure that individuals did not accrue employment rights)'.[93] The unsocial working hours caused by tight schedules increasingly exclude people with young children, and entry-level work on below-subsistence pay can mostly be accepted only by young people with parents sufficiently well-to-do to support them financially. One effect of the marketisation of the industry is thus that the next generation of senior programme makers is liable to be a good deal less socially diverse than the last, with potentially significant implications for the kinds of programme that get made.

Some companies have begun to recognise the costs of overworking

their staff and have marginally reversed their downsizing policies, but it
is now a fully accepted fact of life that most people are working very
hard to produce profits for someone. As the example given above
shows, while Channel 4 pays its own staff comparatively well it too drives
hard bargains with some of its programme suppliers, as does the BBC,
which now also relies extensively on casual workers. Even these two
broadcasters, with no shareholders and strong public service mandates,
have been unable to resist the transformation of the working conditions
of most of their workers that government pressure and competition
from commercial broadcasting have entailed.

The role of the state in reducing risk

There was no shortage of capital keen to enter the broadcasting field
in Britain, either in 1954 when commercial television was first authorised, or in the 1980s and 1990s when it was made competitive. What it
did seek at the outset of each stage of the process, though, was to
minimise its risk.

The only two significant exceptions to this were the creation of the
independent production sector, where the capital at risk was very small,
and Rupert Murdoch's big gamble on breaking into the field with pay-
TV via a foreign-based satellite. Yet Murdoch was arguably saved from
disaster by Mrs Thatcher's sympathetic inaction over Sky's takeover of
BSB and its ITC licence – because Murdoch, as a non-EU citizen, was
not entitled to hold one. The IBA objected, indicating that it would
remove the licence, and a fight might well have precipitated a fatal turn
in Murdoch's relations with his creditors, which were by then critical
(Sky was losing £2 million a week in 1998 before the merger with BSB).
But the IBA failed to carry out its threat. It was widely suspected that
the timing of the takeover had been planned, with Thatcher's knowledge, to exploit a loophole caused by the fact that while the provisions
of the 1990 Broadcasting Act were coming into force there were a few
days when neither the outgoing IBA nor the incoming ITC had
authority to act; but this will probably never be resolved.[94]

Another example of sympathetic inaction concerned the protection
of major national sporting events. After BSkyB's raid on Premier League
football, which meant that the top matches of the nation's most popular
sport could only be watched live by paying £300 a year to BSkyB, the
question arose whether all popular spectator sports would become

progressively privatised in this way. Neither the Conservatives nor Labour were willing to intervene; it fell to the House of Lords in 1995 to force the government to extend very modestly the list of reserved sporting events for which exclusive rights to live television coverage could not be sold. Another contentious issue concerned the so-called 'electronic gateway'. As the 'first mover' in encrypted broadcasting, Murdoch owned the technology that all subscribers were using in their decoding boxes. Critics wanted legislative guarantees of free access for public service broadcasters to (and equal prominence on) the 'electronic programme guide' that would come with this and that would become the programme directory used by more and more viewers; but successive governments refused. Proposals from backbenchers to tax BSkyB – nominally a foreign broadcaster – on the same basis as the terrestrial broadcasters were also resisted.

So although Murdoch took a big risk he also calculated – accurately as it turned out – that the Conservatives would do what they could to help, and their Labour successors were hardly less obliging. In general each major advance into broadcasting by private capital was initially well insured against risk by the terms of the government's regulations. The first ITV franchises had been given free to selected owners who only had to pay a subsequent government levy out of the large profits that their monopoly of advertising airtime ensured. The cable companies were also given their franchises free and, besides, were protected from competition from British Telecom, the privatised but dominant telecommunications company, which was forbidden to transmit entertainment on its phone lines – a protection not removed until 2001. And like Sky, they were given no public service obligations, other than that they must include the terrestrial broadcasters' channels in their subscription packages – which actually gave them valuable added content in the early years. The reasoning was that since people chose to subscribe to their channels, it could be assumed that they were getting what they wanted and needed no protection from a regulator. Channel 5 was given modest public service obligations, and even those were either reduced by the regulator in the channel's early years, or broken at the margin with relative impunity; moreover, the new company was virtually assured of revenue from an advertising industry anxious to break the ITV–Channel 4 duopoly. Finally, when the first digital broadcasting licences were awarded, the auction principle that had been imposed on the ITV companies in 1992 was not applied. All these measures reduced or virtually eliminated risk at the start of each new wave of commercial broadcasting expansion.

'Light-touch' regulation by the ITC was also a factor. As Goodwin has shown, the ITC exploited its role in the 1992 franchise auction to impose what it called 'ITV plus' requirements on the new licensees, letting it be known before the auction that any bid that offered less than the public service obligations of the old franchises would not be deemed to meet the 'quality threshold' and so would not be considered.[95] But enforcing these requirements was a different matter, once the competition for audience share intensified, since unlike its predecessor, the IBA, the ITC only monitored and commented on programmes afterwards. The ITC was able to penalise – mostly rather modestly – breaches of its code of conduct that had widespread public support, on issues such as excessive violence, failure to observe the 9 pm 'watershed' (after which 'adult' material may be screened), lack of impartiality, or professional malpractice such as faking scenes in a documentary.[96] What it was not able to do was withstand changes in the spirit or even the letter of public service obligations that attracted little public interest.

A revealing example of this was the ITV Network's decision in 1999 to move its best-known news programme, *News At Ten*, in order to clear space in its post-'watershed' schedule for popular programmes – especially films – capable of competing effectively for prime-time audiences with the mass-entertainment programmes on Channel 5 and the cable and satellite channels, which were seriously eroding ITV ratings. This was a move disliked by politicians but not greatly disliked by most viewers and the ITC initially felt obliged to accede to it, nominally on a trial basis for a year, after which it would be clear if it meant fewer viewers watching news. This ended badly for both the ITC and ITV, however. After a year the ITC tried to get ITV to move back to 10 p.m. The ITV companies resisted, and while they were arguing the BBC stepped in and moved its own evening news from 9 to 10 p.m. If the ITV did move it news back to 10 p.m it would now have the worst of both worlds – a split prime time, and head-to-head competition for news viewers.

Another illustration of the declining powers of the regulator was the planned merger of Carlton and United News and Media, described above. The two chief executives planned the merger and announced it after 'sounding out' the Director of the ITC, knowing that it broke at

least one if not two of the ITC's regulations limiting concentration. The
feeling in the industry was that the ITC no longer exercised significant
power. Steven Barnett summed it up in 1999 as follows:

> The ITC has powers but increasingly lacks the guts to use them. It is a
> cowed body – cowed by the enormous commercial and competitive
> pressures on their franchise holders, and the fact that the big ones like
> Green and Hollick throw their weight around: 'we're fighting Channel 5,
> Channel 4, Sky, and you want us to fight with our hands tied behind our
> backs.' It has changed radically since 1990. The ITC *were* within a
> favourable environment – there was no political pressure to deregulate
> under Major, the consensus was that the 1990 Act was a bad thing, the job
> was to hold the fort. Now, through mergers, competition, powerful
> moguls, the pressures on them are intense.[97]

At the heart of the issue of risk there was, in addition, the government's treatment of the BBC, which at the end of the 1990s was still the
commercial sector's most formidable competitor. We have already
noted the financial constraints placed on it: a declining budget in real
terms over almost a decade – and from 1993 more severely reduced
than even the Davies Panel recognised, by the requirement that the
corporation should eliminate its £200 million overdraft, implying a real
cut of 5 per cent per annum over the following three years.[98] In
1994–95 the BBC had revenues of approximately £1.2 billion to spend
on running two television channels, while the ITV companies had £1.6
billion – less the dividends it had to pay to shareholders – to spend on
running one.[99]

But the BBC was also required to compete with the private sector on
unequal terms. Under Producer Choice, BBC Resources – i.e. all the
departments providing the facilities used in programme-making – were
obliged to include in all their bids an item to cover their contributions
to the corporation's overhead costs, while their competitors used marginal costs; on the other hand, they were not allowed to compete with
outsiders for non-BBC work. As producers chose more and more
outside contractors, in their efforts to make their own units break even,
BBC Resources' bids became steadily less competitive – since the
overheads still had to be covered, on an even lower turnover – forcing
them to continually lay off staff. The BBC's historic strength, its richness
in talent and experience, and the element of built-in 'redundancy' that

permitted experimentation with innovation, was steadily eroded, along with the *esprit de corps* that all successful creative organisations depend on.

Barnett and Curry quote a remark by Kenith Trodd, a senior BBC drama producer, which makes the essential point very aptly: 'There is a frightening obsession with "the level playing field" – an absurd idea anyway because trade is surely about maximising your unlevel advantages against your opponents' – a view to which the commercial television barons (Michael Green, Lord Hollick, Gerry Robinson and Rupert Murdoch) clearly subscribed. 'Producer Choice is using the concept to penalise the BBC by taking away its natural and peculiar historic strengths.'[100] Pro-market analysts see the BBC's guaranteed income from the licence fee as giving it an unfair advantage vis-à-vis private broadcasters.[101] As a result, those who advocate making up the BBC's increasingly inadequate licence fee income from the commercial profits of the BBC's trading arm, BBC Worldwide, feel obliged to go to elaborate lengths to placate the opposition by prescribing rules to make the BBC's trading operations more and more 'transparent', while those of its competitors remain shrouded in 'commercial confidentiality'.[102] The ultimate irony is that this strategy is in any case self-defeating, as Barnett and Curry point out: to make a significant contribution the BBC's commercial operations would need to become enormous.

> For a commercial division [of the BBC such as BBC Worldwide] to contribute 20 per cent of BBC income, it would need a turnover of around the size of the licence fee revenue. . . . Ultimately . . . an aggressive commercial strategy has an obvious conclusion. The bigger it becomes, the more it challenges private vested interests, and the more opprobrium is levelled at the licence fee.[103]

The global political context was also a factor. Although the Council of Europe affirmed the 'vital role' of public service broadcasting, and the Treaty of Amsterdam secured the right of member states to continue funding it, it was under constant attack from the powerful economic directorates of the European Commission.[104] The commercial broadcasters found a powerful ally in the Competition Directorate, which proposed in 1998 that state-funded public service broadcasters should be prohibited from making programmes of the kinds provided by commercial channels.[105] The recommendation was not adopted by

the Council of Ministers, but like the Multilateral Agreement on Investment (MAI), whose backers simply shifted their efforts to the WTO
after being defeated in the OECD, it could be expected to reappear in
other forms. (It was for instance the central theme of the commercial
broadcasters' lobbying efforts at the end of 2000 to block the BBC's
proposed new children's and youth programmes.)

By now, however, we have moved beyond the issue of risk, convention-
ally defined, to the wider role of the state and political forces in
defining and defending the boundary between non-market and commodified broadcasting. One of the most striking features of the
sequence of events through which British television became increasingly
commodified is that although there were protests from senior BBC
television staff, at no point in the market-fearing 1990s did the BBC's
Director-General or the Labour Party leadership vigorously articulate
the alternative viewpoint: i.e. that the BBC, which had been built up to
a level of pre-eminent excellence over half a century by the financial
contributions of virtually the entire population, should be encouraged
to defend its position aggressively, and should be more generously
funded rather than less, exploiting every accumulated advantage it had,
in the interests of preserving an interpretation of public service broadcasting that British democracy could not do without.[106]

Commodification and public service television

The neoliberal view of broadcasting sees the current proliferation of
channels as recapitulating the early days of the press, assuring freedom
of speech and freedom of choice through a multiplicity of privately
owned channels. It rarely dwells on the fact – predicted by all schools
of economic theory and attested by all students of media history – that
multiplication of channels has been accompanied by a drastic concentration of the ownership of channels, so that freedom of speech
becomes freedom of speech for a few corporations. It takes the view
that whatever viewers want, some channel owner will have an economic
incentive to provide it; nothing essential to a democracy is thereby lost.
As chapter 4 showed, however, this does not address some major
problems thrown up by market theory itself, such as the problem of
negative externalities or the problem of the failure of markets to
provide enough 'merit' goods, of which the knowledge and understand-

ing needed by citizens in a democracy is an important example; not to mention the problems that present themselves to anyone with a less sanitised view of corporations and the outlook and aims of their owners (as Jay Blumler remarks, '[the phrase] "market failure" . . . grossly understates the magnitude of the deficit involved . . .').[107]

In this section, however, we will try to avoid being drawn too far into these issues and confine ourselves as far as possible to asking what have been the effects of the dramatic expansion of commodified television on public service broadcasting in Britain, as it was understood in its heyday, i.e. roughly at the end of the 1970s.

In the first place it is clear that audience fragmentation in itself has ended one dimension of public service broadcasting as it was then – it is now much less likely that everyone will be talking tomorrow about what is shown tonight; and it is clear that no medium-sized country acting alone could have prevented, even if it had wished, the arrival of multi-channel television delivered by satellite more or less throughout the world, propelled by the US television industry and its dominance in the global market-place. In retrospect, the era of two or three channels may be seen as constituting a unique historical moment in which complex modern societies had for a couple of decades something like a single forum for their most important 'formative conversations'; not a forum that offered universal or even broadly representative access to the podium, but one that was at least more or less universally attended.

What remains of this, among the growing throng of commercial broadcasters, is a cluster of established broadcasting organisations with public service remits, and a majority of people who still watch their channels out of habit or preference. At the end of 1999 in Britain over 80 per cent of the population still watched the four truly public service channels, BBC1 and 2, ITV and Channel 4. Even in multi-channel (cable and satellite) homes, the proportion was just under 60 per cent. Projections for the future based on an assumed spread of multi-channel homes still put the total audience share of the four main public service channels at around 50-plus per cent by 2010 or 2012.[108] This would be far from the situation that had existed in 1980, but, given the still greater fragmentation of viewing among all the other channels (both now and predicted in the future), the public service share would still be substantial. Moreover, the 'reach' of BBC1 and ITV, in particular – the fact that in 1998 90 per cent of all viewers still watched each of these at some point every week, a proportion that had fallen much more slowly than audience shares – meant that audience fragmentation had weakened but not completely destroyed the ability of broadcasters to perform their public service function effectively for the population as a whole. The question is, then, how far other changes flowing from commodification may have done this.

Given the importance of this issue, and the superabundance of opinions and anecdotal evidence about it, it is significant that down to 2000 no attempt seemed to have been made to measure the changes that had occurred; certainly none had been published by the ITC or any other public body. So Steven Barnett's and Emily Seymour's careful initial study of trends since the late 1970s, entitled '*A Shrinking Iceberg Travelling South*', is particularly valuable.[109] They focused on drama and current affairs in the five terrestrial channels. On drama, they found that

> The number of hours devoted to single plays has dropped by half over the last twenty years while the time given to soap operas has multiplied by five. Drama series now comprise nearly two thirds of all peak-time drama and there is more emphasis across all channels on police and detective themes. . . .

As regards current affairs, Barnett and Seymour found that its share of peak-time hours was the same as twenty years earlier, but there had been major changes in what 'current affairs' meant, and who covered it:

> There has been a significant decline over the last twenty years in foreign affairs coverage, which is now almost wholly confined to BBC2. Commercial television has effectively vacated political and economic current affairs. . . . Across all channels, there has been a very noticeable rise in coverage of police and crime issues and – to a lesser extent – consumer issues.[110]

Table 5.4 gives a partial summary of the main changes that have occurred – a picture belatedly confirmed by the ITC early in 2001.[111]

Barnett and Seymour pursued two main lines of explanation for the changes in current affairs programming, based on interviews with thirty-four people in the industry. First, the drive for ratings 'appear[ed] to

Table 5.4. Percentages of all peak-time current affairs programming

	Subject matter	All terrestrial TV		BBC1 and 2		ITV	
		1977/78	1997/98	1977/78	1997/98	1977/78	1997/98
Decreased	Industry and business	14.0	6.0	21.6	9.2	–	–
	Home affairs (social issues)	8.9	4.0	10.1	–	6.4	13.7
	Foreign	28.5	19.0	29.8	27.3	25.6	6.8
	Employment	7.6	3.0	9.6	3.8	3.2	–
	Northern Ireland	4.4	–	–	–	12.8	–
	Total	63.4	32.0	71.1	40.3	48.0	20.5
Increased	Crime/Police	5.8	13.4	5.4	9.6	6.4	18.2
	Legal	1.3	5.3	2.0	0.8	–	13.7
	Consumer	–	8.0	–	9.1	–	6.8
	Ethics/Morals	–	6.4	–	6.0	–	9.2
	Total	7.1	33.1	7.4	25.5	6.4	47.9

Source: Steven Barnett and Emily Seymour, 'A Shrinking Iceberg Travelling South': Changing Trends in British Television: A Case Study of Drama and Current Affairs, Report for the Campaign for Quality Television Ltd, London, September 1999, p. 18.

be almost as dominant on the BBC and Channel 4 as ITV', and this drive was frustrated by the erratic sizes of current affairs audiences (which naturally vary with the level of public interest in what happens to be currently in the news). This leads to a search for stories that will attract audiences, rather than stories judged important on other grounds; hence the emphasis on consumer affairs, rather than on foreign affairs, and on crime and police rather than politics or business. Market researchers try to find out what will attract the 'demographics' the advertisers want and producers and scriptwriters are invited to construct programmes to these specifications. In the late 1990s, for instance, Channel 4 initiated a series of meetings with independent programme-makers addressed not just by programme commissioners but also by marketing and market research personnel who explained what was wanted.

The second explanation offered by Barnett and Seymour was budget cuts, which had severely cut back programmes requiring long-distance travel, let alone expensive investigative research that may never produce a story, 'or anything which requires a long-term commitment of time or money'. Cuts had also eroded the working environment, casualising staff, curtailing time for discussion and thought, closing studios and facilities, forcing the pace of 'multi-skilling' and increasing workloads, so that topics requiring more sophistication and experience are avoided. Television journalists also increasingly depend on briefings – including ready-made video clips – provided by government and corporate public relations officers. While the BBC and ITV were slashing their staffs, the public relations staffs of government and companies were expanding at a rate of 25 to 30 per cent a year.[112]

The fact that these two drivers of change had been almost as powerful at the BBC as at ITV is significant. The Charter and the licence fee had not protected the BBC, and to the extent that the declining genres or topics were increasingly only covered by the BBC, their future looked bleak. In the intensified competition for audiences, it is hardly surprising that commercial programme controllers say things like 'we just don't want to see a programme about East Timor going out because it'll do two million and I can't have that';[113] or (on the decision to eliminate *News At Ten*): 'The simple thing behind the new schedule is that we were losing up to two million viewers at ten o'clock every evening, and commercially you can't carry on doing that.'[114] What is significant is that in order to defend its claim to the licence fee the

BBC clearly felt it could not avoid following suit – less drastically but clearly, as table 5.4 shows.*

Budget cuts and the drive for ratings, however, are not the only effects of market pressures. Advertisers have their own ideas of the kinds of programme they would like their products to be advertised on, or which they would like to sponsor, and in the USA it is notorious that programme-makers are made to take these ideas into account. In Britain, by contrast, there was supposed to be a 'Chinese Wall' between advertisers and broadcasters. It is evident that this wall has begun to crumble. For instance, when Paul Jackson became Director of Pro- grammes for Carlton Television in 1992

> he noted two unusual things about his work . . .; the close links he was forging with advertisers and the level of financial information that [Michael] Green [the Chief Executive] required. During more than twenty years as a programme maker and television executive Jackson had rarely had much contact with advertisers. Now . . . he was meeting 'client' groups for lunch or dinner once or twice a month.[115]

Relaxing the rules to permit sponsorship has contributed to this too. Defenders argue that sponsorship so far contributes less than 5 per cent of total commercial television revenues, and that there are more sponsors seeking programmes than the other way round, so that spon- sors have no chance to influence programme content. But most spon- sors don't want to be associated with a controversial programme; and given that programme sponsorship can make a significant marginal contribution to revenues it is hard to see what incentive programme controllers will have not to prefer uncontroversial programmes, or how programme makers will be able to disregard sponsors' wishes.[116]

---

* Some analysts think that the BBC sets standards against which the commercial sector is judged – whether by the regulators or by the public – and that this helps maintain the public service broadcasting commitments of the commercial broadcasters (e.g. David Currie and Martin Siner, 'The BBC: balancing public and commercial purpose', in Andrew Graham et al., *Public Purposes in Broadcasting: Funding the BBC* [University of Luton Press, 1999], p. 77). Others, like the Chief Executive of the ITV Network Centre, Richard Eyre, wanted the BBC and its licence-fee-funded public service remit preserved so that the ITV companies could be relieved of some or all of their public service obligations (*Public Interest Broadcasting: A New Approach*, the 1999 James Mac- Taggart Memorial Lecture [ITV Network Ltd, 1999], p. 10).

Although the ITC tried to limit sponsorship to existing programmes, as a way of preventing the search for sponsorship affecting the schedules, it looked like being a steadily losing battle. In 1996 the Director of the ITV Network Centre was reported as being 'very much in favour of advertisers being encouraged to invest in network programme development', stating that 'if an advertiser can bring me a new *Cracker*, I'd be delighted so long as the deal cleared the ITC'.[117] Although in 1999 the ITC still excluded sponsorship for some kinds of programme, such as national news, it was under strong pressure from the ITV companies to lift this ban, and had already done so for regional news, with immediately debatable consequences.*

As competition increases, pressure also increases to seek income from co-production with foreign partners, which means producing programmes with transnational audience appeal. In 1999 the Department for Culture, Media and Sport added its weight to this pressure in the interests of the television balance of trade, publishing a report that reproached British producers with making too many 'dark', 'slow' programmes, producing series with far fewer episodes than are called for by foreign (mainly American) commercial channels, and failing to cater to foreign tastes.[†] Because the style of UK drama and Britain's literary and dramatic heritage appeal to 'a significant minority of American viewers', the report noted, 'most prestige, "landmark" factual and many drama series made for the BBC are co-funded by a US broadcaster'. What was needed, it implied, was for British producers to start seeking co-funding with European partners and European audience tastes in mind.[118] Programme-makers are increasingly exposed to this demand and the compromises and predictable kinds of programme that it produces.

---

* The ITC decided to permit sponsorship of the 'softer' items in regional television news, such as items on things to do, gardening, etc. 'As trade magazine *UK Press* commented, "The company [Westcountry Television] says that if the gardening slot were looking at conservatories, a double-glazing company might sponsor it. This begs the question of why the regional flagship news programme has decided to look at conservatories . . ."' (Granville Williams, *Britain's Media – How They Are Related*, 2nd edn [Campaign for Press and Broadcasting Freedom, 1996], p. 24).

† David Graham and Associates, *Building a Global Audience: British Television in Overseas Markets* (Department for Culture, Media and Sport, 1999). The authors' views on taste would make a good subject for a satirical television programme, which would, however, almost certainly fail to appeal to the Dutch sense of humour, on which they place a touching reliance (p. 27).

It also sets up an interesting conflict for programme commissioners, since foreign-made programmes have less domestic audience appeal than do domestically made programmes – even if the foreign ones may sometimes be better. In 1999 virtually no foreign programmes, or made-for-television films, could be found on the prime-time schedules of BBC1 and 2, ITV or Channel 4 (Channel 5 was the exception, following the well-established path of using cheap foreign material in the early stages of its market penetration). In many genres, programmes capable of attracting foreign co-financing will not attract large audiences in Britain – unless and until, perhaps, British audiences' tastes become more globalised, through decreasing exposure to anything else. This would of course be a logical market outcome: more and more pro-grammes are designed to be 'generic' or 'global' and are then modified ('repurposed') for different markets, on the basis of market research, just enough to make them appear local (as with cars or perfumes, for example).[119]

By now we have evidently moved away from the quantitative evidence collected by Barnett and Seymour towards more qualitative issues. These range from falling production values to political questions. Even though new technology has lowered some production costs there is general agreement that budget cuts have gone much deeper than the use of new technology can account for; while £600,000 per hour may be a luxury too far, £8,000 per hour – not to mention much lower figures that are not uncommon in cable and satellite television produc-tion – generally means junk television. Some drama producers inter-viewed by Barnett and Seymour thought that even on the main terrestrial channels declining quality due to budget cuts was already evident on the screen.[120] The shift to soap operas means an obvious loss of innovation in both the form and content of television drama; so does the preference for known or 'star' actors over fresh ones (to keep ratings high), a preference for 'feel-good' themes or endings over upsetting ones (also for ratings, but advertisers like them better too), and the search for themes and formats that will appeal to foreign audiences and co-producers. According to Barnett and Seymour, few of their industry respondents romanticised the past; if so, their conclusion deserves attention: '. . . there was a widespread sense that in a short period of time money has become so tied up with programme making that creativity is becoming a form of manufacturing . . .'.[121]

As for politics, there is even more need not to romanticise the past:

the independence and objectivity of the BBC, in particular, have always been limited by the 'establishment' values of the Governors and most Directors-General.[122] These values, however, did not include neoliberalism, and in the mid-1980s the BBC had to be forced to toe the new line. In the course of this several programmes were effectively censored and a new culture of hyper-sensitivity about controversial programmes, especially those critical of the government, understandably developed within a BBC that was more and more closely dependent on the government's willingness to maintain the value of the licence fee.[123] Although for a time ITV was more willing to resist government pressure to trim critical programmes, heightened competitive pressures after the franchise auction of 1991 had somewhat similar effects, including a drastic cut-back in investigative journalism.

In July 2000 Barnett and Seymour published a second analysis of trends in public service television, this time of terrestrial news services over the years 1975–99. Their conclusions were as follows:

We believe there are two stories to tell from this study. First . . . there is a healthy balance of serious, light and international coverage. This is particularly true in comparison to news bulletins in the United States, for example, or some European countries where highly commercialised channels produce news which is dominated by stories about crime, showbiz, trivia or human interest . . . 'big' domestic and international issues are still being covered across the board. . . . The second story is that there has undoubtedly been a shift in most bulletins towards a more tabloid domestic agenda. . . . This shift has been particularly apparent over the last 10 years in the two ITN bulletins. . . .

Is this proof that there is indeed a degenerative process of 'dumbing down' in television news, or is it a much needed injection of accessibility into what 25 years ago was a deeply serious and dull approach to news? Has the increase in channels and competition given us greater diversity or lower standards which denigrate public intelligence? . . . we tend to the conclusion that the UK has maintained a remarkably robust and broadly serious approach to television news. . . . This broadly positive conclusion, however, comes with a major qualification. The rise in sport and consumer stories, combined with a decline in political stories, gives some cause for concern. If it continues as a trend rather than a fluctuation, this could lead to the gradual marginalisation of serious and foreign reporting. . . . It may . . . become increasingly difficult – particularly in the commercial sector – to resist the perceived mass audience appeal of less serious news items . . . we are not wholly optimistic that 10 years from now television news will have maintained its current balanced and diversified approach.[124]

This was perhaps a slight understatement of the authors' concerns.[125] About the time their study appeared there was a sharp intensification of the ratings war, spurred on by Greg Dyke's bold decision in August 2000 to move the BBC evening news into the 10 p.m. slot vacated by ITV, and his announcement of a new medium-term strategy for a revamped BBC, which included reshaping BBC1 to become a primarily entertainment channel competing 'head-to-head' with ITV.* Dyke's new Controller of BBC1, Lorraine Heggessey, did not hesitate to say that she intended the channel to achieve higher ratings than ITV.[126] Popular entertainment programmes from BBC2 were swapped with serious programmes from BBC1 and the traditional ceiling on the amounts of prize money that could be offered in quiz shows was lifted. On 18 October 2000, the first night of the BBC's new 10 p.m. news, the revamped BBC1's peak-time ratings moved up towards ITV's. Dyke clearly believed that political support for the licence fee depended in the end on having as many voters as possible watching BBC1, and few commentators thought he was wrong.†

The ITV Network, for its part, abruptly introduced an extra commercial break in each hour, and planned a significant expansion of spending on programming. It too, however, was suffering from the rampant inflation in 'intellectual property rights' in all its most important genres – high-quality serials, sports and films. It intensified its search for cheaper programming that could be sandwiched between its increasingly costly big-draw items (known as 'hammocking').

---

* In his MacTaggart Lecture *A Time for Change*, at the Guardian Edinburgh International Television Festival, 25 August 2000, Dyke outlined a complex package of savings in administration, earnings from commercial activities, and better funded and reorganised channels. BBC1 and 2 would become more distinct, BBC1 becoming more explicitly popular and BBC2 more serious. The BBC's digital channels would be reorganised into two evening channels (BBC3 and 4) devoted respectively to youth and intellectual interests, and two daytime children's channels, while more funding would be put into the round-the-clock news service, News 24.
† Chris Smith, the Secretary of State for Culture, Media and Sport, made some reproving speeches, warning the BBC not to sacrifice quality for ratings, but these could be read as intended as much to placate the BBC's commercial rivals as to influence Dyke.

All this was happening in the context of intense lobbying by everyone concerned as the government prepared its proposals for the long-term re-regulation of broadcasting in the 'new media' age, which were finally published in a Communications White Paper in December 2000. The key change was that there would in future be a single regulator – an Office of Communications, or 'Ofcom', for all forms of communication including broadcasting, and covering the BBC as well. Although the White Paper reasserted the government's commitment to public service broadcasting, Ofcom would combine several existing market-oriented regulators, and its objectives were framed in competition terms, so that the BBC's performance and needs would in future tend be judged by these criteria. In the same vein, Channel 4 was to remain publicly owned, but its public service obligations would be reviewed; and since the law was to be changed to allow for the formation of a single ITV company, and since ITV's public service obligations were to be lightened, and some of them 'self-regulated', and Channel 5's largely removed, it seemed clear that Channel 4's obligations would also have to be lightened to enable it to compete for ratings. The existing free channels – BBC1 and 2, ITV, Channel 4, Channel 5 and Welsh Channel 4 – would remain free on digital terrestrial, cable and satellite broadcasting; and Ofcom would regulate the electronic programme guide or EPG (the viewer's guide to 'what's on' the 250 potentially available channels) to ensure that the public service channels were not 'buried' in it. On the other hand, Ofcom would also ensure that the BBC 'does not use its licence money unfairly in the market'[127] – and as we have seen, to the commercial broadcasters, this meant using it for anything they could make money from.*

The tensions between the interests of the commercial broadcasters and the BBC, represented respectively by the Department of Trade and

---

* DTI/DCMS, *A New Future for Communications: Communications White Paper* (Stationery Office, 2000). The wide scope of the White Paper precludes full discussion here. Its proposals also included more cross-media ownership, allowing one company to own both the weekday and weekend London licences, and allowing an ITV company to have a controlling interest in Independent Television News (ITN), the main commercial news provider, which had previously enjoyed a degree of protection from owner influence. There would be a new 'consumer's panel', but, as its title implied, concerned with the consumption of television as a commodity, not as a component of democracy (see Steve Barnett, 'A surprising win for quality over quantity', *Guardian*, 17 December 2000).

Industry (DTI) and the Department for Culture, Media and Sport (DCMS), were thus obvious in the White Paper, and the ground yielded to the DTI was limited – but it was significant. Barnett and Seymour's idea that the negative trends they had observed in television news might be a 'fluctuation' seemed even less plausible than before. The signs pointed to a further commodification of broadcasting, rather than the reverse.

There is, however, an alternative way of viewing the changes that have occurred or are in prospect: namely that even if competition had not made ratings so crucial, audiences have changed, and 'it is no good making programmes that no one wants to watch'. It can be argued that as global market forces came to be seen as the perceived determinants of economic life, and as Thatcherism – and then New Labour – reshaped life in Britain, individualising and privatising it, public interest in current affairs necessarily changed too – broadly, shifting from politics to business. On this view television broadcasters have been responding to changes in the wider culture, as much as to changes in the regulatory environment; the changes in broadcasting are also 'audience-driven'. As Goodwin remarks, 'the idea of a collective project for changing society has been declared unnecessary, so why should anyone watch political programmes?';[128] and Barnett suggests that 'we have perhaps returned to a sort of political consensus, like that of the late 1950s only this time with a right wing core', and that broadcasters are responding to this as much as to regulatory changes or commercial pressures.[129] An independent producer summed it up by saying that in the 1980s programmes were still

> informed by what you might characterise as a liberal-humanistic agenda. There was a presumption that you were on the side of the poor, the disadvantaged and the voiceless against the rich and those with a voice . . . there is to some extent a perception that the viewers are not interested in this, they're not interested in poor people, they're not interested in failures, it's not what they want to watch on television and in the end you've got to deliver the viewing figures, that's what counts.[130]

It is also significant that newspapers, which have always been unregu-lated, exhibit similar trends, with a sharp decline in the number of stories on international subjects and a sharp rise in the ratio of photographs to text and other changes aimed at holding on to their readers in competition with television.[131] The editor of the *Times* said, about the readers he needed to attract, that 'many of these young people do not read if they can avoid it, they are not interested in politics or current affairs; they do not go to the opera or the theatre . . .'[132]

There is no reason to disagree. The system of cause and effect in which changes of taste occur is always circular. The regulatory and commercial forces that have been changing public service television are part of a wider set of changes that have also been changing audiences. But it must always be remembered that broadcasting, and especially television, plays a crucial role in representing and normalising these other changes. To attribute all the changes that have occurred in broadcasting to changes in the audience would be as absurd as to say that changes in the audience play no role in changing broadcasting. But there is also a crucial one-way dynamic at work here:

> The cultural differences between the over-30s and the 20-somethings are wider than ever. . . . The different attitudes are beginning to be apparent in programme-makers as well. But then it is not surprising that a generation that has grown up in the casualised and ratings-dominated world of today's television has not imbibed the values that came automatically to their equivalents in the secure broadcasting organisations of the 70s and 80s. Public service television may be hollowed out from within. It would be ironic if, in a few years' time, millions of pensioners and middle-aged viewers who want public service television can't get it because the people who make programmes have no idea how to provide it.[133]

From this point of view it is interesting to compare television with health care (discussed in chapter 6), where government efforts to commodify public services have encountered a good deal of public opposition, which official rhetoric has not significantly reduced, and a good deal of resistance from within the system, which public opposition has reinforced.

Whatever the final analysis of causes, the main changes in public service broadcasting during the last two decades of the century are clear and measurable: (1) audience fragmentation; (2) a decline in the volume of programming relevant to making informed decisions about political, economic and social issues, as opposed to programming relevant to coping with life as a consumer; (3) a narrowing of the scope of such political and economic programmes as are made, and – significantly, in the epoch of globalisation – an almost complete absence of foreign topics from current affairs programming on the most-watched channels; (4) an avoidance of controversial topics or critical analysis that falls outside the narrow political spectrum defined by the main political parties; (5) a decline in the volume and quality of research for current affairs programming, a greatly increased dependence on government and corporate sources of information, and a drastic decline in investigative journalism; (6) the increasing displacement of serious drama by soap operas; (7) the subordination of artistic and creative aims to commercial ones, including a growing standardisation of the product.

To this list should be added the already weakened regulatory structures of public service broadcasting, and an impending single regulator of communications – the so-called 'Ofcom' – likely to be more rather than less market-oriented in outlook. The 2000 Communications White Paper removed the threat of privatisation from Channel 4, at least for the next parliament, but it also envisaged largely removing Channel 5's public service obligations and allowing ITV to 'self-regulate' its own performance of them. It was hard to see how Channel 4 could avoid responding in kind to the intensified drive for ratings this would permit, since it also depended on advertising. ITV would in any case consolidate into a single company, too powerful for any regulator to control; and the BBC, by adopting so much of the neo-conservative agenda from the late 1980s onwards, had given up some of its greatest assets, especially some of its institutional memory and *esprit de corps*. Finally, the new subscription media were not subject to any public service obligations, so that 'the traditional areas to which the public service principle is now confined will become progressively smaller parts of the broadcasting landscape'.[134]

Conclusion

In the absence of a well-established doctrine about the role of broadcasting in a democracy these departures from public service broadcasting as it used to exist in the 1970s can be dismissed as of no consequence.[135] For instance, Richard Eyre, the Chief Executive of ITV in 1999, attacked the idea of public service broadcasting as inherently paternalistic ('giving the public what it ought to have') and out of date ('an idea that belongs to yesterday'). Instead he proposed, as the natural task for commercial broadcasters, the concept of 'public interest' broadcasting – which he defined, in Murdoch's notorious terms, as offering the public what interests it. Eyre argued that the advertisers' interest in higher-income viewers prevents them from pursuing the lowest common denominator of taste, while the need for mass audiences forces them to broadcast programmes of wide appeal. But it is interesting to compare this with what he envisaged for the BBC, which he said should do 'the things the commercial sector cannot' do: '. . . the provision of something really good, regularly and for all its licence payers . . . astonishing creative ambition . . . massively creatively ambitious, risk-taking, very large-scale programme enterprises . . . research and resource-intensive projects . . .'.[136] In other words, Eyre accepted that ITV would not be very ambitious or tackle big, risky or expensive projects. This did not bother City media analysts like Mathew Horsman, who wrote that while 'free TV was on its way to the museum' there was 'still reason to believe that the UK broadcasting industry would continue to make quality television, however it is paid for' – since 'story-telling is, after all, what most of us still want'.[137] Behind both Eyre's impossibly idealised mission for the BBC and Horsman's bluff reduction of television to 'story-telling' lies a shared recognition that market forces have already seriously eroded television's capacity to fulfil the function of a public service, on any realistic definition.

It is widely held that British television (at least BBC1 and 2, ITV and Channel 4) remains more critical than the press of governments and corporations, and that in many other countries the process of subordination to commercial aims is further advanced; but this is hardly grounds for satisfaction unless there are reasons to think that the recent trend is likely to be reversed.[138] In 2000, however, all the signs were that regulation was in retreat, that the commercial sector was consolidating, and that no government would risk unpopularity by granting the BBC the expanded resources needed to compete effectively across the whole range of the new media, let alone to bid for scarce rights and talent in face of rising costs. It was more likely that the BBC would be forced to narrow its focus, that its audience share would fall, and that the legitimacy of the licence fee would be increasingly challenged, while ITV's public service obligations would be increasingly eroded or ignored, and Channel 5's would become minimal, forcing Channel 4 and the BBC to skimp on theirs.

Meanwhile the process of commodification was rapidly transforming broadcasting in the same way that fast-food outlets had transformed eating. Television production was being industrialised, and multi-channel audiences were learning to accept the cheap standardised product that, increasingly, was all that was available free (or for the lowest subscription 'package'); higher-value programmes, costing more in terms of skilled labour, were increasingly available only at premium prices. One could even argue that audiences were increasingly collaborating in their own commodification, as 'demographics' for sale to advertisers and targets for 'e-commerce' and 't-commerce' (interactive television shopping services).

The sale of things was replacing the sale of services too. Video recorders, DVD recorders and more sophisticated 'time-shifting' devices like TiVo were forerunners of the normal end-result of industrialisation, substituting material goods for services and transferring labour to the final consumer: in the last example the work of schedulers is replaced by the work done by consumers at home. (It even took no huge feat of imagination to conceive that before long a growing number of people would be buying equipment and software not just to record programmes but to make them for themselves.)

Be this as it may, at some point along this continuum the idea of television as a medium of the public sphere, a forum for the 'main formative conversations of society', would come to seem as quaint and outdated as the stagecoach. And then where, if anywhere, would such conversations occur?

6

The National Health Service

At first sight it may seem that health services could hardly be more different from broadcasting. No giant global corporations seem to be muscling in on the public sector here; in the UK it still appears as a vast field of public service, provided by 1.2 million workers (about 5 per cent of the national workforce and two-thirds of all public employees) and accounting for 7 per cent of the United Kingdom's GDP – a tax-funded, non-profit domain, whose privatisation both its workers and the public have vigorously resisted. In reality, however, health services have been undergoing a similar process of transformation under market pressures.

Although medicine has been practised from time immemorial, health care as we know it dates from roughly the same time as broadcasting. Before the 1920s medicine had made significant progress in diagnosis but could offer few effective treatments for most illnesses. In the next three decades, however, new drugs and other scientific advances transformed the situation, making more and more conditions amenable to cure and virtually eliminating the major epidemic diseases in the industrialised countries. Access to medical care now really mattered, and the injustice of the unequal access to it that market-based provision afforded became less and less acceptable. In Britain, health insurance had been developed during the first half of the twentieth century but it was mainly for industrial workers and offered incomplete coverage. Meantime the Second World War had shown that collective provision was practicable in virtually all fields, and the case for universal health care was particularly compelling. Most people experience serious health problems in old age, while a small minority suffer from them earlier. Few people can afford the costs individually, and who will be stricken is broadly unknowable in advance. The logical response is to provide health care equally for all. It was this logic that led to the post-war adoption of systems of state-funded and largely state-provided medical care throughout most of the world – with the significant exception of the USA.

The National Health Service, 1948–79

The NHS was among the first of these systems and, for a while, one of the best. From 1948 onwards it provided comprehensive medical care (including eye and dental care) for all, free at the point of delivery, financed out of general taxation. Hospital doctors became salaried. General practitioners (GPs), while remaining formally self-employed 'independent contractors', were contracted to work for the NHS for a mixture of tax-funded capitation payments (a fixed sum per patient registered) and – increasingly, over the years – fees geared to serving public health needs or particular health targets (such as specified rates of innoculations against contagious diseases). In this way neither hospital doctors nor GPs had an incentive to over-treat (as in fee-for-service systems), which kept costs down.[1] Costs were also controlled by the fact that, apart from accidents and emergencies, specialists would only see patients referred to them by a GP – i.e. GPs were gatekeepers for access to more expensive specialist care.

In spite of periodic reorganisations, for the first forty-two years of its life – from 1948 to 1990 – the main features of the NHS remained basically constant. A hierarchy of regional and district health authorities, acting as agents for the Department of Health, channelled funds to some 2,000 hospitals and to a parallel system of Family Practitioner Committees through which the country's 26,000 GPs were paid. Policy-making power was shared in practice between the Department of Health and the hospital consultants and their professional Colleges (and to a lesser degree, the Royal Colleges of GPs and nurses). The local democratic element was minor: district-level Community Health Councils, consisting of appointed (not elected) lay members, represented the interests of local residents but had no policy-making or executive powers, and a local government representative sat on the board of each District Health Authority.

In 1990 the NHS was still very successful. Britain's national health statistics were roughly at the OECD average; indeed life expectancy and infant mortality rates in Britain were, as we saw in chapter 4, better than the USA's.[2] It was also spectacularly economical. Britain spent only two-thirds as much as Canada on health services, per head of population, and only a third as much as the USA.[3] To some extent this reflected underspending on the NHS's capital stock, and comparatively low wages for many of its workers, especially nurses and support staff, which its monopoly position allowed it to pay. But another significant reason was exceptionally low administrative costs. Before 1990 these were estimated at 6 per cent of total health-care spending, compared with over 20 per cent in the USA.[4]

Unlike the BBC, until the 1980s the market forces surrounding the NHS were comparatively weak. Doctors' resistance to the introduction of the NHS was strident but ultimately half-hearted. Most GPs came to see that they could make a better living and do more satisfying work in a publicly funded nation-wide system, and opposition by hospital consultants was overcome by offering them relatively generous salaries, topped up by peer-awarded 'merit awards' and the freedom to engage in private practice alongside their NHS work (in the notorious words of the Minister of Health, Aneurin Bevan, he 'stuffed their mouths with gold').[5] Just as important, perhaps, they were also given a dominant position in hospital management and hence in medical policy-making. Most independent voluntary hospitals and all local authority hospitals were absorbed into the NHS, the for-profit acute care sector was minute, and the for-profit long-term care sector was also small and fragmented. As late as 1986 non-NHS providers accounted for only 9 per cent of all hospital-based health-care spending. At that time no private health-care lobby existed on a scale comparable to the advertiser and private broadcasting lobbies that had been forcing open a market in broadcasting.

The transition to commodified health services

The NHS presented a big challenge to the neoliberal project. It occupied a major sphere of potential capital accumulation from which capital was excluded, and as the virtually sole purchaser of drugs, equipment and other medical supplies it could drive hard bargains with suppliers. In addition, as medicine advanced, expectations rose, and as the population aged, needs increased, so that the NHS needed constant budget increases. In the late 1970s it accounted for 11 per cent of government expenditure and this share seemed set to rise inexorably at a time when reducing taxes was a top neoliberal priority. Moreover, the NHS was easily the largest single employer in the country, with a strongly unionised and mainly Labour-voting nursing and non-clinical workforce; and even most senior doctors were by then strongly identified with it. Finally it remained extremely popular. In spite of being housed in increasingly run-down buildings, understaffed, bureaucratically run and effectively unaccountable it was still infused with a strong spirit of public service and equality. By and large people received good treatment in NHS hospitals, regardless of their income and social class. It represented a legacy of socialist, or social-democratic, ideals, largely identified with the Labour Party. Mrs Thatcher had declared that 'there was no alternative' to market capitalism, but the NHS showed that there was. It was the strongest pillar of the social-democratic temple that she wanted to pull down – 'a prime test for the assault on collectivism'.[6]

In 1982, the third year of Thatcher's first administration, the cabinet began to consider various options for privatising health care, including making part of the population take out private health insurance. An internal document from the government's Central Policy Review Staff was leaked to the press and there was a huge public outcry. Thatcher was forced to make a famous disclaimer, declaring that 'the NHS is safe with us'.[7] Thoughts of wholesale privatisation were abandoned. Instead the government proceeded incrementally, with three main policies: (1) ancillary hospital services such as cleaning, catering, laundry, pathology tests, etc., were increasingly 'contracted out'; (2) from 1984, on the advice of Roy Griffiths, the Managing Director of Sainsbury's supermarket chain, a new hierarchy of general managers was installed in the hospitals, backed up by businessmen appointed to hospital management boards, with the aim of supplanting the power of senior doctors (consultants) who had hitherto run them by 'consensus' (i.e. chiefly among themselves); (3) spending was cut back below the growth of needs, forcing the NHS either to deliver the same for less, or to reduce services. Experts thought the NHS needed about a 2 per cent real annual increase in spending just to maintain services in face of growing needs, but throughout the 1980s the real annual increase averaged less than half of this.[8] (The parallels with the Thatcher government's treatment of the BBC at the same period are obvious.)

From the point of view of the staff, work got harder while conditions got worse. Hospital consultants, in particular, found their views increasingly overridden by general managers on short-term contracts and 'performance-related pay' who were strongly focused on the 'bottom line' and sometimes seemed to have little understanding of health care.[9] Nurses no longer had enough time to give patients the care they thought necessary. Support staff like cleaners and cooks found themselves transferred to outside firms on lower wages and inferior terms of employment, typically non-unionised; between 1981 and 1991 the number directly employed by the NHS fell by over 40 per cent.[10] As for patients, unless they were acutely ill – when they almost always continued to praise hospital staff for the care they received – they encountered stressed and demoralised nursing and support staff and longer and longer waiting times just to see a specialist. By 1994, for example, the average wait to see an ear, nose and throat surgeon was three months, and an orthopaedic surgeon six months – and sometimes the subsequent wait for an operation could be even longer.[11] People lived with increasing pain and/or disability and occasionally died before they were treated.

Comprehensiveness and equality of access were reduced as well. Universal access to dental care was removed by simply 'capping' the dental budget from the late 1980s onwards, which effectively cut dentists' incomes from NHS work. Dentists increasingly responded by declining to treat patients 'on the NHS'. By the mid-1990s, while most dentists continued to treat children as NHS patients, fewer and fewer adults could get dental treatment on NHS terms, which in any case also now included user fees covering up to 80 per cent of the cost. Regular eye examinations were no longer provided by the NHS, glasses were no longer provided free to children and fees were raised for prescription drugs.*

Lengthening waiting-times – and occasional well-publicised and not wholly atypical cases of acutely ill patients waiting on hospital trolleys because of bed shortages – boosted interest in private health care and led to a rapid expansion of private medical insurance (PMI) in the

* Charles Webster, *The National Health Service: A Political History*, (Oxford University Press, 1998), pp. 156–8. NHS income from 'user fees' for dentistry rose from £65 million in 1979 to £340 million by 1990. By 1998 it totalled £475 million, compared with £396 million from prescription charges (*Compendium of Health Statistics*, 1999, table 2.19). Prescription charges were trebled in the 1980s but this proved self-defeating: the charge of £5.90 per prescription in 1999 covered only 8 per cent of the cost but was still too high for pensioners and people on social security benefit, to the point where 85 per cent of prescriptions made up were exempt from charges.

1980s. Companies now routinely offered PMI to senior executives and their families and the proportion of the population covered by PMI – mainly through such corporate plans – trebled, from under 4 per cent in the mid-1970s to 11.6 per cent in 1990.[12] Between 1981 and 1990, while NHS bed numbers fell by 21 per cent, private hospital bed capacity expanded (with various forms of government encouragement, such as the removal of planning restrictions) by 53 per cent, from 7,035 beds to 10,739;[13] and most of the increase was in hospitals owned by for-profit companies. Virtually all of the treatment provided in the private sector was given on a fee-for-service basis by NHS consultants – especially surgeons with part-time NHS contracts.[14]

The funding squeeze eventually led to a revolt within the NHS as well as protest by the all-party parliamentary Select Committee on Health. Unprecedented industrial action by the nursing unions, with equally unprecedented support from senior doctors, culminated in December 1987 in a joint open letter to the Prime Minister from the Presidents of the three senior Royal Colleges of medicine declaring that the NHS was in crisis. Mrs Thatcher's response was to set up a committee consisting of a small group of ideologically 'sound' ministers and civil servants, chaired by herself and meeting in strict secrecy, to review the financing of the NHS. It rejected the option of moving to either vouchers or an insurance-based scheme, but adopted instead the 1985 proposals of an American management consultant, Alain Enthoven, for creating a so-called 'internal market' by splitting the NHS into 'purchasers' and 'providers'.[15] The resulting 'reforms' radically changed the service's orientation and structure.

NHS hospitals became self-financing 'trusts', run by government-appointed boards of directors, providing services to patients in return for payments by 'purchasers'. The purchasers were of two kinds. The principal purchasers were the roughly one hundred health authorities (or in Scotland and Northern Ireland, boards) that 'purchased' all hospital-based health care for the patients in their areas. A much smaller but significant group of purchasers were GP group practices that opted to become 'fundholders'. These 'fundholding' GPs received a portion of their local health authority's hospital services budget, out of which they, rather than the authority, 'purchased' the more routine kinds of hospital-based care their patients required.* In theory hospital

---

* Although there were experiments in 'total fundholding', most fundholding general

trusts were to compete with each other for patients, i.e. for the 'contracts' that the purchasers had to offer. (They could also raise money by selling services to small numbers of private patients, as some already did – offering them faster access, in more comfortable and better-staffed rooms, with better food.)

This 'internal market' was introduced in 1991, without any formal public debate or, indeed, any electoral mandate. The idea was that it would make the NHS more cost-effective by making hospitals respond to customer demand (the latter being exercised on behalf of patients by health authorities or fundholding GPs), and become much more cost-conscious – while the government still controlled total spending. The name 'internal market' was really a misnomer, however, in two senses. Insofar as it was internal, it was not really a market. In a real market financially successful hospitals would have expanded and unsuccessful ones closed. Since this was socially and politically unthinkable, the 'internal market' functioned at best as a 'shadow' market and was tightly controlled from the centre by directives to the health authorities and a stream of what were euphemistically called 'guidelines' to the trusts. The contracts the purchasers made with the trusts were not legally enforceable, and neither the purchasers nor the providers were actually free to follow market logic.[16] And insofar as it *was* a market it was not internal – health authorities purchased services from private hospitals (especially when trying to cut waiting times), NHS Trusts competed for private patients with for-profit hospitals, and NHS consultants also worked in the private sector.

Both qualifications are important. The first meant that people were set to behave in a market-oriented way, but not really allowed to, while the second opened up the system, fragmented initially into over 400 trusts and several hundred 'purchasers', to a wide range of external market influences. Such as it was, however, the system was more or less fully operational by the mid-1990s; by 1997, when Labour replaced the Conservatives in office, virtually all NHS hospitals, clinics and other

---

practices were only responsible for the cost of secondary care of up to a maximum of £5,000 a year for any one patient – enough to cover, say, an appendectomy or a hip replacement, but not heart bypass surgery. Costs above £5,000 were met out of the local health authority budget – i.e. the risks continued to be effectively pooled for populations of around half a million.

'provider units' had become 'trusts', and almost 60 per cent of all GPs had become 'fundholders'.

Coupled with these 'reforms' was another equally significant change. Under the NHS and Community Care Act 1990, which established the 'internal market', responsibility for the long-term care of the chronically ill, the frail elderly and mentally handicapped (people with 'learning difficulties') was transferred from the NHS to local authorities – the elected local government councils. Local authorities got additional funding to cover this, but whereas care in the NHS was free, local authorities could charge people for some of the costs of their care and were under strong central government pressure to do so. So these patients were now means-tested, and expected to dispose of all but a small residue of their savings (including their homes) to pay for their own care before it would be covered by public funds.[17] Second, local authorities were obliged to use 85 per cent of the transitional funding given them for this purpose to place patients in *privately* owned nursing or residential care-homes. The private long-term care sector had already been expanding rapidly thanks to the Thatcher government's policy, formalised in 1983, of allowing poor people in private care homes, but not in local authority-run homes, to claim social security payments, which came from the central government budget. Cash-strapped local authorities had therefore encouraged people to move out of local authority homes into private sector homes, and now the 1990 NHS and Community Care Act channelled further public funding into the private sector. On the other hand the 1990 Act also terminated the practice of allowing patients in private homes to claim social security benefits; from 1993 everyone in private care homes would be funded from local authority budgets, and be subject to means-testing. In effect, long-term care ceased to be a health-service responsibility and was no longer free, except for the very poor; by 1996 almost 69 per cent of all residential care for the long-term ill and infirm was provided by the private sector.[18] A multi-billion-pound long-term care industry had been created, using public funds; publicly-provided care had been drastically curtailed; and then the public funding had been reduced as well.

These changes drove a large bridgehead into the psychological defences of the NHS by removing equal access to health care from the members of the population who were, in general, most in need of it, but least able to fight – the old and chronically sick. The change was represented as moving them out of 'faceless institutions' into 'the community'. The reality was an often abrupt, budget-driven move from fully-funded care in one institution – a hospital, which for many elderly people had long been their home, and by no means always a bad one – to means-tested care in another institution, a private home, usually less well staffed and not necessarily even located in a 'community' with which they had any connection at all.*

The government refused to pilot or test these 'reforms', or to undertake or fund any evaluation of them; the idea was to impose them and minimise opposition by limiting objective discussion. The weight of the evidence collected by experts in the field, however, is that they did not achieve any of their proclaimed goals.[19] They did not reduce costs significantly except by cutting services, while – ironically enough – they more than doubled administrative costs.[20] They did not make good hospitals better, or push bad ones towards either improvement or bankruptcy; there were hospital closures and trust mergers, but these were mainly a result of the way capital assets happened to be distributed among trusts, and did not reflect or, usually, enhance the productivity of the trusts concerned, or the quality of services they offered.[†] They did not improve hospital care, because budget pressures took pre-cedence over patient needs. They did not enhance 'patient choice', even when this was exercised in reality by fundholding GPs, but reduced it, since GPs could now only send patients to providers with whom either they or the local health authority had made contracts.[21] Nor is there any evidence that fundholding made GPs more efficient or, in general, able to secure better hospital care for their patients than non-fundholding GPs (although the latter was widely believed).[22] The one clear change, a further loss of power by hospital consultants, was seen by some as a gain, although it is not self-evident that either managers

---

* In one instance, aged patients were shipped from a London hospital to a private nursing home in Yorkshire. In a number of such cases, only some of which were subsequently investigated, the death rate among these old people, abruptly displaced from their familiar surroundings, rose sharply in the immediately following weeks.
† All trusts had to pay the Treasury a capital charge of 6 per cent a year on the value of their capital assets. If a trust inherited a large inner-city site and many buildings, this could create an unsustainable burden on its revenues, necessitating the sale of some of the capital stock. On capital charges and their effects see Jean Shaoul, 'Charging for capital in the NHS trusts: to improve efficiency?', *Management Accounting Research* 9, 1998, pp. 95–112; and Allyson M. Pollock and Declan Gaffney, 'Capital charges: a tax on the NHS', *BMJ* 317, 1998, pp. 157–8.

or GPs are preferable to consultants when it comes to deciding how best to use health-care resources.

Alongside these disappointed promises must be set some major negative consequences. One was the creation of a 'two-tier' service, if not a three-tier one: immediate *de luxe* service for private patients in NHS hospitals; fast-track service for the patients of some fundholding GPs (in cases where the latter had successfully bargained for this in making their contracts with hospitals); and consequently longer waiting-times and worse service for everyone else – i.e. a further general erosion of the principle of equal access based on health needs alone. A second major problem was the impossibility of rational planning for services to meet local health needs, when hospital trusts struggling for financial survival were making plans solely with a view to cutting costs and developing services in which they thought they had some advantage. Third, specialist services were sometimes suspended regardless of need, to meet hospital 'bottom lines', because the funds provided for these services in the current year's contracts had already been used up, even if many of the costs involved – for staff and premises – would have to be met anyway, implying a further loss of public access to treatment, and a rise in average costs.

Although the Labour Party had consistently pointed out these defects when it was in opposition, when it took office in May 1997 it retained the 'purchaser–provider split' (renamed 'the separation between "planning" and "provision"') while abolishing the detailed financial transactions on which it was supposed to have been based. The Labour government said it expected to save £1 billion a year in administrative costs by replacing detailed annual contracting with the 'commissioning' of specified categories of services for periods of several years – although informed observers were sceptical.[23] Otherwise the structure of health authorities and independent trusts was left intact, as was the power of hospital managers vis-à-vis senior hospital doctors.

The chief reason given for abandoning the party's stance in opposition was that the NHS had undergone so many changes in the previous decade and a half that it needed a period of stability. It soon became clear, however, that the real reason lay elsewhere, in 'New' Labour's overriding preoccupation with City opinion. The modernisers shared some of Thatcher's preference for central control, and her dislike of public sector professionals, including doctors;[24] but what immediately governed the decision to retain Thatcher's NHS reforms was New Labour's pre-election pledge to stay within the Conservatives' existing public spending plans. Undoing the NHS reforms would have been incompatible with this pledge. Pre-election discussions in the City had also convinced New Labour of the need to push ahead with the Conservatives' Private Finance Initiative, under which the public sector would lease capital assets from the private sector rather than undertaking major capital investments itself. The most important early application of the PFI would be a major new hospital building programme, which decisively broke the barrier between public and market provision.

And far from giving the NHS a period free from additional structural change, the Labour government soon introduced additional changes that portended a further shift to market-based health care. The main thrust of the government's 1997 White Paper, *The New NHS*, was to make the NHS 'primary care led'.[25] Control over all NHS spending on secondary (general hospital) care was to be gradually transferred from health authorities to Primary Care Groups (PCGs), each covering an average population of around 100,000, run by boards on which GPs – who, it will be remembered, were mostly self-employed small business-men and -women – would predominate.[26] The separate category of fundholding GPs would be phased out by 2000. Moreover, in a relatively short period of years – in some cases, as early as April 2000 – PCGs were able to graduate to the status of Primary Care Trusts (PCTs), which, like the hospital trusts, would be legally and financially independent and have the same freedom to engage in for-profit activities.

More innovations, less dramatic but still important, were also foreshadowed in *The New NHS*, including the establishment of a National Institute for Clinical Excellence, charged with establishing and defining good and cost-effective clinical practice across the NHS, and a Centre for Health Improvement, charged (in effect) with enforcing it; 'NHS Direct', a nation-wide free telephone 'help' line; and NHS 'walk-in' primary care clinics. But to grasp the significance of the whole sequence of changes made to the NHS over the last two decades of the twentieth century, of which these were a quite logical continuation, a brief review is needed of the health-care system as it stood at the end of this period.

176   MARKET-DRIVEN POLITICS

Figure 6.1.   The NHS since 1980: a chronology

1980	Contracting out ancillary work and financial squeeze imposed on NHS
1981	Social security budget made available for fees for patients in private but not local authority-owned nursing and residential care homes
1983	Roy Griffiths recommends general management for NHS hospitals
1987	Financial crisis. Royal College Presidents write to Prime Minister
1988	Thatcher sets up committee to review NHS financing
1990	NHS and Community Care Act introduces internal market: 'purchasers' (health authorities and GP fundholders) split from 'providers' (NHS trusts)

Responsibility for long-term care devolved from NHS to local authorities but 85 per cent of transferred transitional funding to be spent on placements in private care homes |
| 1991 | Private Finance Initiative (PFI) introduced |
| 1993 | Funding of long-term care from Social Security budget ended All long-term care becomes local authority-financed and means-tested |
| 1997 | New Labour government
'Internal market' abolished
PFI legislation passed for NHS
White paper outlines 'primary care-led NHS' |
| 1998 | 'First wave' of PFI hospitals approved |
| 1999 | Primary Care Groups (PCGs) established
NHS Direct, National Institute for Clinical Excellence (NICE), and Centre for Health Improvement (CHI) established
'Second wave' of PFI hospitals approved |
| 2000 | NHS spending increases announced
First wave of PCGs become Primary Care Trusts
NHS Plan published in July
Concordat with Independent Healthcare Association finalised in October |

Table 6.1.   NHS spending 1991/92 and 1997/98 (%)

	1991/92	1997/98
Hospital services	60.3	52.9
Community Health services	9.5	9.5
Pharmacy service	11.0	13.1
General Medical services[a]	8.1	7.9
Dental services	4.5	3.5
Opthalmic services	0.5	0.6
Other[b]	6.0	12.4
Total	100.0	100.0

[a] GPs
[b] Central administration, ambulance services, mass radiography, etc.
Source: Compendium of Health Statistics 2000, table 2.16.

The NHS quasi-market and other health care markets, 1999–2000

While the NHS was still the predominant provider in the acute sector, it was no longer a monopoly provider of health services in the UK. Substantial new market forces had been unleashed and encouraged to penetrate the domain of health-service provision.

The NHS

In 1999 total expenditure on the NHS in Great Britain was approximately £52 billion, accounting for 14 per cent of all government expenditure and 7 per cent of GDP.[27] Just over half of this was spent on hospital services, which, as table 6.1 shows, represented a sharp drop since the beginning of the decade, while the share of spending on drugs had risen, and the share of spending on administration had doubled. Policy and the budget for the NHS were set by the Department of Health and Parliament. Spending the budget and implementing policy were the responsibility of the NHS Executive, located in Leeds.

Figure 6.2. The NHS in 2000

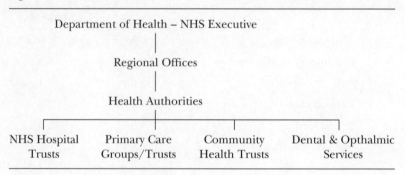

Department of Health – NHS Executive

Regional Offices

Health Authorities

| NHS Hospital Trusts | Primary Care Groups/Trusts | Community Health Trusts | Dental & Opthalmic Services |

The Executive parcelled out the budget to the health authorities and boards that commissioned services from about 500 'self-financing' hospital and community health 'trusts' (see figure 6.2).* Both health authorities and trusts were run by Chief Executives and management teams, with non-executive directors and chairpersons appointed by the government. Doctors enjoyed 'clinical independence' but had to work within budgets and administrative policies set by general management.

The NHS acute (short stay) hospital sector
In 1998/99 the total bed capacity of all NHS hospitals in the UK was about 248,000, down 45 per cent since 1981. This huge drop was due partly to the transfer of long-term care out of the NHS and partly to a steady decline in length of stay for acute admissions, the latter being accelerated in the early 1990s by the substitution of day surgery for inpatient surgery (by 1996/97 about a quarter of all 'finished consultant episodes', or FCEs, were day surgery cases, double the 1990 share). But while bed numbers had fallen, clinical staff numbers had risen, to cope with increased patient 'throughput'. Directly employed support staff numbers had fallen dramatically (from a peak of 280,000 in 1981 to under 100,000 in 1997) due to outsourcing, but all other categories had increased. In 1998 there were about 76,000 doctors and dentists,

---

* Mergers of both health authorities and trusts had reduced their number – in the case of UK hospital trusts, from a peak of 536 in 1995/96 down to 400 in late 2000. Many trusts managed several hospitals.

128,000 professional and technical staff and 442,000 nurses in NHS hospitals – together with non-clinical staff, a total of some 909,000. Together with the 'outsourced' support workers they were responsible for 14 million FCEs – an increase of 100 per cent since 1980. Over nine million people – about 16 per cent of the population – attended a hospital outpatient clinic in 1998. A total of 5.1 million people – equivalent to 9 per cent of the population – were admitted to hospital as inpatients. Almost six million operations were performed.

Perhaps the most striking feature of all this is that it worked as well as it did. Discharge rates per thousand population still compared favourably with those of most other OECD countries, in spite of the UK's relatively low hospital bed:population ratio, as did infant mortality rates and other indicators. Health-care coverage remained, if not comprehensive, extensive, and access remained – in theory at least – universal and equal. But the fact that it remained publicly provided and free was increasingly anomalous in a world inundated with the ideology of individualism and choice.

Primary care

Family health services were mainly provided by GPs, now numbering 30,000 and almost all working as self-employed 'independent contractors', even though their NHS contract provided them with virtually all their income.[28] From April 1999 they were were organised into 481 new Primary Care Groups (or in Scotland, Cooperatives). The total number of patients covered by PCGs ranged from about 50,000 to about 250,000.

Initially PCGs might merely advise the health authority on its commissioning of secondary care, but they could also assume responsibility for up to 60 per cent of the authority's overall budget; and beginning with a 'first wave' of PCGs in April 2000 they could opt to become Primary Care Trusts, responsible for commissioning all secondary (i.e. specialist) care for their patients; and in a final stage, take responsibility for the community care budgets for their areas too.*

A 'primary care-led' NHS had been the ostensible aim of successive

---

* Community health trusts, providing public and preventive health services, occupied a space between the acute and primary care sectors. In the long run they seemed destined to be merged with PCTs into a new kind of all-round local level health service organisation.

governments seeking to shift spending from expensive inpatient secondary care to cheaper outpatient and home-based care, and this was clearly the main aim of the new structure. But it was also intended to level up the standard of GP services, which varied quite widely, especially in big cities; to oblige GPs to take collective responsibility for their drug budgets, curbing the high-spending prescribers among them; and to allow new services, or new ways of providing existing services, to be developed without running into resistance from the vested interests of hospitals, community health trusts or GPs. These innovations were to include new service models run by salaried GPs or 'nurse practitioners' working in larger primary care centres; as well as 'walk-in clinics', unconnected with patients' places of residence, and 'NHS Direct', the phone service mentioned earlier.

In 2000 the new PCG/PCT structure was still embryonic and its implications could only be speculated about. A lot would depend on as yet unstated government 'guidelines'. But what was clear was that the new PCTs would have the same financial obligations and legal rights as NHS hospital trusts, including the freedom to raise capital from the private market, to outsource activities to for-profit providers (from accountants to physiotherapists), and to raise revenue by undertaking profit-making activities such as pharmacies or the sale of private medical insurance. A number of companies were already active in seeking to build and lease premises to GPs and were developing PFI projects.[29] Whatever else it implied, a 'primary care-led NHS' meant an NHS led by the one element within it that had remained in the private sector from its inception and that would be free to integrate itself more fully than before with the corporate health industry.

Dentistry
Almost all the 20,000 dentists in the UK were, like GPs, self-employed, contracted to work with the NHS but not employed by it. In 1999 it was estimated that about a third still worked solely within the NHS, mostly in underprivileged inner-city areas.[30] Between 5 and 10 per cent did only private work; the remainder did both NHS and private work. Thanks to the government's capping of the dental budget the trend was steadily away from NHS work. In most places it was now hard to find a dentist prepared to take on adults as NHS patients. By 1998 about 57 per cent of dentists' total income came from fees paid by patients.[31] So a part of the NHS had been substantially privatised

without serious public resistance, and the remaining public revenues assigned to it were only enough to provide what dentists considered a cut-price service for children and those unable to afford more than NHS dental charges – and even these charges were beyond the reach of anyone dependent on social security, for example. This was not unlike the American model for health care in general. In 1997 Bruggen summed up the effects on dentistry done 'on the NHS' as follows:

> The total money put into NHS dentistry has remained the same. But dentists must now fit more into it and there are many restrictions, for example on the frequency of certain procedures. Work on children is paid per capita. . . . Work on adults is paid per item. Both of those decisions are in keeping with the service being managed for cost rather than for quality. A time restriction means that, for example, the calculation of fees and income are on the assumption of 17–18 minutes per NHS root filling. This is very little time for a well done job, except for very fast practitioners. This means risks are taken. . . . Apart from increasing registrations, the way to get more money was to do a large number of service items on adults. Thus dentists were encouraged to increase their rate of work by reducing the time spent on any item, and this encouraged them to cut corners.[32]

The private acute (short stay) hospital industry[33]

In 1998 total spending on patients in private hospital beds was estimated at £2.5 billion, equivalent to about 10 per cent of total spending on all NHS hospitals. About 60 per cent of this went to private hospitals and clinics, 10 per cent to NHS hospital private beds, and 30 per cent (an estimated £683 million) in fees to surgeons, anaesthetists and physicians (nearly all of whom were part-time NHS consultants).[34] There were also about 150 private pathology laboratories in the UK in 1995, earning a total of £84 million, accounting for 8 per cent of total spending on pathology nation-wide.

There was considerable concentration of ownership, with just three organisations – General Healthcare Group, BUPA Hospitals and Nuffield Hospitals – owning 53 per cent of all private hospital bed capacity. BUPA was a provident (i.e. non-profit) association, and Nuffield Hospitals was a non-profit 'charity' (in quotation marks because although BUPA and Nuffield enjoyed charitable status for tax purposes, they

catered exclusively to people able to pay their fees – in effect they
enjoyed a state subsidy). Overall, 67 per cent of all private hospital beds
were owned by for-profit companies and accounted for 72 per cent of
all private hospital revenue.

Over-capacity in private hospitals was extreme. Capacity had been
increased when new medical technology was rapidly reducing the
average time patients needed to stay in hospital, and by 1998 average
bed occupancy rates in private hospitals were under 50 per cent. The
PMI companies began to develop 'preferred provider' schemes, offering
patients (and in one case also doctors) financial incentives only to use
hospitals on a restricted list. The aim was to cut costs by concentrating
business in fewer hospitals, allowing these hospitals to secure greater
economies of scale and the insurer to drive harder bargains. This
accelerated an already significant process of concentration and hospital
closures. By 1998 the top ten providers accounted for 84 per cent of
acute care revenues.

By now, however, the private acute care industry faced a number of
major constraints on further expansion. The chief one was that the
number of people covered by PMI had remained more or less static
throughout the 1990s. This was mainly due to rising PMI premiums,
which deterred both individuals and companies (see the following
section). It was also due to the fact that the main incentive to seek
private insurance was not the quality of treatment offered by the NHS
for serious illness, but the waiting times for surgery, including elective
surgery for non-life-threatening but painful or disabling conditions like
cataracts and arthritic hips. Even Conservative governments, which
wished to encourage PMI, felt obliged to respond to electoral pressure
by periodically diverting funds to 'reduce waiting lists', with some
success (however temporary).

Laing observes that 'the additional resources that the Labour government would have to commit to providing an elective surgery service
which is as timely and accessible as the private sector's is, will probably
prove well beyond what is politically feasible'.[35] This conclusion is surely
correct – except that for the great majority of people elective surgery in
the NHS will always remain much *more* accessible than in the private
sector. The private sector will continue to cater for those lucky enough
to have PMI, but cannot expand beyond the 13 per cent of employees
for whom employers are able or willing to pay the increasingly costly
premiums involved. So although private hospitals had begun to expand

the range of operations they would do, they still tended to concentrate on the 'minor' or 'intermediate' kinds of surgery that are for non-life-threatening conditions and have the longest NHS waiting times.[36] Very few offered the full range of specialties found in a typical NHS General Hospital.*

To expand out of this market niche they needed a larger stream of revenues than the PMI market could produce.[†] From 1997 to 1999, however, during the first two years of the new Labour government, health authorities were discouraged from making contracts with private hospitals – to reduce waiting times for elective surgery, for example – to the extent previously allowed by the Conservatives, and it was hard to see how the private acute sector could expand much further unless this changed. But the private acute hospital sector was no longer a negligible political force. Laing's observation that 'by the time the new Labour government came to power in 1997, the private healthcare sector was much more firmly established than it had been two decades earlier, and less vulnerable to political change',[37] could have been phrased more strongly: it was now much better placed to get the market boundaries shifted further in its favour. Events would show, moreover, that the new Labour government was much more willing to comply than it initially appeared.

Private medical insurance (PMI)

The demand for treatment in private acute hospitals has depended entirely on the growth of PMI, and company-paid PMI subscriptions have been its mainstay. In 1998 6.8 million people were covered by PMI, and another half a million had private medical cover from non-insured funds – altogether 12.4 per cent of the population. These people were overwhelmingly professionals, employers and managers (about 20 per cent of whom had PMI) and their families, and to a

---

* NHS hospitals were not only left to provide most of the more expensive treatments, but also had to admit any private hospital patients who developed complications that could not be handled in the private hospital concerned – in a word, the NHS was subject to 'adverse selection' by the private hospital industry.
† There was the further constraint that even consultants with part-time NHS contracts could not do all their private work during day-time hours: a 1992 survey showed that 33 per cent of private surgery was done in 'unsocial' hours for this reason (*Laing's Healthcare Market Review*, 1999–2000 [Laing and Buisson, 1999], p. 81).

much lesser extent intermediate or junior non-manual staff (9 per cent of whom were covered, almost all by company schemes) and their families, heavily concentrated in the south-east of the country.

Seven non-profit provident associations accounted for half of all PMI, and seventeen for-profit companies for the other half, but concentration was high, with two provident associations (BUPA and WPA) and one commercial company (PPP, owned since 1999 by a French insurance TNC, AXA) earning between them 76 per cent of all premium income. But throughout the 1990s PMI revenue stagnated, in spite of every effort to win new business. The value of the claims made by patients rose faster than the retail price index, forcing profit margins down and premiums up. While the premium increases did not lead to equivalent reductions in insurance cover on the part of companies, self-paying individuals did tend to respond by 'downgrading' their policies – accepting reduced coverage, covering fewer dependants, or agreeing to bigger 'co-payments', in order to keep the premium down – further reducing the attractiveness of PMI. The insurers responded to rising costs and falling margins by introducing the 'preferred provider' schemes already mentioned, by making tentative efforts to introduce 'managed care' on American lines for some medical conditions, by trying to reduce consultants' fees, and by vertical integration (BUPA and PPP both acquired substantial holdings of hospitals) and 'product innovation'.[38] Taken together these measures might succeed for a while in containing the threat that PMI faced from relentless cost inflation – 'Baumol's disease'. But they also tended to underline the limitations of PMI; it was affordable only by a fortunate minority with very large personal incomes or senior jobs in companies with PMI schemes, and retaining even these subscribers was proving difficult.

On the other hand the 'product innovation' engaged in by the insurers broke some significant new ground, at least ideologically. Besides offering cheaper plans with more restricted coverage, insurers also offered plans that, for example, restricted cover for private treatment to conditions for which the NHS waiting time was more than six weeks, or more than twelve weeks. Schemes were also advertised that provided lump-sum cash payments, rather than paying for treatment, or cash payments for agreeing to accept NHS treatment rather than private treatment when treatment became needed, and so on. In 1997/ 98 it appeared that about 5 per cent of the population who did not have PMI had such cash plans, so that all told some 16–17 per cent of the population now had some sort of private provision. The fact that private medical cover had become more and more common could prove politically significant later on. Tax relief on PMI premiums, for example, introduced by the Conservatives for people over sixty in 1989 but withdrawn again by Labour in 1997, could be reintroduced and extended by a government disposed to use it as an incentive for further privatisation.

The for-profit long-term care industry

In 1999 there were 554,000 places in 'care homes', of which 380,600 (69 per cent) were for-profit, with total annual revenues of £5,390 million, most of which came from public funds (social security, local authorities, or – in a very small minority of cases – the NHS). About 29 per cent of the patients or residents were paying for themselves. A further £670 million worth of non-residential or domiciliary services (16 per cent of the total) was also provided by for-profit agencies.[39]

Although the private care home sector accounted for the bulk of this very important segment of health service provision, it remained over-whelmingly a cottage industry. A 'major provider' in this sector is defined as owning just three or more homes, and yet only 30 per cent of the total for-profit capacity was owned by 'major providers'. The three largest providers owned just 7.9 per cent of capacity between them; the top ten, only 13.8 per cent. The great majority of the country's 15,000 homes, especially residential (as opposed to nursing) homes, were small companies operating a single home in converted premises. Nursing homes, which required larger investment and had higher staff costs, had a somewhat more concentrated ownership pattern: 'major providers' accounted for 40.8 per cent of these, and 47.2 per cent of dual-registered (i.e. residential and nursing) homes, but even in this sub-sector no single provider had significant market power.

This compounded the problems faced by the for-profit care-home owners when in 1993 the Conservative government finally 'turned off the tap' of central government funding, as described above. The resources given to local authorities to replace this funding were both smaller and less 'ring-fenced' (i.e. they could be and were partly diverted to other uses, such as children's care, which attracted more media attention). For the rest of the decade care-home owners found they had to accept static real fee levels while facing rising costs.

Although the Labour government that took office in 1997 retained the Conservatives' system, and continued to press local authorities to divest themselves of their own long-term care homes, the private care-home sector continued to be squeezed.* Costs were raised by the introduction of a minimum wage, by the EU Working Time Directive, which raised holiday entitlements, and by an 8.2 per cent nation-wide increase in nurses' pay in 1999–2000. Occupancy rates also fell from the very high levels of the 1980s. The small units typical of the industry could not achieve economies of scale and many homes closed. One solution, particularly attractive to 'major' providers, was to sell the premises to finance companies and lease them back, releasing capital for expansion. Six finance companies, three of them American- or partly American-owned, were active in this field, attracted by the relatively low risk (thanks to the virtually guaranteed government funding that made up the bulk of the homes' revenues).[40] Some concentration of ownership could be expected to ensue from all these developments, but the essential weakness of the industry vis-à-vis the purchasers – the local authorities – seemed unlikely to change significantly.

The pharmaceutical industry

In 1997 British-based pharmaceutical companies produced 6.7 per cent of total world pharmaceutical output – the fifth largest after the USA, Japan, France and Germany. The world's largest pharmaceutical company, Glaxo Wellcome, was British.[41] The industry employed 60,000 people in the UK and generated an annual trade surplus in drugs of £2.4 billion. The drug industry was thus a major force, in relation to which the government had conflicting interests. Sixty-three per cent of its total output was sold in the UK, of which the NHS bought 80 per cent; so the NHS had the power to drive hard bargains and to restrict the adoption of expensive new drugs until their long-term value had been well established. On the other hand the government wanted to

---

* The Labour government abolished the Conservatives' requirement that local authorities spend 85 per cent of the funds transferred to them from the social security budget on for-profit homes; but 'contracting for residential care was by then sufficiently rooted in local authority culture and procedures not to need protection through budgetary ring fencing' (*Laing's Healthcare Market Review*, 1999–2000 [Laing and Buisson, 1999], p. 170). In practice further pressure was put on local authorities to divest themselves of their remaining homes.

foster the industry because of its contribution to national income and the trade balance. Its solution, which favoured the drug industry more than taxpayers, was the Pharmaceuticals Price Regulation Scheme (PPRS), whereby it agreed to fixed prices for the branded prescription drugs bought by the NHS, subject to the manufacturers' books being inspected by the government to ensure that their resulting profits remained within an agreed range. The drug companies could promote their new drugs to NHS doctors but health authority budgets imposed a major constraint on their adoption, even though doctors nominally remained free to prescribe what they judged best for their patients. (As we have seen, one of the motives behind the creation of PCGs with 'unified budgets' was to curb GPs' spending on drugs by making them deal with the financial consequences.)

The creation in 1999 of the National Institute for Clinical Excellence (NICE) foreshadowed in the government's 1997 White Paper, *The New NHS*, and the related Centre for Health Improvement (promptly dubbed CHIMP by irritated or alarmed clinicians), added a new dimension to the relationship between the government and the pharmaceutical industry. NICE was mandated to examine the evidence on both the clinical and the cost effectiveness of treatments, including drugs, and CHIMP was mandated to oversee and if necessary enforce good performance based on such evidence. Whether NICE would avoid 'capture' by the pharmaceutical industry, which was represented on all its key committees, was a key issue in the debates surrounding its first year of operation. The industry's interest was to stop NICE being persuaded by the Department of Health to make adverse judgements on its products.* Besides stressing the value of the industry to the economy, the industry's lobbying organisation argued that spending money on medicines was much cheaper than treating people in hospital:

> Hospital costs make up a significant proportion of the total cost of health care. While medicines expenditure may have risen, these costs are more than matched by the rising costs of health care. Research has shown that

* In October 1999 NICE provisionally recommended that Glaxo Wellcome's influenza drug Relenza not be adopted by the NHS, on the grounds that clinical evidence did not show it to be generally effective. As we have already noted, Glaxo's Chairman wrote to the Secretary of State for Health threatening to move the company abroad. In the summer of 2000 the company resubmitted its case to NICE, which eventually agreed to recommend it for a limited range of cases, a manifest compromise.

medicines save the NHS as much as £10 billion every year through
replacing inpatient treatment with medicines.⁴²

Of course these are not really alternatives, but the argument shows how
the pharmaceutical industry was a major force – in health care, certainly
the most important – pushing to substitute the purchase of goods for
the purchase of services.

These relationships between the pharmaceutical industry and the
NHS were at the national level. After the NHS 'internal market' was
introduced in 1990, however, pharmaceutical companies approached a
number of health authorities, NHS trusts and GP practices individually
with proposals for 'disease management' schemes on US lines. Esen-
tially the companies offered free services (or even cash contributions)
to enable these NHS purchasers or providers to develop standardised
treatment plans for specified chronic diseases, using the companies'
products.⁴³ These initiatives were banned in 1994, but were later allowed
again under strict limits that in particular excluded any contract that
specified a particular branded drug. By 1999 a number of initiatives
were being developed within this constraint. For some illnesses the drug
of choice is so well known as not to need to be specified: in other cases
a few manufacturers may benefit together from expanding the use of
drugs for a particular condition. While it is illegal to advertise prescription drugs directly to the public, the manufacturers have many other
means at their disposal, from 'disease awareness' advertising, which
encourages patients to ask doctors for drug treatments, to lavish conferences for doctors and financial support for patients' groups that
demand that drugs be made available.⁴⁴

With the NHS, where these activities are well known, distrust of the
pharmaceutical industry's motives and claims is quite widespread, but
hospital consultants' research often depends heavily on participation in
industry-financed drug trials, and many NHS managers and GPs are
quite sympathetic to the pharmaceutical industry.⁴⁵ Moreover, another
obstacle to the adoption of 'disease management' in the NHS has been
the institutional separation between hospitals and GPs. If this separation
is significantly reduced in the new 'primary care-led NHS', and if
governments see political and economic advantages in closer links, the
pharmaceutical industry could well find itself playing a larger role in
NHS-provided treatment. In 2000 a new *NHS Plan* seemed to point in
this direction.

The commodification of health care

Before we look at the crucial year 2000, however, we need to pause briefly and ask: how did all these for-profit providers come to surround and penetrate the NHS? To see this it is easiest to return again to the four conditions that need to be fulfilled: (i) the services must be commodified – broken down and 'reconfigured' as discrete units of output that can be packaged in such a way that they can be produced in quantity, to some extent interchangeably, and priced; (ii) patients must be persuaded to want these services as commodities; (iii) the existing workforce of service providers must be redefined as producers of commodities, producing a surplus for the owners of the assets they work with; (iv) where risk, in one form or another, confronts would-be entrants into the field, it must be underwritten by the state.

The transformation of health care into commodities

This was probably the most important long-run effect of the 'internal market'. The so-called 'contracts' between 'purchasers' and 'providers' were at first rather vague, but since money was changing hands they were apt to become more detailed and precise over time. To deal with this, hospital trusts needed to know what each 'procedure' cost, which meant trying to standardise them and assign them a share of fixed costs, which also had to be calculated. In practice few had the resources to do this and contracts were priced largely on the basis of overall past costs. In some cases health authorities led by Conservative-appointed business-men drove harder and harder bargains, forcing trusts to reduce their prices and seeking to impose penalties for non-performance. By 1997 two-thirds of NHS hospital trusts had financial deficits.[46] In the search for economy clinical directorates (i.e. specialist departments) in hospitals were given separate budgets and set to meet given performance targets (in terms of FCEs per £1,000 spent). A new culture of cost-consciousness and economy was inaugurated in making policy decisions, competing with a professional culture using purely clinical criteria. The removal of long-term care from the NHS accelerated this shift. *Care* was increasingly replaced by *treatments*, which could be individuated, standardised and priced: e.g. seventy-five hip replacements at, £3,755 each.* It was harder to determine a standard price for taking the best possible care, week by week, of an older person with several chronic interacting illnesses, but NHS hospitals no longer cared for such patients.

After 1997 the Labour government ended the full 'internal market'. Beginning in 1998, instead of price competition a list of 'reference costs' of a wide range of procedures was published, compiled from the range reported by all NHS trusts, the idea being to identify costly 'outliers' – trusts whose costs were much higher than average. Few people in the NHS who were familiar with statistics took the 'reference costs' seriously because they rested on data much too crude to support the interpretations placed on them by politicians. To have adequately adjusted them for local variations in 'case-mix', the costs of equipment for different specialties and innumerable other differences would have called for more resources to be devoted to data collection and analysis than trusts or health authorities could afford. Nonetheless a new culture had been established in which patients were liable to be looked at not just in terms of clinical need, but also in terms of the potential demands they would make on the budget.

Cost-watching was reinforced by cost-cutting, which took various forms. One was the accelerated shift from inpatient surgery to day surgery. Day surgery may be better for some patients, although this is not the experience of others, especially those who have no family carer at home to take care of them during their recovery; and in the USA the adoption of some new surgical techniques that permit surgery to be done on an outpatient basis has been criticised for being adopted prematurely.[47] The great economic benefit of day surgery, however, is that it avoids the so-called 'hotel costs' of hospitalisation. To the extent that this is made possible by less invasive surgery, these costs are certainly reduced, but those that remain are mainly labour costs that are simply shifted from hospitals to patients' families and friends, or to the patients themselves.

A variant of cost-cutting by day surgery was experiments with 'hospital

* The figure is taken from *The New NHS 1999 Reference Costs* (Department of Health, 1999), p. 10. In what must surely be an unconscious illustration of the ideological effects of commodifying health care (who would have dared to mean it ironically?), the authors add: 'For comparative purposes, the NHS provides four primary hip replacements for the cost of a new medium-sized family saloon.' I am indebted for this gem to James Lancaster at University College London.

at home' schemes, in which non-surgical patients are treated by hospital doctors and nurses, but in their own homes. A trial in Leicester reported in 1999 found that compared with hospital admissions, patients treated at home had no significantly different health outcomes, but did have significantly shorter 'stays' in care. The overall cost, however, was only slightly less, even though the inputs of care made by relatives or friends, or by the patients themselves, were not counted;[48] it seems clear that if almost any cash value had been put on these inputs it would have tipped the cost advantage back in favour of hospital admission.*

Another form of cost-cutting that applied the economic logic of 'day surgery' to non-surgical treatments was to 'downsize' the whole acute hospital sector in favour of primary care, because primary care is cheaper (see table 6.2). In this the PFI played a major role. Not only was the cost of financing the new PFI hospitals higher than if they been built using public capital, but the funds to lease the new buildings now had to come out of the revenue budgets of the trusts involved – budgets that were not increased correspondingly. This meant new buildings with fewer beds – on average 30 per cent fewer. Even though the new hospital plans assumed dramatically – many doctors thought unrealistically – increased rates of 'throughput' of patients, 30 per cent fewer beds still implied a big drop in hospital admissions, and more people needing community-based or primary care – both those who would otherwise have been admitted to hospital but no longer could be, and those discharged from hospital earlier than in the past (in order to achieve high patient 'throughput').[49] Yet the PFI plans made no provision for a corresponding expansion of community or primary care in the areas affected, since the health needs of the local population were a problem for the health authorities, not for the trusts. The health authorities responsible for the overall health needs of the local population were of course aware of all this, but were not given additional

---

* This did not prevent the government awarding a 'special' grant of £10 million to a newly privatised military policy research company, the Defence Evaluation Research Agency, to try out a 250-patient 'hospital at home' scheme by 2002. Contrary to the findings in the Leicester study, DERA stated it as its belief that the scheme would save the NHS 'a lot of money' and that 'it could prove a model for the future for the entire NHS' – and perhaps equally significantly, that 'the project [would] be a money-earner for the UK "through deploying leading edge, shop window technology in the UK"' (*Guardian*, 26 April 2000).

Table 6.2.   NHS pay and the 'skill mix'

(a) NHS pay scales, January 2000	(£)
Consultant with A-plus distinction award	124,100
Typical consultant, basic	63,640
GP, intended average net income	54,220
Senior house officer (hospital doctor) top of scale	40,265
Typical senior house officer, basic	24,425
Nursing sister, top of main scale	24,090
Experienced staff nurse, top of scale	19,220
Newly qualified nurse	14,890
Nursing assistant, top of basic scale	11,010

Source: Department of Health and BMA data, *Guardian*, 18 January 2000.

(b) 'Taylorisation' of nursing staff in Durham hospitals under PFI plans: full-time equivalent staff numbers

Grade	1996	2000	Change	% change
Nurse manager	4.68	3.0	−1.68	−35.9
Sister/Charge nurse	159.58	147.28	−12.30	−7.7
Staff nurse	493.40	430.27	−63.13	−12.8
Team assistant	216.97	260.21	+43.24	+19.9
Team housekeeper	0	81.49	+81.49	n/a
Total	874.63	922.25	+47.62	+5.4
Total qualified nurses	657.66	580.55	−77.11	−11.7

Source: Declan Gaffney and Allyson Pollock, *Downsizing for the 21st Century: A Report to UNISON Northern Region on the North Durham Acute Hospitals PFI Scheme*, Health and Health Policy Research Unit, School of Public Policy, University College London/UNISON, n.d., p. 15.

money to expand community or primary care services. However, by September 1998 mounting expert criticism and protests from the medical profession forced the government to undertake a 'national beds inquiry', and in 1999 it determined that the decline in bed numbers needed to be reversed.* The drive to cut back the acute sector had overshot the limits to the rate of productivity growth in acute care.

Yet another form of cost reduction involved shifting clinical responsibilities from doctors to nurses, who earned on average half as much, and from qualified to less qualified and lower-paid nurses or nurse assistants (see Table 6.2). Within hospitals a new category of 'nurse consultants' was created in selected priority hospital sectors, senior hospital nurses were given some rights to prescribe drugs and, in some cases, control of the capital budgets for hospital wards, while a variety of schemes were encouraged to upgrade or requalify nurses and nursing assistants. In the primary sector practice nurses were given representation on PCG governing boards and increasingly entrusted with consulting and prescribing in place of GPs; two trials in England found that patients mostly preferred consulting nurses to consulting their GPs, and benefited as much from it.[50] The nurse-managed telephone help line, NHS Direct, was also designed to reduce the demand on doctors, largely by reassuring patients and encouraging them to look after themselves (about 35 per cent of callers received advice to 'self care'), or diverting them directly to hospital emergency services.[51] All these trends are, of course, recognisable effects of the standardisation and rationalisation characteristic of commodity production, in this case induced by the 'shadow' market forces of the internal market.

Ironically enough it was the public sector NHS that was forced to embark on this process, substituting treatments for care, limiting the

---

* The National Beds Inquiry, (reported in *Shaping the Future NHS: Long Term Planning for Hospitals and Related Services* Department of Health, 1999),'showed not only that there is little scope for productivity gains but also that there is no spare capacity in the NHS', and projected that 'up to 2003–4 an increase of 2000 (1.4%) general and acute beds and 2000 intermediate care beds will be required for the NHS . . .' (A. M. Pollock and M. G. Dunnigan, 'Beds in the NHS', *BMJ* 320, 19 February 2000, pp. 461–2). Pollock and Dunnigan note that, remarkably, the report referred only to the loss of bed capacity that had already occurred, and not to the impending new losses of bed capacity that would occur as the new PFI hospitals opened. The government's position was obscure if not self-contradictory.

number of treatment 'models' on offer, shifting work to cheaper employees, and getting patients and their families to bear more of the costs and perform more of the necessary labour themselves. It was noticeable, however, that the emphasis remained mainly on raising productivity through 'Taylorisation', i.e. by substituting less expensive for more expensive labour (under the rubric of 'changing the skill mix' and 'reconfiguring' or 're-engineering' services), and by transferring the most labour-intensive services out of the NHS, especially by making long-term care 'the responsibility of individuals until they are too poor to pay'.[52] Apart from the gradual expansion of the drugs budget, little progress had been made towards substituting goods for services on a large scale; the mass-produced 'diagnostic and prescribing machine' envisaged by John Gershuny still seemed far away.* Short of that, however, industrialisation in the NHS was relatively well advanced.

The private acute sector, in contrast, although represented by its proponents as inherently more efficient than public provision, appealed to PMI subscribers precisely because it offered health care that did *not* exhibit these features, and was consequently afflicted with Baumol's disease – the inexorably rising costs of skilled personal services – and hence with stagnation and the threat of decline. Of course, if private health care were to become the norm, all the characteristics of commodity production manifested in the NHS would immediately appear in the private sector, together with higher costs, loss of comprehensiveness, inequality and the other disadvantages familiar from the USA. Unless and until that happens, the private acute care industry will serve precisely to provide a high-cost residual supply of expensive, skilled labour-intensive health care for those privileged enough to be able to afford it, or to have employers willing to pay for it.

---

* John Gershuny, *After Industrial Society? The Emerging Self-Service Economy* (Humanities Press, 1978), p. 90; see chapter 4 above, p. 94. Various factors seem to be involved in any plausible explanation for the difference between health services and television broadcasting in this regard, including the risks involved in self-treatment, and ironically, 'quasi-market failures', which meant that the returns to the many experiments in 'telemedicine' that have been attempted in Britain seldom accrued to the part of the NHS that bore the costs involved (see, e.g., Michael Cross, 'As not seen on TV', *Health Service Journal*, 9 March 2000, pp. 26–8). Since market-based medicine in the USA has not produced dramatic changes in this regard either, there may well be other limiting factors. A major one, suggested by Dr Joel Lexchin, is perhaps that so much diagnosis still depends on experienced hands-on physical examinations.

Creating a demand for health-service commodities in place of health care

Part of the appeal of commodified health care – the 'carrot' – lies in the aura of science. The conception of health care as an armoury of 'magic bullets' is popularised by media stories of new drugs and reinforced by TV programmes that present hospital treatment (usually surgical) as a set of fast-moving 'episodes' of high-tech care delivered on the run by teams of doctors and nurses whose efforts, when they are not pursuing romances, bear a distinct resemblance to those of the kitchen staff in a McDonald's. Further, the actual experience of hospital treatment that most people have – in outpatient clinics and day surgery – consists of visits to various specialist departments with the general industrial characteristics of car exhaust repair shops, and this gradually becomes the norm. *Care* largely ceases to be associated with hospitals and becomes associated for most people only with home, where it is usually provided by female relatives (if patients are lucky enough to have any), or with staff in long-term care homes.* As fewer and fewer people remember what it used to be like to be cared for in hospital (just as a growing number will barely remember home cooking), we can expect the concept of commodified health services to be gradually accepted, along with the idea of a range of models, as with cars, the more upscale only for those who can afford them. And as on the privatised railways the word 'passenger' was officially replaced by 'customer', so in the NHS 'patient' was gradually giving way to 'service user' or 'client'. The Patients' Charter, introduced in 1992 – a list of (unenforceable) 'rights' (such as not to be kept waiting more than thirty minutes after the appointed time in an outpatient clinic) that patients are supposed to have as individual consumers – was part of an ideological project to make the supply of health services seem not essentially different from that of any other commodity.

The counterpart of all this – the 'stick' – was to give people reasons to become disenchanted with the existing free, state-provided service, above all by systematically underfunding it. A useful comparison here is

---

* In Britain in 1992 an estimated 1.3 million people, nearly all women, one third of whom were themselves ill as well as elderly, devoted twenty hours a week or more to providing unpaid care to others, nearly all relatives, who were unable to look after themselves. The situation had not changed significantly since Hart's summary of the situation in the mid-1980s (Julian Tudor Hart, *A New Kind of Doctor* [Merlin Press, 1988], pp. 266–9), which makes painful reading.

with Canada, where the social-democratic tradition is much weaker than in Britain, but where more people express satisfaction with their publicly provided health service. There are no doubt many reasons for this, including the fact that Canadians see the US alternative at close quarters and overwhelmingly reject it;[53] but the fact that Canada spends 30 per cent more per head on health care is surely important too. Down to 1992, for example, Ontario hospitals had come to expect a 'traditional 10 per cent annual increase' in their budgets.[54] In Britain, by contrast, forty years of underfunding had pushed the NHS close to the limits of viability. By 1994 Britain had only five hospital beds of all kinds per 1,000 population, compared with seven per 1,000 in Canada, and only half as many acute care beds per 1,000. Waiting times for consultations and elective surgery were far longer. The often dilapidated premises of the NHS contributed to the problem. Why should seriously ill people be expected to step into antiquated and shabby accommodation at the very moment when they need the best?

Besides the pressure to cut costs that came from the purchasers in the 'internal market', all hospital trusts were required by the Department of Health to find 'productivity savings' of 3 per cent a year. Increasingly no such savings were to be had; the only practical way to save was to reduce the services offered – i.e. ending comprehensiveness and reducing access. The chief reason many GPs gave for deciding to become fundholders during the 1990s was to protect their patients against being disadvantaged in the intensifying competition for scarce hospital services.[55] With the end of a separate category of fundholding GPs after 1999, the 'two-tier' service that fundholding had been seen as generating within the NHS came to an end; but this only drew more attention to 'waiting lists', 'post code rationing', and the ever-diminishing attention that over-stretched NHS staff could provide.* Throughout

---

* 'Post code rationing' refers to the fact that different health authorities made different decisions about the services they could afford, so that how long one had to wait to see a consultant oncologist, or whether one could get an MRI (magnetic resonance imaging) scan or a new expensive drug at all, depended on where you lived. The issue of waiting lists has been extensively debated. No policy that does not significantly expand provision will reduce waiting times for specialist attention and treatment (see Anthony Harrison and Bill New, *Access to Elective Care: What Should Really Be Done About Waiting Lists*, [The King's Fund, 2000]). There is a telling obiter dictum in the report of one of the experiments in substituting nurses for GPs for same-day appointments, mentioned above: 'The slightly longer time spent on consul-

the 1980s and 1990s people became more and more aware that the NHS no longer provided access to the best possible health care. Those who could afford it turned to PMI. The rest told pollsters that they wanted more public funds devoted to the NHS.[56]

Public disenchantment with the NHS was aggravated by the privileges given to senior hospital doctors to overcome their initial resistance to it. Their original control over the hospital service meant that the pre-existing hierarchical and class-conscious culture of the medical profession was continued in NHS hospitals. Over time this was modified by fresh generations of doctors influenced by the more democratic – or at least consumerist – culture outside it, but the somewhat hermetic institutional culture of hospitals always tended to lag behind that of the wider world. Patients who were becoming used to a more market-oriented culture, and who were no longer grateful for health care newly and wondrously available free, as their parents or grandparents had been, increasingly found some clinicians' attitudes arrogant and unacceptable: '. . . forty years is a long time to go on feeling grateful for gifts you have already paid for with taxes'.[57] And in 1999 and 2000 a series of highly publicised cases of malpractice stimulated an overdue public critique of the profession's apparent arrogance, and its questionable ability to regulate itself.[58]

For all these reasons the public's image of the NHS had significantly altered. The NHS was still popular, but in a more conditional way, increasingly tolerated rather than loved.

Redefining the medical workforce as producers of a surplus

This is first of all a problem of doctors. In the USA, for-profit Health Maintenance Organisations stepped in and in effect took over most of the profitable small businesses that the self-employed, fee-for-service American doctors had built up, increasingly employing doctors on salary to generate profits for HMO shareholders. This result remains harder to achieve in Britain, where the NHS made consultants into senior partners in a huge sort of monopolistic guild, deriving satisfac-

---

tations [i.e. by the nurses, who took on average ten minutes compared with the eight minutes taken by the GPs] is potentially a cause for *concern*' (Chau Shum et al., 'Nurse management of patients with minor illnesses in general practice: multicentre randomised controlled trial, *BMJ* 320, 2000, pp. 1042–3 (italics added).

tion from a distinctive blend of high social status, professional autonon-omy, unchallenged administrative authority, a sense of vocation and relatively high salaries (for most of them at first only modestly supple-mented by private practice). From the mid-1980s onwards, however, this structure of motivations was progressively undermined by subordi-nating consultants to general managers, curtailing the time allowed for consultations, limiting the time and funding available for research, forbidding the sharing of information with either the 'purchasers' or even their colleagues in other – competing – hospitals, and in many other ways. One NHS Trust chairman notoriously said a doctor's duty to the employer (the trust) came 'before the professional duty to the patient'.[59]

Moreover, from 1999 onwards the NHS was supposed to become 'primary care-led' – i.e. hospital policy would have to follow priorities set by GPs. It was unclear how hospital consultants would respond, but the evidence that they were turning more and more to private practice was significant. NHS consultants had from the first been allowed to do private practice alongside their work in the NHS. Although about 20 per cent of consultants, mostly physicians, were on full-time contracts and did little if any private work, consultants on 'maximum part-time' contracts could draw nine-tenths of a full salary (later raised to ten-elevenths) for doing half a week's work in the NHS, and earn as much more from private practice as they liked. This led to some abuse, especially in certain surgical specialties (eye, heart and hip operations); the longer it took to see a surgeon in any given NHS surgical specialty, the more private practice surgery the surgeons in question did, and the more private hospital beds were available in the area.[60] In 2000 a few surgeons were said to be making as much as £1 million a year, with incomes of £500,000 not uncommon, and 'maximum part-time' consult-ant surgeons and anaesthetists were, on average, deriving more than 50 per cent of their income from private work.[61] If some private hospitals could find ways to offer some consultants a varied range of full-time work, while more and more of the others increased their part-time private practice, a medical career more or less wholly outside the NHS would again become an accepted alternative to one fully within it, as it had not been for half a century.

Similar issues arise with nurses. Declining job satisfaction, overwork and low pay had already created a serious staff shortage. In 1997 the annual rate of turnover among NHS nurses reached 21 per cent;[62] to reduce stress and get more flexible hours many switched to work for nursing agencies, which then 'leased' them back to NHS hospitals to cover shortages (with obvious costs to patients in terms of continuity of care).

In spite of these changes some doctors and many nurses, as well as unionised NHS staff of all kinds, seemed likely to continue for some time to oppose the transformation of a comprehensive, free, equal access service into one offering partial, fee-paid services and unequal access. Understanding the dynamics of this ideological contest is an important research task, full of fascinating twists and paradoxes. For instance, in 2000 multiple-bed rooms were normal in NHS hospitals (and larger open wards were still not uncommon), with the result that they remained places where people of quite different class backgrounds met and watched television together, and where they were treated more or less equally, affecting the outlook of staff as well as patients. Significantly enough Laing comments that one of the competitive disadvantages of NHS 'pay bed' units relative to beds in private hospitals 'is believed to be the difficulty of achieving a change in culture among NHS nursing and other staff and altering staff attitudes to reflect the demands of paying customers'.[63] (What demands are these, one wonders? For the painstaking, personal approach that everyone should receive, but that underfunding and market-driven reorganisation make the NHS less and less able to provide? Or for greater deference to patients who are 'paying customers'?)

The role of the state in underwriting risk

Unlike broadcasting, there was in the 1980s no large block of capital ready and able to enter health service provision, partly thanks to the NHS's monopoly but also because the state's intervention was needed to limit the financial risks inherent in entering a new field in which a demand for commodified health care was being created, but in which *effective* demand – demand backed by money – remained limited.

The Conservatives tackled this problem in several ways, some of which have already been mentioned. Companies were given tax breaks for private health insurance premiums for their less highly paid employees; individuals over sixty were allowed to offset individual health insurance premiums against income tax; private non-profit hospitals registered as charities were exempt from tax, even though they admitted only patients able to pay their very high fees.[64] NHS hospitals were required to fund savings through annual 'efficiency increases' and to pay the Treasury a 6 per cent annual 'capital charge' on the current value of their plant.[65] These requirements were supposed to encourage cost consciousness and dynamism but they were also intended to 'level the playing field' for competition with private sector hospitals. The private sector also put pressure on the government to forbid NHS hospitals to 'cross-subsidise' the services they offered to private patients in competition with the private sector, even though they themselves were free to cross-subsidise as well as indulge in 'cream skimming'.

Two of the Conservative government's measures to boost private health care were, however, more important than all the rest. One was the earmarking of 85 per cent of the transitional funding for long-term care to the private sector via local authorities. It showed that the real key to privatisation was diverting public funds to for-profit companies. This precedent having been established (thanks to the fact that long-term care affected a politically weak group of patients, at a time when the opposition in parliament was divided and weak as well), the principle could be extended piecemeal to other parts of the NHS.

The other big boost to the private sector was the PFI (officially remamed Public–Private Partnerships or PPP after 1997), which also diverted substantial public funds to for-profit companies. The new PFI hospitals would be owned by private consortia (of builders, facilities management companies and bankers), who would also employ all the non-clinical staff; the NHS trusts would sign leases of up to thirty years. This largely eliminated the private sector's risk; the credit rating agencies assigned the first NHS PFI projects 'triple-A' ratings, treating them as in effect underwritten by the state, even though the 'transfer of risk' to the private sector was the chief justification officially advanced for the higher cost of PFI projects compared with publicly funded projects.[66] By late 1999 thirty-one new privately-financed hospital building projects had been approved, with a forecast capital cost of approximately £2.2 billion.

But the PFI signified more than a way of diverting a significant share of the NHS revenue budget to the building and 'facilities management' industries. It implied another shift in the public–private sector boundary. The PFI consortia would not only want a voice in major management issues, but would also be free to sell health insurance policies, long-term care and other health service products such as rehabilitation and convalescence to the patients using their facilities.[67] As Pollock and her colleagues note, 'A new type of corporation almost wholly dependent on government contracts has arisen,' with the potential to start re-aligning the NHS and integrating it into adjacent markets on a large scale.[68]

Effects

The health impact of the trend to commodification in health care is impossible to distinguish from that of many other factors. Even the data on service provision are difficult to interpret, as provision varies from place to place and reflects complex differences in both needs and resources. What most concerned politicians and the public were waiting times. The waiting time to see even a GP was often several days, and the average GP consultation lasted about eight minutes.[69] The waiting time to see a specialist, after referral by a GP, had fallen significantly since 1995, but in 1999 about a quarter of those seen had still had to wait for more than three months. When they finally got an appointment, it might last as little as last four minutes; and the average subsequent wait for admission to hospital, if needed, was over four months.[70] 'Initiatives' to reduce waiting times by improving waiting-list management or hospital discharge systems or record-keeping constantly fell foul of the service's fragmentation into several hundred NHS trusts that were overwhelmingly preoccupied with balancing their inadequate budgets. Staff morale had been sapped by constant cuts, making work more stressful and less satisfying, while the pay of NHS staff, which accounted for over 60 per cent of the total NHS budget, was well below that of their European counterparts. To raise service standards to what patients had a right to expect, staff numbers and their pay would need to be increased. Moreover, by 1999 NHS premises were severely run down. The backlog of repairs to the capital stock had reached £2.6 billion, equivalent to about 5 per cent of the total NHS annual budget.[71]

'Rationing' in various forms was endemic. One was the practice by some health authorities of placing strict limits on prescribing certain expensive drugs, perhaps the most publicised kind of 'rationing by post code'. Another, much less common but significant, was witholding hospital treatment from old people. A survey in 2000 showed that three-quarters of GPs thought this practice was widespread, even though it contradicted the NHS's official policy of equal access for all – apart from being ethically dubious, to say the least, and probably in breach of human rights legislation.[72] Sixteen per cent of GPs said they decided not to refer older patients because they suspected that 'they won't get treated because of their age'; 10 per cent 'fail[ed] to refer because they [knew] of age barriers'. Eight per cent seemed to endorse the practice by agreeing with the statement that older patients 'had already had a good innings'. Health economists had, of course, provided a rationale for such thinking by developing the concept of 'quality adjusted life years' or 'QUALYs', purporting to allow the 'health gain' from various treatments to be measured and compared with their cost. This logic seemed to underly the practice of placing a 'DNR' – 'Do Not Resuscitate' – instruction on some older patients' case notes, as hospital doctors were found to have done on a number of occasions without the patients' knowledge.[73]

As Mullen has cogently argued, however, the idea that neoliberals and health economists have assiduously fostered, that 'rationing is inevitable', and that 'hard choices' have to be made, has no validity. Even a modest increase in the resources provided makes the choices less hard, and 'there is no reason to suppose that any particular percentage of GNP is the correct amount to spend on health'.[74] The fundamental reason why 'rationing' had become such an issue in the NHS was severe underfunding, relative to other comparable countries, and relative to the degree of choice most people were getting used to having in other areas of their lives.*

* In 1997 the average share of GDP devoted to health care in fifteen EU countries was 8.7 per cent, or £1,109 per capita. Britain spent 6.8 per cent of its GDP or £907 per capita; France spent 9.6 per cent of its GDP or £1,397 per capita; Germany spent 10.7 per cent of its GDP or £1,666 per capita (*Compendium of Health Statistics* 1999 [Office of Health Statistics, 2000], tables 2.2 and 2.3). As Mullen notes, 'one reason why the NHS delivered a relatively large amount of health care for, by international standards, a relatively low share of GDP, was that lower quality was accepted in non-clinical areas (for example long waits, shabby buildings, restricted choice)' (Penelope M. Mullen, 'Is it necessary to ration health care?', *Public Money and Management* 18/1, 1998, p. 57).

The *NHS Plan* and the *Concordat* with the private sector

In the winter of 1999–2000, during the annual 'winter beds crisis' (when patients suffering from 'flu and pneumonia overwhelm hospitals already operating at the limits of their capacity), it finally became clear to the 'New' Labour leadership that the NHS was a key electoral asset they were in danger of throwing away. Having accumulated an unexpectedly large budget surplus (thanks to the combination of the US-led boom and two years of staying within the Conservatives' spending plans), the government abruptly announced a major expansion of the NHS budget, promising to increase it by an average of 6.1 per cent per annum in real terms each year for four years (i.e. from 2000 to 2004). The prospect of a 30 per cent increase in real current spending by 2003–4 was certainly dramatic, and the government made it clear that it expected equally dramatic changes in the NHS in return. In April 2000 it appointed a task force of 133 'leading and frontline doctors, nurses, patients, managers and other NHS staff', organised in a series of 'modernisation action teams', to draw up a plan 'to revitalise the NHS – by July' (as the *BMJ* ironically put it).[75]

The *NHS Plan* was duly published in July 2000 and was endorsed in general terms by leaders of the various components of the NHS, whose representatives had been coopted into its preparation – the presidents of the royal medical colleges, nurses, NHS managers, patients' groups and UNISON, the NHS staff union. Its main thrust was reform in every sector of the NHS, to make it more accountable to patients and the public, increase staff numbers and pay, break down inter-professional barriers, reduce waiting time, improve hospital food and facilities – the list was very long, and accompanied by numerous quantitative targets. The *NHS Plan* also proposed a new consultants' contract specifying a minimum of 'sessions' to be worked each week, and barring newly appointed consultants from undertaking private practice for 'perhaps' the first seven years of their careers, in return for higher salaries – an idea promptly rejected by the British Medical Association (and presumably likely to lead to a compromise along the lines indicated by that 'perhaps'). Thus far, however, the *NHS Plan* looked like a valiant (if curiously under-researched and rushed) effort to galvanise everyone concerned into agreeing to all possible ways of using the new funding to make the NHS both more efficient and more user-friendly.

Nevertheless at almost the same time as it announced the preparation of the *Plan* the government also announced that it was negotiating a new 'concordat' between the NHS and the Independent Healthcare Association (IHA). Presented largely as a formalisation of existing practices, the 'concordat' was in fact much more far-reaching. It arose from a chance discovery by Tony Blair that his first Secretary of State for Health, Frank Dobson, had instructed NHS trusts that they should only make contracts with private sector providers as a last resort and after securing authorisation from the Department of Health. The Prime Minister had the instruction revoked and went on to encourage Alan Milburn, who replaced Dobson as Secretary of State in 1999, to make a much broader policy change, which the 'concordat' eventually embodied.[76]

Its main thrust could have been predicted by anyone reading the report of the 1999 National Beds Inquiry, in which the government foresaw that private nursing homes might be used to provide 'inter-mediate' care beds for patients who were not yet well enough to be discharged, but who no longer required acute care and so were 'block-ing' hospital beds needed for acute admissions. Since, as we have seen, private nursing homes' margins had fallen sharply, they would clearly be keen to fulfil this function. At the same time, as we also saw earlier, the private acute hospitals were severely under-utilised, and an injec-tion of NHS funding was just what they needed. The main difficulty was that most of the under-used private hospitals were unable to provide NHS standards of treatment for more than a narrow range of conditions, and even fewer private nursing homes were able to provide acceptable 'intermediate care' for patients just discharged from acute hospital care.[77] In fact research commissioned by one health authority (Barking and Havering) suggested that the standard of medical care in its private nursing homes was scandalously low.[78] Accordingly, when the *Concordat* was published in October, its key provision was section 2.3:

> The concordat . . . signals . . . *a commitment towards planning the use of private and voluntary care providers, not only at times of pressure but also on a more proactive longer term basis* where this offers demonstrable value for money and high standards for patients. These, like NHS contractual arrange-ments, can where appropriate be reflected in Long Term Service Agreements.[79]

In other words, the private sector was being encouraged to *invest* in the facilities and staff that would permit it to become a regular provider of 'NHS' care; for the first time the private sector would provide acute clinical services, nominally 'within' the NHS, and receive revenues from public sources, as the private long-term care sector already did.*

The *Concordat* was made with the IHA, which represented private acute hospital and long-term care home operators. The *NHS Plan*, however, envisaged that the same policy would extend to other services previously defined as clinical, stating that 'the NHS will explore with the private sector the potential for investment in services – such as pathology and imaging and dialysis', and that 'the task force has agreed that pharmaceutical industry involvement in the development and implementation of national service frameworks would benefit both the NHS and industry' – i.e. 'disease management' was officially back on the agenda.[80] While the statements in the *NHS Plan* and the *Concordat* were general, they were categorical enough. Almost every segment of the private health-care industry was potentially being offered a new share of the NHS market.

The significance of this policy shift was clearly huge, and seen to be so by the IHA, which itself acquired an entirely new level of legitimacy in the process. Whatever the fate of the rest of the *NHS Plan*, the *Concordat* seemed destined to have long-lasting effects. The *NHS Plan*, devised hastily, was a gamble. Whether the promised funds would really prove sufficient 'to transform the NHS from a Third World to a First World service' (as one commentator put it) was bound to be doubtful.[81] The spending increase, while substantial, was still relatively limited, especially when adjusted for the rate of inflation in health care, as opposed to the general retail price index. It would still leave the absolute amount spent per capita substantially below the EU level. The backlog of needs was enormous, and the *NHS Plan*'s central idea, that the NHS would be fine if all its parts came up to the standards of its best, was very problematic: it would be extremely difficult to get a huge organisation that had been deliberately balkanised to 're-standardise'

---

* An IHA spokesman thought the *Concordat* could lead to a 10 per cent increase in private hospital operations. In the long term increased private bed provision might be planned to handle increased NHS demand; in the short run any new private hospital bed provision was expected to consist of small satellite facilities on or beside NHS hospital sites (Peter Fermoy, interview, 6 September 2000).

itself in this way. Meanwhile a stream of media stories of fatal delays, mistaken diagnoses, 'failures of communication' and arrogant doctors continued to appear and could confidently be expected to go on doing so – the implication invariably being that unless the 'NHS crisis' could be overcome, the NHS should give way to the market. This was clearly the unspoken meaning of the statement by the President of the Royal College of Physicians, Sir George Alberti, that the funding increase was the NHS's 'last chance'.[82]

The idea that the market was the only alternative was meantime being made to seem more and more 'natural' by the government's constant stress on 'partnership' with the private sector, of which the *Concordat* was only the latest and most far-reaching expression. Almost all primary care and dental care, and most long-term care, was already provided by self-employed or corporate providers in privately-owned premises with privately-employed nursing and support staff; and this would be the case with more and more hospitals too, as the PFI hospitals came on stream. There were already 3,000 private beds in existing NHS hospitals in 1999, half of them in 'dedicated' Private Patient Units, separate from the accommodation of 'non-paying NHS patients' and offering 'single rooms with en-suite facilities and stand-alone catering'.[83] The new spending on primary care premises promised under the *NHS Plan* would also be PFI-financed. GPs, like hospital managers in the early 1990s, realised that the PFI was 'the only game in town' and were encouraged to take a stake in the equity with one or other of the various types of company that were positioning themselves to make money from primary sector PFI projects.[84] The same was true of dentists, who were now deriving almost two-fifths of their total income from private practice. Only hospital doctors, medical technicians and most (but not all) hospital nurses were directly employed by the NHS, and many consultants were earning more from private practice than from the NHS. For their part, NHS patients, responding to the ideology of commodification and encouraged by lawyers, were suing doctors and NHS trusts in record numbers.[85] In revenue terms, by 1998 for-profit providers were receiving about 20 per cent of all expenditure on hospitals and nursing homes, almost 60 per cent of all expenditure on long-term residential care, and 16 per cent of spending on home care services (not to mention 100 per cent of all spending on pharmaceutical and other medical supplies).[86] Many PCTs were likely to offer private health services alongside 'free' ones. Under the *Concordat* private nursing homes were to become providers of NHS 'intermediate' care, and private acute hospitals were expected to perform up to 150,000 more operations a year on NHS patients – a roughly 15 per cent increase in surgical activity and income. The *NHS Plan* also left open the possibility of inviting private health-care firms to bid to take over 'failing' NHS hospitals.[87] Tim Evans, the IHA's Chief Public Relations Officer, envisaged that the NHS would eventually become a mere brand, or 'kitemark', affixed to a wide range of private clinical institutions.[88]

In short, since 1980 the scope of the NHS had become much more narrowly defined, and more and more oriented to financial considerations and commercial values, and increasingly 'industrialised'. It was also much more integrated with the numerous commercial markets surrounding it; it remained publicly funded but was less and less publicly provided, and seemed likely to become steadily more integrated with the private sector. It was not difficult to foresee that it was destined to reach a point when resistance to privatisation had been sufficiently weakened and disheartened, and the market forces surrounding it sufficiently strengthened and emboldened, that further, more radical measures would became practicable. The conjuncture of a pro-market government and an economic downturn, and media always keen to highlight public sector problems, would provide the context. Then the inequalities that globalised market forces produced in the distribution of personal income and wealth would be reflected in health services. The link between medicine and science, which was briefly glimpsed at the high point of publicly-provided health-care systems (and which points so clearly in the direction of the equalisation of work, status and income, as well as health-care), would be displaced by the link between medicine and profit.[89]

Global market forces and the NHS

The role of global market forces has been touched on at many points in this account, yet the case of the NHS still differs noticeably from that of public service broadcasting, where external market forces early on established commercial television in competition with the BBC and then gradually opened up the field to more and more extensive occupation. Of course private sector lobbies were also at work seeking to influence health policy, like the Association of the British Pharmaceutical Industry and the IHA; and the construction industry, with its close historical links to the Conservative Party, had played a major role in lobbying for the PFI, and all had significant global dimensions. There were also intellectual parallels: the impact of the American global market advocate Alain Enthoven, referred to earlier, on the design of the NHS 'internal market' parallels that of the Scottish global market advocate Alan Peacock on broadcasting policy at the same time. Another significant influence was the role of management consultancies, particularly after 1990, in transmitting market concepts and values to policy-makers in NHS trusts and health authorities. The so-called 'big six' consultancies of that time were transnational firms with large American offices, but many of the smaller firms that worked closely with NHS trusts also admired the US model and had ties to American consultancies working in the US health-care market.[90]

In Britain, however, successive governments adopted market solutions to all policy problems, so that it might be thought that there was little for the private health-care industry lobby to do. But this was not how the US health-care industry saw things. The bulk of health-care expenditure everywhere still consisted of the direct provision of services, and HMOs and health-care consultancy companies, medical insurance companies and companies specialising in leasing and managing hospitals and clinics all wanted to be able to provide these services anywhere in the world. American HMOs were particularly anxious to find more profitable fields, as the US market had become saturated and profits had collapsed from the mid-1990s onwards.[91] They moved aggressively into Latin America, rapidly reshaping health-care provision in Brazil, Argentina, Chile, Peru and Mexico, as well as several smaller Latin American countries, and making very large profits from the secure revenues provided by these countries' social security funds.[92] In relation to the EC, however, they felt unfairly excluded. European companies could compete with them in the US market, but most West European health-care systems were not open markets, so the traffic was all one way.[93] In their view, all these publicly financed and run systems, including the NHS, were potential markets that in a world committed to free trade ought to be open to competition.

In the case of Britain, the NHS 'internal' market, the PFI, the privatisation of long-term care and the contracting-out of non-clinical work of all kinds provided some scope for foreign firms, but most American companies that had tested the waters in the 1980s – for instance in long-term care – had withdrawn by the end of the 1990s. They found the market still too narrow and controlled to be attractive, and the same was true in the EU generally. It therefore became a major policy objective of the US health-care industry to break down these barriers, with support from the US government and the World Bank.

The first step was to extend free trade in goods to free trade in services. This was accomplished in 1995 in the General Agreement on Trade in Services (GATS). National governments, however, were allowed to define health care and social services as 'government services' and exempt them from the Agreement, and about a quarter of the WTO's 134 member states did so. To overcome this the WTO secretariat, at the urging of the US trade delegation, argued that the exemption should not apply to government services that were already a mix of public and private provision, like Britain's and those of most other OECD countries:

> ... according to the WTO, wherever there is a mixture of public and private funding, such as user charges or private insurance, or there are subsidies for non-public infrastructure, such as public–private partnerships or competitive contracting for services, the service sector should be open to foreign corporations.[94]

The British government repeatedly declared that this would not affect the NHS, but this was not the understanding of the US negotiators at the WTO, who intended that a foreign state should be able to oblige any member government to open its public services up to private investors in the name of free trade. When the breakdown of the WTO summit meeting at Seattle in 1999 prevented this issue from being resolved there, the US and the European Commission put it at the top of the agenda for the 'GATS 2000' negotiations that WTO members were committed to starting in May 2000, and that were supposed to produce agreed new regulations by May 2002.

The details of these negotiations need not occupy us but their significance needs stressing. All the signatories to the GATS are bound to agree on rules that will reduce barriers to trade, and when the rules are agreed the GATS gives states the right to oblige any other state to change any policy found by WTO adjudicators to be in conflict with the rules. The explicit aim of the US trade delegation and the European Commission at the WTO has been to make the economic principle of maximum freedom of trade prevail over social principles such as the right to universal health services or higher education.[95] The effect could be, among other things, to oblige the British government to invite foreign companies to compete for the right to run hospitals or to take over Primary Care Trusts, or to 'unbundle' services like health services that pool risks and 'cross-subsidise' service recipients so that foreign companies could operate the most profitable of them:

> ... governments that currently use non-market mechanisms and struc-
> tures such as risk-pooling, social insurance funds, block contracts and
> cross-subsidisation for the delivery of universal health-care services could
> be required to switch to ... market mechanisms [and to show that] ... a
> government control did not impose unreasonable control on commercial
> providers ...[96]

Pollock and Price, the authors of the careful analysis from which this quotation is drawn, note that in the view of the Inter American Development Bank the requirement to provide services universally, regardless of cost, constitutes just such an 'unreasonable' control.[97]

How far any of this would prove acceptable to public opinion in Britain is hard to guess, not least because the negotiations have been kept from public debate. Much would depend on the immediate context, and on presentation or 'spin'. On the evidence of the 1990s, however, it is hard to envisage the British government strongly resisting US pressure to secure a more and more pro-business interpretation of the GATS. The 'new reality' of global market forces made New Labour decide to accept most of the Thatcher legacy. This logic still applies. If market-driven domestic politics have not already led to the abandonment of the NHS's founding principles of universality, comprehensiveness and equality of access, transnational politics could still do so.

7

Market-driven politics versus the public interest

Suffice it that the disease has been pointed out: goodness knows how to cure it.[1]

From a book as wide-ranging as this it seems best, on the whole, to leave conclusions to be drawn by the reader. In politics there is always a superfluity of causes, and it would be absurd to claim that every political event of note that has occurred in Britain since 1979 is a result of the economic globalisation that the abolition of capital controls in that year decisively accelerated. But it would be just as absurd to deny that from then onwards British politics underwent a fundamental change, and that by 2000 their dynamics were very different from those of the decades before 1980, when markets were to a significant degree still politically controlled. Now, to an equally significant degree, politics are market-driven. I think it is reasonable to draw that much of a conclusion, but beyond this there is certainly plenty of room for debate.

What follows, then, is not a list of my conclusions. Instead, following a short recapitulation of the argument – but this time, working back to causes from the effects we have just been examining – I comment briefly on a series of questions that the argument has prompted.

The argument recapitulated

Market-based provision of services is not just another way – allegedly more efficient – of providing public services. To be marketed they must be commodified, and commodification first transforms them into 'products', and then further transforms these into different products, serving different ends. Public service television and the National Health Service were both considered important for, if not essential to, democratic citizenship. Under market-driven politics, both are being displaced by the profitable production of commodities. Television programming is seen less and less as a contribution to public education and debate and is devoted more and more to entertainment. The hospital service is stripped of its role as a provider of care and 'reconfigured' as an increasingly industrialised provider of treatments; more and more NHS functions are privatised and commodified; the boundaries between it and commercial medicine are blurred and increasingly breached. While clinical services remain formally free and universal, they are no longer all publicly provided, and further instalments of 'marketisation' are confidently expected by the commercial health-care industry.

On both public service television and health care the government of Tony Blair has been ambivalent, torn between its attachment to the BBC and the NHS and its need to be seen as 'a party of business'. It wanted the BBC to provide a public service and set standards but it also wanted to foster a globally competitive commercial television and communications industry, so the BBC was exhorted to set public service standards while being kept on such short rations that it was in danger of losing the critical viewing share on which the legitimacy of the licence fee depended. In 1999/2000 the government realised, belatedly, that the NHS was a key electoral asset and decided on a major expansion of its budget, but at the same time the private health-care industry was encouraged to expect that it would receive significant shares of this new income stream through 'public–private partnerships', outsourcing (the *Concordat*), 'disease management', and so on. A future Conservative government – or the next Labour one – will have no shortage of precedents and rationales for the next significant transfer of NHS functions to the market-place, or for narrowing still further the BBC's effective presence in television broadcasting.

Public service television and health care are not exceptional in this respect. The same process is at work in public education, public transport, social services, public libraries, the arts, prison services, policing. David Marquand writes persuasively:

> ... the public domain of citizenship and service should be safeguarded from incursions by the market domain of buying and selling. ... The

goods of the public domain – health care, crime prevention, education – should not be treated as commodities or proxy commodities. The language of buyer and seller, producer and customer, does not belong in the public domain; nor do the relationships which that language implies. Doctors and nurses do not 'sell' medical services; students are not 'customers' of their teachers; policemen and policewomen do not 'produce' public order. The attempt to force these relationships into a market mould undermines the service ethic, degrades the institutions that embody it and robs the notion of common citizenship of part of its meaning.[2]

But this is where market-driven politics leads. Even if the Thatcherites had not made 'marketising' the public sector into an ideological crusade it would still have occurred (though more slowly and with less publicity), for three main reasons. First, because global corporations look upon the public domain as an unexploited potential market that they now have more and more leverage to pry open – thanks to their formidable lobbying resources, frequently backed by the US state and its dominance in the IMF/World Bank and the WTO. Second, because eighteen years of Thatcherism had convinced the Labour leaders – and would have convinced any politician as exclusively focused as they were on returning to office – that it was now impossible to win and keep office without business support. Even if the 'modernisers' had not happened to share Thatcher's taste for centralised control, for scapegoating public sector institutions and workers, as well as her sometimes uncritical respect for business, much of what happened under New Labour in broadcasting, health care, education and the rest would still have occurred. There was no powerful body of public opinion to which a less market-oriented government could have appealed against the pressure from market forces, backed by the bulk of the press. For decades Labour had not cultivated such a body of opinion, and market ideology had become hegemonic. At the very least major compromises would have had to be reached. The refusal of successive governments to raise the BBC's licence fee significantly, for instance, and the acceptance of concentration in ITV, would have been necessary even if the Labour government had valued the BBC's public service mission much more highly than it did. The same could be said about Labour's acceptance of PFI and its extension throughout the NHS.

The third main reason why the marketisation of the public sector would have occurred, even if the Thatcherites had not made it a crusade, was the widely shared concern to drive down costs, raise productivity and reduce the public sector tax bill. Labour politicians attached almost as much importance to this as did Conservatives, and convinced themselves that no significant political or social cost would be incurred by it. They were also enthusiasts for new technology. Tony Blair attached great importance to the NHS's telephone service, NHS Direct, and to linking all schools to the internet, without inquiring closely into the costs and benefits of either. If competition led to the substitution of consumer goods for personal services, then exposing public services to competition seemed to most politicians desirable. (Most of them would probably have been surprised, for example, to learn that the hours devoted to housework had not declined with the introduction of vacuum cleaners, washing machines and refrigerators, as the labour formerly involved in cleaning, washing and food storage services was shifted to the consumers of these goods – in this case, women.[3])

The initiation, or acceleration, of the commodification of public services was thus a logical result of governments' increasingly deferential attitude towards market forces in the era of the globalised economy. The four prerequisites for the conversion of non-market spheres into profitable fields for investment, however – the reconfiguration of services into commodities, the creation of a demand for the commodities, the conversion of the public servants concerned into profit-oriented workforces, and the underwriting of risk – did not call for constant government intervention. A good deal of what was needed was accomplished by market forces themselves, with only periodic interventions by the state, which then appeared as rational responses to previous changes.

For example, the development of television as a means of producing audiences for sale to advertisers, or saleable products for sponsors, went on independently in the USA; authorising commercial television in Britain in the 1950s was a response to this. The subsequent decision to approve an eventual merger of the remaining ITV companies was similarly a response to the fact that markets for these commodities had by then become global and very much more competitive. Similarly for the creation of effective demand: given the balance of social forces in the 1990s, probably no government could have greatly increased the BBC's funding at a time when BSkyB was flourishing, the cable companies were getting close to recouping some of the investment that had been made, and ITV's revenues were stagnating. There would have been violent attacks by the ITV companies, the cable companies and the Murdoch-owned press, not to mention BSkyB itself. So the BBC remained starved of cash, its programming budget shrank and its sports coverage was bid away by the commercial broadcasters, reinforcing the demand for subscription television. The dialectic between market-led changes and state interventions is less obvious in the case of the NHS, because its monopoly lasted much longer than the BBC's. But the government-sponsored growth of the private acute and long-term care sectors in the 1980s produced similar effects in the 1990s, when a cash-starved NHS confronted a well-established private sector with considerable excess capacity. The point is only that the dynamism of markets is a constant with which political analysis needs to reckon much more than it has in the past.

We can trace the causal mechanism of market-driven politics back a further step: commodification of public service television and health care was also strongly influenced by the transformation of the British state and party system that both accompanied and followed from the deregulation of capital, and by the changed political culture in which politicians of all parties were operating, at least by the time New Labour took office in 1997. It is hard to imagine that Labour backbenchers, for example, or delegates to the party's annual conference, would have accepted the leadership's volte-face on PFI as meekly as they did after 1997, had Labour not been radically de-democratised by Kinnock and Blair. The party was strongly identified with the NHS, and the NHS's million-strong workforce were mostly Labour supporters and opposed to the PFI. But the centralisation of party decision-making and the weakening of the trade unions had put the party leadership in unchallenged control. Also important was the fact that the public had grown used to privatisation and commodification, from privately-operated social security offices and GP house-call services to subscription television. As Greg Dyke put it (referring to the not entirely mythic anonymous letter-writer to the *Times* in years past), ' "Disgusted of Tunbridge Wells" is disappearing, and being replaced by "Not bothered of Newcastle." '* Labour Party conference delegates knew this too, and no revolt occurred inside the party.

* Greg Dyke, *A Time for Change*, MacTaggart Lecture, Guardian Edinburgh Inter-

There is no need to stress this further. The higher civil service had been successfully infused with market values through changes in organisation, accounting practices and promotions. Local government had lost its autonomy. Not only the 'nationalised industries' taken into public hands after 1945 but a vast range of traditional public sector activities, from airports to prisons, were now private businesses. Everything now happened in a world where market forces ruled, and this in turn reflected the fact that these were no longer national but global forces, represented by the credit-rating agencies, the lobbyists of the TNCs and the financial markets that never sleep.

Is the UK an 'outlier'?

Long before economic globalisation the UK had an unwritten constitution and a highly centralised, unitary system of government, with a non-proportional electoral system; it also had historical cultural and political ties to the USA. Its highly outward-oriented economy, its imperial legacy (symbolised by the Commonwealth) and its powerful financial services sector all likewise predate economic globalisation. All these factors contributed to Britain's late and somewhat equivocal membership of the EU, and also played significant roles in the capture of the Conservative Party by Thatcherism, and the relative ease with which Thatcher was subsequently able to reshape British politics on neoliberal lines. The result is that from the point of view of mainstream European social democracy the UK is something of an 'outlier' – outside the typical EU pattern in some important respects, such as its low level of state pensions, its low level of spending on health care, its weak employment protection and trade union rights, and so on.

For these reasons it would be a mistake to conclude that what has happened to British television or health care or any other field of policy is likely to be repeated in other EU countries. On the other hand, from the point of view of some other EU countries such as Greece, or of countries like the Czech Republic (soon to join the EU), Britain might well appear atypical in the opposite sense – with stronger trade union

---

national Television Festival, 25 August 2000. Of course 'Disgusted of Tunbridge Wells' was never a Labour voter. The proper equivalent for our example would be 'Concerned of Hampstead', but he or she has never made much of an impression.

rights, better state pensions, and so on. What seems important to ask is whether the tendencies at work in the other major EU countries are similar to those observed in Britain. It is not part of the argument of this book that they are, but the fact that Britain has been unlike them in the past does not mean that they are immune to the forces that have produced such rapid and dramatic changes in Britain. There is some evidence that market forces are pushing Germany, Sweden and other centrally coordinated economies towards the Anglo-American model. Marx told German readers of *Capital* not to assume that his analysis of capitalism in England did not apply to them, because it did (*'de te fabula narratur'* – the story concerns you).[4] He was right then. Whether this is also true in the era of globalised capitalism is a matter for investigation.

Does it matter that politics are market-driven?

The argument so far has only been that market-driven politics expose society more and more to market forces – and in particular, that this changes the purposes ultimately served by public services – not that the effects are disastrous. Polanyi's thesis on this point, however, has never been refuted: left to themselves, market forces will destroy society. It has always been the function of states to prevent this; but economic globalisation has made states market-driven, rather than market-control-lers, and left societies more fully exposed to market forces than ever before.

We have documented the gradual undermining of the original form and purpose of public service broadcasting and a less advanced but still far-reaching transformation in the National Health Service. I would maintain that both services are important, arguably essential, elements in the healthy functioning of democracy today, where policy reflects shared values and the agenda is set by collective reflection and debate about the kind of society people want to live in. To that extent the erosion of these two services alone is not a minor but a major loss to democracy.

But it is not hard to point to even more obviously serious conse-quences. For most countries, the accumulation cycle can no longer be ironed out by the action of the state acting alone. The growing inequalities resulting from the power of financial capital and global labour-market restructuring will not be significantly compensated by redistributive fiscal policies, because these are unacceptable to the financial markets and a deterrent to foreign investment. Environmental degradation will not be prevented or reversed by state regulation because of the risk to exports or jobs or both. There are also accumulating psychological costs: rising rates of mental illness linked to unemployment and loneliness, insecurity and family breakdown caused by casualisation, and the emergence of a new 'under-class' of unemployed young people with high rates of drug abuse and crime. Some painful reckoning with reality lies ahead.

Social class will, evidently, be central to this reckoning. Globalisation has produced turmoil in the traditional class identities and class relations in industrialised countries like Britain, as market forces sort people out into those with some global market power and those with little or none. (Indeed, looked at from this angle, the so-called new 'under-class', for example, presents striking similarities to the so-called 'lumpen-proletariat' of the mid-nineteenth century; the computer engineers and software designers of areas like Silicon Valley in California and the 'Cambridge–Reading crescent' in England stand in a direct line of succession to the boilermakers and other 'labour aristocrats'; and so on.) But from a global viewpoint what stands out is the way the interests of those who own and control the world's productive assets have been forcefully reasserted at the expense of everyone else. A renewed democratic socialism in the era of global capitalism will undoubtedly be very different from social democracy in late nineteenth-century Europe, but to be effective it too will need ultimately to be grounded in the basic realities of class interest and class power.

In the current ideological climate any analysis that starts out from this elementary truth is apt to be automatically dismissed, which is presumably one reason why Karl Polanyi's *The Great Transformation* has enjoyed such a vogue recently, since he correctly identifies the threat presented to society by 'self-regulating' capitalism but is silent on the subject of the class character of capitalist countries. Yet the state, which in his model regularly reasserts the interests of society against those of capital ('the self-regulating market'), itself rests on class forces, and his disinclination to specify these forces leaves this salutary historical function of the state ultimately unexplained. I have touched earlier on the way in which economic globalisation has exposed this weakness in Polanyi's account; the underlying weakness, however, is really the one referred to here. I have nonetheless not hesitated to use Polanyi's theory as a reference point because it has helped to keep the threat that 'deregulated' capitalism presents on the intellectual agenda, and because in that respect it is valid.

Why has there been so little resistance?

Some of the reasons why resistance to the commodification of public service broadcasting and health care has been relatively weak and unsuccessful have already been given. The broadcasting unions were defeated by the end of the 1980s, just as the print unions had been. The viewing public enjoyed the gradually widening choice of channels and the Labour Party was ambivalent about the BBC and afraid of the commercial media, and especially Murdoch's newspapers. A stronger fight seemed likely over the NHS, on account of its much larger workforce, the public's strong attachment to it, and its special place in the history of the Labour Party. But the imposition of general management on the NHS hospital service, and the 'contracting out' of non-clinical services to private firms, took place during the mid-1980s in the context of an intense campaign by the Thatcher government against the trade unions, both through legislation stripping them of rights and protections, and through deliberately raised levels of unemployment (the peak was reached in mid-1986). Tens of thousands of mainly women cleaners, laundry workers and cooks, who were transferred by outsourcing into non-unionised jobs in private firms with lower pay, fewer benefits and heavier work schedules, could do little to prevent it. Then the 'internal market' balkanised the hospital service into several hundred independent trusts run by general managers whose careers depended on supporting the policies adopted by their boards of directors, and who were then told their only hope of getting new hospital premises lay in the PFI, about which the Labour leadership had meantime changed its mind. Hospital consultants were ambivalent; even many of those who saw the threat to the NHS's founding principles still wanted the better premises and equipment promised in the PFI plans. The main NHS trade union, UNISON, had to balance its general opposition to PFI against the need to secure its members' jobs in the downsized clinical structures of the new PFI hospitals as their plans came up for final approval. Local communities mobilised sometimes unprecedented opposition to hospital closures resulting from PFI projects. Very few carried any weight with the New Labour government, however, which counted on winning support from voters elsewhere who were glad to be getting long-overdue replacements for their run-down local hospital facilities.[5]

To anyone close to these events, the question why there was not more resistance may well seem misplaced. If the Labour Party was unwilling to back resistance, all other forces were placed at a severe disadvantage. The exception which proved the rule was the ultimately successful popular resistance to the poll tax in 1987–90, which turned on two significant points: the tax touched everyone in the country and was manifestly unjust. The Labour Party also opposed it, though without backing the widespread refusal to pay. Where an issue did not clearly affect everybody, or create such a clear sense of injustice, or have Labour's support, resistance could be isolated and defeated.

Do public services matter?

The main reason why this study has focused on public service television and the NHS is that they are major fields of non-market service provision under active encroachment by market forces, where the mechanisms of market-driven politics can be studied most easily as they impact on everyday life. It might be argued that this has led to these services – and by implication public services in general – being given undue prominence in this book. I maintain that, on the contrary, public services are defining features of a civilised society, which capitalist market production, if it persists at all, should exist to pay for, and to which it should be subordinate.[6] Many of the things that are primary requirements of genuine democracy (as opposed to a cynical conception of democracy as the sale to voters by political elites of 'political products', to be marketed like all other commodities) are goods that markets will not provide, such as general education, objective information, universally accessible media of communication, public libraries, public health and universal health care. Markets provide these things at best unequally, if at all, so they have to be provided collectively instead. They are anything but secondary.

In this connection it is instructive to look once again at William Baumol's work on the so-called 'cost disease'. In one of his last articles on this question Baumol pointed out that there was nothing objectively 'unaffordable' about labour-intensive public services like education and health care.[7] In the first place some productivity increases do occur in them all the time, if only as a result of rising productivity in the inputs into these services, such as transport, so they do actually become cheaper. In the second place, rising productivity in other sectors means that we could afford more and more public services even if their productivity were completely stagnant – and still have more of everything else as well. All it entails is that a steadily growing share of total income is devoted to them. Taking the USA as an example, and assuming that the historical productivity growth rates of the different sectors of the economy were maintained for another fifty years, Baumol showed that by 2040 total consumption would have more than tripled. If the consumption of education and health care (each of which accounted for 10 per cent of total spending in 1990) expanded at the same rate as all other consumption, however, by 2040 they would account for about 21 per cent and 35 per cent of total GNP respectively, because productivity would have gone on rising more slowly in these sectors than in the rest of the economy.

Of course, given the American New Right's success in persuading voters to favour tax cuts and a 'smaller' state, Baumol could not imagine them agreeing to spend 56 per cent of GDP – much of which would have to be financed by taxation – on these two sectors alone! He envisaged that the reaction to the growing monetary cost of education and health care would be to privatise them still further, and merely pointed out, very mildly, that this would give privatisation a bad name, because private firms would not be able to deliver productivity increases without degrading the educational and medical services people really wanted. (How right he was is evident from the widespread hatred of the for-profit HMOs that had developed in the USA by the end of the 1990s.)

Even in Britain, where social-democratic ideas and ideals still have some popular support, it is hard to imagine voters agreeing to an ever larger share of GDP being taxed to support public services, even if the total real outlay on them was actually declining. Overcoming the 'money illusion' will always be very difficult.* In one way or another,

---

* Baumol remarks that 'the task of explanation to the public [of the money illusion that makes it hard to see the real relationships involved] should not be beyond the most skilled of journalists and others who specialize in the art of effective communi-

however, it must be overcome if a genuine form of democracy is to survive. The problem is, perhaps, a new form in which Rosa Luxemburg's famous dilemma – socialism or barbarism – presents itself.

In the meantime progressive democrats need to be concerned with raising productivity in public services, as much as (or more than) market fundamentalists. But the kinds of productivity sought must be at least compatible with the purposes the services exist to fulfil, and preferably enhance their fulfilment. Productivity increases should not be pursued for their own sake, or, as they have been so often, at the cost of inferior services, and the public should be the judge of whether or not this is the case. Ursula Huws' questions from the 1980s have lost none of their relevance: 'Do elderly people really want more sophisticated alarm systems, or would they rather have more contact with human beings? Do pregnant women want more foetal monitors, or would they rather have more or better-trained midwives?'[8]

On what basis can public services flourish?

British experience suggests three broad conclusions about the necessary basis of public services: (1) the public domain needs to be based on a clear philosophy, and a set of practical principles to secure its funding and its internal health; (2) the interests of the public domain need to be promoted and defended across the whole range of public policy; (3) the boundaries between the public domain and the market sector need to be effectively policed and the scope of the public domain from time to time extended.

(1) The mid-twentieth century social-democratic concept of the 'mixed economy' had two fatal shortcomings: first, the public sector was conceived in the image of the private sector, but with the state as the sole shareholder; and, second, its relationship with the private sector was conceived of as fixed and stable, when in fact it was from the outset subject to erosion. In a globalised economy the erosion is speeded up. To resist this the public domain needs reliable increases in funding, well-formulated professional ethics and mechanisms for devel-

---

cation.' (Willliam J. Baumol, 'Health care, education and the cost disease: a looming crisis for public choice', in Ruth Towse [ed.], *Baumol's Cost Disease: The Arts and Other Victims* [Edward Elgar, 1997], p. 519). It is hard to know if he is being serious.

oping and enforcing them, and principles of internal organisation and operation appropriate to its public service function, including principles that assure dynamism, a capacity to change, corresponding to public wishes and needs. British public services have been notoriously weak on all fronts – frequently underfunded, saddled with ill-considered mixes of professional, civil service and business values, hierarchical rather than horizontal, lacking the incentive or the means to seek and take advantage of either self-criticism or public opinion. Resources for research and development are as important for public services as they are for firms. So are functional equivalents of the need to keep market share. The one potential general source of dynamism that does not mimic market incentives and the distortions they produce in public services is a thoroughgoing democratisation, something that has rarely been seriously explored.

(2) Responsibility for supporting the public domain must be shared by politicians and the whole state apparatus across the entire field of public policy. Its achievements must be honoured and its initiatives treated with respect. The non-market principles on which it rests must be widely understood and celebrated. Its pay and conditions must match those of the market sector. It must not be expected to subsidise the market sector nor to absorb the costs of markets' negative externalities (for example cleaning industrially polluted water or providing health care for victims of unsafe industrial practices, free of charge). And its tax revenues must be treated as a matter of common sense, not a problem. If it can be done for the army it can be done for the health service.

(3) The boundaries between the public domain and all the adjacent markets need to be well policed. The tendency of market forces to weaken and penetrate these boundaries has to be recognised and preventive mechanisms put in place. Legislation is always open to pressure for amendment, and the public domain needs the means to counter the lobbying and advertising and other forms of influence that are used to weaken it. It might for instance have its own advertising budget (financed, perhaps, by a tax on private sector advertising). The conflict of interest between the two domains needs to be acknowledged and priority given to the public domain.[9]

Is this relevant?

A strong non-market domain, providing various core services, as the common sense of a civilised and democratic society may sound far-fetched in the era of market-driven politics. But it is debatable whether it is really as far-fetched – as hard to imagine or as absurd – as the world towards which market-driven politics is tending, in which more and more of the workforce is absorbed in ever-intensified competition for ever-higher output and consumption, while the collective services on which democracy depends gradually decay. That is, in any case, the debate to which this book is intended to be relevant.

Notes

1 Introduction

1. Kenichi Ohmae, *The End of the Nation State* (HarperCollins, 1995); John Gray, *False Dawn: The Delusions of Global Capitalism* (Granta Books, 1998); Michael Hardt and Antonio Negri, *Empire* (Harvard University Press, 2000); Thomas L. Friedman, *The Lexus and the Olive Tree*, 2nd edn (Anchor, 2000); Helen V. Milner and Robert O. Keohane (eds), *Internationalization and Domestic Politics* (Cambridge University Press, 1996).
2. In the first two decades of the twentieth century the American Frederick Winslow Taylor popularised the detailed breakdown of tasks into their component parts and the assignment of the latter to the least expensive labour capable of performing them.
3. See especially Geoffrey Garrett, *Partisan Politics in the Global Economy* (Cambridge University Press, 1999).
4. Karl Polanyi, *The Great Transformation: The Political and Economic Origins of Our Time* (Beacon Press, 1957 [1944]), p. 73. Polanyi pointed to the colonies – perhaps with King Leopold's Congo especially in mind – as an example of what happened when no state protected the population from the impact of market forces (p. 214).

2 The global economy and national politics

1. David Held, Anthony McGrew, David Goldblatt and Jonathan Perraton, *Global Transformations: Politics, Economics and Culture* (Stanford University Press, 1999), p. 170.
2. *World Investment Report* 1999 (UNCTAD, 1999), p. 95. The process was, however, not symmetrical; while Japan was a major source of outward FDI, it accepted hardly any inward FDI.
3. Stephen Thomsen, 'Regional integration and multinational production', in Vincent Cable and David Henderson (eds), *Trade Blocs? The Future of Regional Integration* (Royal Institute of International Affairs, 1994), pp. 109–26.
4. Richard J. Barnet and John Cavanagh, *Global Dreams: Imperial Corporations and the New World Order* (Simon and Schuster, 1994), pp. 394–5.

5. Eric Helleiner, *States and the Reemergence of Global Finance* (Cornell University Press, 1994), pp. 136–8. The opposition was led by the Bank of England and the Swiss National Bank, both of which benefited from the Euromarket.

6. Philip Cerny, 'The deregulation and re-regulation of financial markets in a more open world', in Philip G. Cerny (ed.), *Finance and World Politics: Markets, Regimes and States in the Post-hegemonic Era* (Edward Elgar, 1993), pp. 51–85.

7. *World Investment Report: Transnational Corporations, Employment and the Workplace* (UNCTAD, 1994), p. 123.

8. Many British manufacturers, for example, would be hard hit by deregulation, but nonetheless backed Mrs Thatcher's neoliberal policies as the only way to defeat the trade unions and the Labour left. See Colin Leys, 'Thatcherism and British manufacturing: a question of hegemony', *New Left Review* 151, 1985, pp. 5–25.

9. Eric Hobsbawm, *Age of Extremes; The Short Twentieth Century 1914–1991* (Abacus, 1995), p. 15.

10. Paul Hirst and Grahame Thompson, *Globalization in Question: The International Economy and the Possibilities of Governance* (Polity, 1996). Bob Sutcliffe and Andrew Glyn make a broadly similar argument in 'Indicators of Globalization and their Misinterpretation', *Review of Radical Political Economics* 31/3, 1999, pp. 111–31. They stress, however, that no general conclusions follow from their demonstration that many claims about the novelty and scale of transnational investment, production and trade are greatly exaggerated, and they agree that financial globalisation is on an altogether novel scale.

11. Leo Panitch, drawing on the work of Robert Cox, in 'Globalisation and the state', in Ralph Miliband and Leo Panitch (eds), *Between Globalism and Nationalism: Socialist Register 1994* (Merlin Press, 1994), p. 64.

12. Strictly speaking there was actually a three and a half hour gap between the close of the stock exchange in New York and the opening of the exchange in Tokyo, and another hour-long gap between closing in Tokyo and reopening in London.

13. Held et al., *Global Transformations*, pp. 204–8. On derivatives and risk see Adam Tickell, 'Unstable futures: controlling and creating risks in international money', in Leo Panitch and Colin Leys (eds), *Global Capitalism Versus Democracy: Socialist Register* 1999 (Merlin Press, 1999), pp. 248–77.

14. Peter Gowan, *The Global Gamble: Washington's Faustian Bid for World Dominance* (Verso, 1999), pp. 95–100.

15. John M. Stopford and Susan Strange, *Rival States, Rival Firms: Competition for World Market Shares* (Cambridge University Press, 1991), p. 15; Peter Dicken, *Global Shift*, 2nd edn (Paul Chapman, 1992), p. 57. The proportions of the various commodity markets controlled by TNCs were: over 80 per cent, wheat, maize, coffee, cocoa, tea, pineapples, forest products,

cotton, tobacco, jute, copper, iron ore, bauxite; 70–80 per cent, rice, bananas, natural rubber, crude petroleum, tin; 50–70 per cent, sugar, phosphates.

16. *World Investment Report* 1993 (UNCTAD, 1993), pp. 130 and 134.

17. Held et al., *Global Transformations*, p. 247.

18. François Chesnais, 'Globalisation, world oligopoly and some of their implications', in Marc Humbert (ed.), *The Impact of Globalisation on Europe's Firms and Industries* (Pinter, 1993), pp. 15–16.

19. Susan Strange, 'The defective state', in *What Future for the State? Daedalus* 124/2,1995, p. 59.

20. Chesnais ('Globalisation', p. 17) thinks that 'the entry of the Japanese keiretsu as major competitors in the late 1970s and their large-scale penetration through investment into the US economy gave the onset of global oligopoly its irreversible character and made international cross-investment an imperative strategy for the survival of large firms'. On 'networks' see also Gunther Teubner, 'The many-headed hydra: networks as higher-order collective actors', in Joseph McCahery, Sol Piciotto and Colin Scott (eds), *Corporate Control and Accountability* (Clarendon Press, 1993), pp. 41–60.

21. A 'back-of-the-envelope calculation' by the editors of the Economist cited in Barnet and Cavanagh, *Global Dreams*, p. 423.

22. Ibid., p. 135.

23. *World Investment Report* 1999, p. 6.

24. Dicken, *Global Shift*, p. 49. Of the world's 100 largest TNCs in 1992, 29 were American, 16 were Japanese, and 44 European (World Investment Report 1994, [UNDP, 1994], p. 8).

25. *World Investment Report* 1999, p. 17. Britain was twice as dependent on foreign TNCs as France, and three times as dependent as Germany or Italy. All the other equally 'transnational' economies were much smaller.

26. George Monbiot, *Captive State: The Corporate Takeover of Britain* (Macmillan, 2000), pp. 188–9.

27. Susan Strange, 'The name of the game', in N. X. Rizopoulos (ed.), *Sea-Changes: American Foreign Policy in a World Transformed* (Council on Foreign Relations, 1990), p. 247; Barnet and Cavanagh, *Global Dreams*, p. 386; *Guardian*, 30 January 1996.

28. For instance Vivien A. Schmidt, writing about the European Union, notes that 'business' privileged access to supranational decision-making ensures that policy interactions have shifted from an almost exclusive reliance on national government bargaining [i.e. bargaining between the member governments] to one that includes, if it is not dominated by, business actors in the transnational sector' ('The New World Order, Incorporated', in *What Future for the State?*, p. 80).

29. Susan Strange, 'Rethinking Structural Change in the International Political Economy: States, Firms and Diplomacy', in Richard Stubbs and

Geoffrey R. D. Underhill (eds), *Political Economy and the Changing Global Order* (Macmillan, 1994), p. 111.

30. Monbiot, *Captive State*, pp. 254–61.
31. Held et al., in *Global Transformations*, p. 277, cite an estimate by Rousslang that transfer pricing saves MNCs (multi-national corporations) 'around $8 billion' in taxes, but add that 'this is only around 4 per cent of worldwide taxable income of manufacturing MNCs' and 'of secondary importance to profits and government tax revenues'. The significance of the word 'only' is not clear. If MNCs' average tax rate were, say, 10 per cent, the tax 'saved' in this way would presumably be equal to 40 per cent of their tax obligations.
32. Teubner, 'The many-headed hydra', p. 58, quoting H. Collins, 'Ascription of legal responsibility in complex patterns of economic integration', *Modern Law Review* 53, 1990, p. 731.
33. Sol Picciotto, 'Transfer pricing and corporate regulation', in McCahery et al., (eds) *Corporate Control*, p. 387. Picciotto's major study *International Business Taxation* (Clarendon Press, 1992) describes in dispassionate detail the elaborate ways whereby corporations avoid tax, and the hitherto rather ineffectual responses of international cooperation between tax authorities.
34. Michael Wallerstein and Adam Przeworski, 'Capital taxation with open borders', *Review of International Political Economy* 2/3, 1995, 425–45. The authors criticise the view that this flowed necessarily from capital mobility, arguing that, provided the full cost of investment is tax deductible, as it usually is, only fear of tax changes, and not the absolute level of tax on profits, affects investment flows.
35. Anthony Ginsberg, quoted in Barnet and Cavanagh, *Global Dreams*, p. 389. In a survey of the capital income tax situation in the EC in the early 1990s, Peter B. Sorenson concluded: 'Governments in Europe should seriously consider whether they wish to retain personal taxes on income from capital in reality and not just on paper. If the answer is in the affirmative, they must soon take steps to ensure that such taxes can actually be enforced in an integrated European market. This will be a very difficult task, involving sensitive issues such as bank secrecy laws, and requiring a cooperative attitude from non-EC countries. If EC governments refuse to face this challenge directly, the days of the personal income tax as we know it may be numbered' ('Coordination of capital and income taxes in the Economic and Monetary Union: what needs to be done?', in Francisco Torres and Francesco Giavazzi [eds], *Adjustment and Growth in the European Monetary Union* [Cambridge University Press, 1993], p. 378). The problem remains largely unaddressed.
36. Vincent Cable, 'The diminished nation-state: a study of the loss of economic power', in *What Future for the State?* p. 37.
37. Held and his colleagues conclude that 'the capacity of environmental

globalization to create potential risks and threats ... greatly exceeds existing capacities to address them ...' (*Global Transformations*, p. 413).

38. For a survey of this development see Monbiot, *Captive State*, chapter 10.

39. British enthusiasm for American policies is of course long-standing, reinforced in this case by heavy pressure by the Clinton adminstration on the incoming Blair government; see Gregory Palast, 'Tony rushes in where Bill fears to tread', *Guardian*, 25 May 2000.

40. Monbiot, *Captive State*, pp. 310–11 and 329.

41. Ben Steil, 'Competition, integration and regulation in EC capital markets', in Cable and Henderson (eds), *Trade Blocs?*, p. 155.

42. Hamish Macrae, '1996's financial markets', *The World in 1996* (Economist Publications, 1996), pp. 124 and 127.

43. Cerny, 'The deregulation and re-regulation of financial markets', pp. 79–80.

44. Timothy J. Sinclair, 'Passing judgment: credit rating processes as regulatory mechanisms of governance in the emerging world order', *Review of International Political Economy* 1/1, 1994, pp. 133–59. Whether the credit agencies or their clients make intelligent use of the data they collect may be doubted, in view of the failure to foresee either the Mexico crisis of 1994 or the East Asian crisis of 1997–98.

45. For a discussion of proposals concerning pension funds see, e.g., Robin Blackburn, 'The new collectivism: pension reform, grey capitalism and complex socialism', *New Left Review* I/233, 1999, pp. 3–65, and the subsequent exchange between Blackburn and Henri Jacot in *New Left Review* II/1, 2000, pp. 122–36.

46. In a study of fifteen countries from 1967 to 1990 Garrett found that 'the financial markets always attached interest rate premia to the power of the left and organized labor' and that these premia appeared to increase with greater capital mobility. 'Presumably, these results reflect the market's skepticism about the willingness of governments to pursue "prudent" macroeconomic policies where the left and organized labor are powerful' ('Capital mobility, trade, and domestic politics', in Robert O. Keohane and Helen V. Milner [eds], *Internationalization and Domestic Politics* [Cambridge University Press, 1996],p. 95).

47. Held et al., *Global Transformations*, p. 165, citing S. Page, *How Countries Trade*, (Routledge, 1994), chapter 4.

48. Ronald Dore, 'World markets and institutional uniformity', in Geraint Parry (ed.), *Politics in an Interdependent World* (Edward Elgar, 1994), pp. 59–60. American companies could not get orders from the Japanese *keiretsu* (or corporate groups), which did business with each other based primarily on long-term relationships of trust, and only secondarily on price. Japan's Large Retail Store Law – which protects small Japanese retailers from elimination by supermarket chains in order to maintain employment in the retail sector and preserve a pedestrian-based local

shopping culture – was also targeted, because of the desire of US retailers like Toys-R-Us to open branches in Japan. The Japanese for their part were concerned with reform of the American education system, the adoption by the US of metrication, and improving US savings behaviour.

49. John H. Dunning, *Globalization: The Challenge for National Economic Regimes* (Economic and Social Research Institute, Dublin, 1993), p. 15.

50. Jeanne-Mey Sun and Jacques Pelkmans, 'Regulatory competition in the Single Market', *Journal of Common Market Studies* 33/1, 1955, pp. 67–89. In one case Britain and Ireland banned the sale of upholstered furniture that was not impregnated with flame retardants. Ten other EC states took them to the European Court of Justice but in the end the matter was left to be sorted out politically. In another case France prevented Barclays Bank from offering French customers interest-bearing current accounts, which were legal in Britain, but Barclays accepted the ban rather than pick a fight with the French government; i.e. the decisive consideration was again political, in spite of Barclays' apparent legal rights.

51. Cable, 'The diminished nation state', pp. 39–41. In spite of the inconsistency involved, most neoliberal politicians also advocate curbs on immigration.

52. For a survey of the environmental threat posed by the globalised capitalist economy see Held et al., *Global Transformations*, chapter 8.

53. For a comprehensive review of the Tobin tax idea and the problems it raises, see Mahbub ul Haq, Inge Kaul and Isabell Grunberg (eds), *The Tobin Tax: Coping With Financial Volatility* (Oxford University Press, 1996). One of the contributors, Peter B. Kenen, calculated (p. 110) that a tax of 0.05 per cent on spot transactions would have been feasible (i.e. would not have provoked excessive evasion) and would have yielded $100 billion in 1992 and $150 billion in 1996 – figures that both explain some of the opposition, and form a useful contrast with the level of official development aid for those years of $54 billion and $35 billion respectively. At this 'feasible' level of taxation, however, Kenen assumed the tax would have no effect on the volume of transactions – apparently, if it were large enough to reduce volatility it would be evaded.

54. See Wolfgang Streeck, 'Neo-voluntarism: a new European social policy regime?', *European Law Journal* 1/1, 1995, pp. 31–59. Streeck's analysis of the impact of global market forces on EU states in relation to social policy is very like the one adopted more generally here, although more nuanced. His thesis that the EU states have retained their sovereignty, however, seems to me somewhat formal, given his recognition that it no longer covers domestic economic and social policy.

55. John D. Stephens, Evelyne Huber and Leonard Ray, 'The welfare state in hard times', in Herbert Kitschelt, Peter Lange, Gary Marks and John D.

Stephens (eds), *Continuity and Change in Contemporary Capitalism* (Cambridge University Press, 1999), pp. 189–92.

56. Peter Hall, in a valuable survey of the political science literature, notes that some organisation theorists have tried to conceptualise sets of ideas as institutions; but the degree of reductionism involved seems more than usually heroic. See Hall, 'The role of interests, institutions, and ideas in the comparative political economy of the industrialized nations', in Mark I. Lichbach and Alan S. Zuckerman (eds), *Comparative Politics: Rationality, Culture, and Structure* (Cambridge University Press, 1997, p. 194).

57. Will Hutton, *The State We're In* (Cape, 1995).

58. David Soskice, 'Divergent production regimes: coordinated and uncoordinated market economies in the 1980s and 1990s', in Kitschelt et al., (eds) *Continuity and Change*, pp. 133–4.

59. The summary given here is drawn from references throughout the new institutionalist literature, but see especially Geoffrey Garrett and Pater Lange, 'Internationalization, institutions and political change', in Keohane and Milner (eds), *Internationalization*, pp. 72–3; and Desmond King and Stewart Wood, 'The political economy of neoliberalism: Britain and the United States in the 1980s', in Kitschelt et al. (eds), *Continuity and Change*, pp. 371–97. It should be added that there are aspects of the British political system that are omitted from the stylised account provided in this literature. In particular, American analysts tend to ignore the class character of constitutional arrangements. The House of Lords, the judiciary and the higher civil service remain significant 'veto points', but only in the general interest of capital

60. On the second point see, e.g., Andrew Graham, 'The UK 1979–95: myths and realities of Conservative capitalism', in Colin Crouch and Wolfgang Streeck (eds), *The Political Economy of Modern Capitalism* (Sage, 1997), pp. 117–32; and David Coates, *Models of Capitalism: Growth and Stagnation in the Modern Era* (Polity, 2000), pp. 244–7.

61. Herbert Kitschelt, 'European social democracy between political economy and electoral competition', in Kitschelt et al. (eds), *Continuity and Change*, pp. 343 and 334.

62. Streeck, 'Neo-voluntarism', p. 58.

63. 'As governments try to match the efforts of their rivals in order to allow their own TNCs to compete on, at least, equal conditions, they "match the low bidder".... Thus a democracy with a docile electorate, or an autocratic government, will be able to implement low-bidder policies more easily than a democracy featuring fierce competition among political parties and an electorate likely to punish a non-performing government. John H. Dunning described a failure to match the "low bidder" as "an unaffordable luxury"' (H. Peter Gray, 'The modern structure of international economic policies', *Transnational Corporations*

4/3, 1995, p. 53). Gray and Dunning both taught at Rutgers School of Business.

64. On the creation of millionaires by corporate executive stock options see Wally Seccombe, 'Contradictions of shareholder capitalism: downsizing jobs, enlisting savings, destabilising families', in Panitch and Leys (eds), *Socialist Register 1999*, pp. 76–107. Merrill Lynch estimated that the nearly six million High Net Worth Invididuals (i.e. owning a million dollars or more), who collectively owned $21.6 trillion in 1998, would own $32.7 trillion by 2003 (Merrill Lynch/Gemini Consulting, World Wealth Report, www.ml.com/woml/press_release/ 19990517.htm). The 1995 figure of 358 billionaires is taken from the UN *World Development Report 1996* (UNCTAD, 1996). In 1997 *Forbes Magazine* reported that the 225 richest people in the world owned a total of $1 trillion between them, an average individual fortune of $4.5 billion each (*Human Development Report* [UNDP, 1998], p. 30).

65. Cable notes the emergence in the older industrial countries of what used to be the hall-mark of 'third-world' societies: '. . . for the educated and moneyed section of the population, the opportunities presented by globalization – travel, wider experience, promotion – are great. We thus have one, potentially large, disadvantaged, alienated and powerless element in society, and another which is flourishing but has less of a stake in the success of any particular country' ('The diminished nation state', p. 43).

66. Amos A. Jordan and Jane Khanna, 'Economic interdependence and challenges to the nation-state', *Journal of International Affairs* 48/2, 1995, p. 443. The NETs studied in the article are Greater China (Taiwan and the PRC), Northeast Asia (Japan, North and South Korea, northeast China and far eastern Russia), and four southeast Asian NETs: the Indonesia–Malaysia–Singapore Growth Triangle; the Indonesia–Malaysia–Thailand Growth Triangle; and the Golden Quadrangle embracing northern Thailand, Yunnan Province in China and northern Myanmar and Laos. A nascent fourth NET is also referred to, linking Brunei to parts of Indonesia and the Philippines.

67. *The Manifesto of the Communist Party*, in Karl Marx, *The Revolutions of 1848* (Penguin, 1973 [1848]), pp. 70–71.

3 British politics in a global economy

1. In an article in the *Daily Mail*, 26 March 1997. An alternative version appeared in Blair's foreword, as Prime Minister, to the 1998 White Paper on employment law: 'the most tightly regulated labour market of any leading economy in the world'.

2. In 1980 the interest rate on US Treasury Bills averaged 14.91 per cent; the rate on US dollar deposits in London averaged 17.75 per cent.

3. From 44 per cent of GDP in 1980 to less than 40 per cent in 1990; Ron Martin, 'Has the British economy been transformed? Critical reflections on the policies of the Thatcher era', in Paul Cloke (ed.), *Policy and Change in Thatcher's Britain* (Pergamon, 1992), p. 151.

4. Based on four variables (the share of FDI gross capital formation, FDI stock as a percentage of GDP, value added by foreign 'affiliates' as a proportion of GDP and employees of foreign affiliates as a percentage of total employment), the UK's 'transnationality index' was 16, France's 9 and Germany's 6 (*World Investment Report* [UNCTAD, 1999], 1999 p. 17).

5. Colin Hay, *The Political Economy of New Labour: Labouring under False Pretences?* (Manchester University Press, 1999), chapter 4. On the problematic nature of Labour's attempt to gain market approval both before and after the election see Mark Wickham-Jones, 'The ties that bind: Blair's search for business credibility', unpublished paper, Bristol University, 1996.

6. Michael Moran and Elizabeth Alexander, 'The economic policy of New Labour', in David Coates and Peter Lawler (eds), *New Labour in Power* (Manchester University Press, 2000), pp. 108–21.

7. George Monbiot, *Captive State: The Corporate Takeover of Britain* (Macmillan, 2000), p. 262.

8. Wickham-Jones, 'The ties that bind', p. 21.

9. On the economic weaknesses of the UK economy and the economic achievements of Thatcherism see Martin, 'Has the British economy been transformed?'; and Andrew Graham, 'The UK 1979–95: Conservative capitalism', in Colin Crouch and Wolfgang Streeck (eds), *Political Economy of Modern Capitalism* (Sage, 1997), pp. 117–32.

10. Unless otherwise indicated all the data in this and the following section are from *Social Trends 30*, 2000 edn (The Stationery Office, 2000).

11. Contrary to a common misrepresentation, most of the men on temporary terms, and a quarter of the women, were in this 'precarious' employment because they could not find permanent work (see *Social Inequalities*, 2000 edn [Office of National Statistics, 2000], p. 77).

12. According to Richard Reeves, 'the average dual-income household in London spen[t] £5,000 a year on cleaners, gardeners, dog walkers and so on' ('All change in the workplace', *Observer*, 30 January 2000).

13. Christopher Hird, Fulcrum Productions, interview, 2 December 1999.

14. David Saunders, 'Goodbye to all that', *Guardian*, 3 July 2000.

15. The idea was that if a majority of MPs voted to ban hunting with dogs, and the House of Lords rejected the ban, it would be an issue in the next general election, though not one that the government would feel obliged to adopt.

16. The Labour government's attempt to repeal the discriminatory Section 28 of the Local Government Act, passed by the Conservatives in 1988,

which prohibited the 'promotion' of homosexuality in schools in England and Wales, was eventually defeated by homophobic members of the House of Lords.

17. See Monbiot, *Captive State, passim.*

18. On the growth of PR in Britain see Aeron Davis, 'Public relations campaigning and news production', in James Curran (ed.), *Media Organisations* (Arnold, 1999), pp. 173–93; 'Public relations, news production and changing patterns of source access in the British national press', *Media, Culture and Society* 22/1, 2000, pp. 39–59; and 'Public relations, business news and the reproduction of corporate elite power', *Journalism: Theory, Practice and Criticism* I/2, 2000, pp. 282–304.

19. The speech was greeted by slow hand-clapping, a novel experience for Blair, who had significantly misjudged the politics of the WI's fifty-something middle-class women activists (Kamal Ahmed and Gaby Hinsliff, 'End of the affair for Tony and his women', *Guardian,* 11 June 2000).

20. Roger Jowell, John Curtice, Allison Park and Katarina Thomson (eds), *The British Social Attitudes Survey: The 16th Report: Who Shares New Labour Values?* (Ashgate, 1999), pp. 25 and 28.

21. Philip Cohen, 'Teaching enterprise culture: individualism, vocationalism and the new right', in Ian Taylor (ed.), *The Social Effects of Market Policies* (Harvester Wheatsheaf, 1990), 49–91; Oliver Fulton, 'Consuming education', in Russell Keat and Nicholas Abercrombie (eds), *Enterprise Culture* (Routledge, 1991), pp. 223–40.

22. In 2000 the annual loss from social security fraud and error combined was estimated by the Public Accounts Committee at £4bn. In the nature of the case such estimates are highly unreliable and how much was due to error and how much to fraud (much of which is said to be landlords fraudulently claiming rent for tenants on income support) is impossible to know. Estimates of losses from tax evasion are equally problematic.

23. On the shifting of the tax burden see Margaret Wilkinson, 'British tax policy 1979–90: equity and efficiency', *Policy and Politics* 21/3, 1993, pp. 207–17. Estimates of the size of the 'black economy' are notoriously unreliable; the estimate of £50–80 billion – 'up to 8 per cent of GDP' – is from the report by Lord Grabiner, QC, *The Informal Economy,* published by HM Treasury, March 2000.

24. Jowell et al., *British Social Attitudes: Who Shares New Labour Values?,* pp. 5–6, 9.

25. Data on litigation against the police are not centrally collected but large payments were regularly reported in the press. The National Audit Office found that in 1998–99 NHS trusts paid out £1 billion in legal claims – equivalent to about 2 per cent of the total NHS budget – while in 1999 the Medical Defence Union paid out £77 million in cases against individual doctors, almost double the figure for 1996.

26. For the dependence of scientific research in universities on corporate funding see Monbiot, *Captive State*, chapter 9.
27. *Guardian*, 2 August 2000.
28. *The Future Funding of the BBC* (the Davies Report: Department for Media, Culture and Sport, 1999), p. 179.
29. Wyn Grant, *Pressure Groups and British Politics* (Macmillan, 2000), p. 217
30. Several of the case studies in David Marsh and R. A. W. Rhodes (eds), *Policy Networks in British Government* (Clarendon, 1992), note the growing power of business interests during the 1980s, but only one covering those years (on EC technology policy) transcends the national level. The book's conclusions did not register the radical shift in the relations between government, professional elites and companies that globalisation was producing and that would result in the 'Captive State' described in Monbiot's case studies in 2000.
31. Grant, *Pressure Groups*, pp. 69 and 95. The chief executive or chairman of a big enough company, such as News Corporation, will often deal with the Prime Minister.
32. Ibid., p. 69.
33. *Guardian*, 8 October 1999, 3 and 26 June and 21 November 2000. The Glaxo chairman's threat appeared to produce a concession: in its final decision in November 2000, NICE recommended the use of Relenza for a narrowly restricted category of patients, implying predicted sales to the NHS of between £2.3 and £11 million, rather than the figure of up £100 million reportedly expected.
34. Monbiot, *Captive State*, pp. 262–6.
35. Cf. Sam Whimster, 'Yuppies: a keyword of the 1980s', in Leslie Budd and Sam Whimster (eds), *Global Finance and Urban Living: A Study of Metropolitan Change* (Routledge, 1992), p. 315: 'It . . . has to be admitted that no overall social science paradigm has yet emerged which is sufficient to explain the complexities of the move towards post-industrial societies that has occurred over the last two decades. Using a popular acronym, like yuppie, is in no way a simplifying device, for the word brings together a range of sociological issues [among] which number social structural change, social status, social class, consumerism, lifestyle, social mobility, personality, political and social values, and career.'
36. '. . . the old is dying and the new cannot be born; in this interregnum a great variety of morbid symptoms appear' (Antonio Gramsci, *Selections from the Prison Notebooks* [International Publishers, 1971], p. 276).
37. See especially Budd and Whimster (eds), *Global Finance*; Stuart Corbridge, Ron Martin and Nigel Thrift (eds), *Money, Power and Space* (Blackwell, 1994); and Andrew Leyshon and Nigel Thrift, *Money/Space* (Routledge, 1996).
38. On the politics of the Big Bang see Michael Moran, *The Politics of the Financial Services Revolution* (Macmillan, 1991).

39. The various regulators were ultimately brought together in 2000 in a single Financial Services Agency.
40. Will Hutton, *The State We're In* (Vintage, 1996), pp. 298–318.
41. Nigel Thrift and Andrew Leyshon, 'In the wake of money: the City of London and the accumulation of value', in Budd and Whimster (eds), *Global Finance*, pp. 282–311, reprinted in Leyshon and Thrift, *Money/Space*, pp. 164–84.
42. Leyshon and Thrift, *Money/Space*, pp. 144–5.
43. Ibid., p. 181.
44. Alan Clark, *Diaries* (Phoenix, 1994), pp. 162–3.
45. See Judith Cook, *The Sleaze File and How to Clean Up British Politics* (Bloomsbury, 1995); David Leigh and Ed Vulliamy, *Sleaze: The Corruption of Parliament* (Fourth Estate, 1997). Jonathan Aitken, a junior defence minister, had 'commercial relations' with Saudi Arabian arms purchasers; Neil Hamilton, a backbencher, took money for asking parliamentary questions.
46. Peter Riddell, *Honest Opportunism*, 2nd edn (Imago, 1996).
47. Whimster, 'Yuppies: a keyword of the 1980s', p. 328.
48. On parties of notables see Maurice Duverger, *Political Parties: Their Organization and Activity in the Modern State* (Methuen, 1954); also Andrew Gamble, *The Conservative Nation* (Routledge and Kegan Paul, 1974), and A. J. Davies, *We, the Nation: The Conservative Party and the Pursuit of Power* (Little, Brown, 1995).
49. The transformation of the Labour Party is the subject of an enormous literature. For a useful survey see Steve Ludlam, 'New Labour: what's published is what counts', *British Journal of Politics and International Relations* 2/2, 2000, pp. 264–76. For the changes in Labour's constitution see Leo Panitch and Colin Leys, *The End of Parliamentary Socialism*, 2nd edn (Verso, 2001), chapters 10 and 13.
50. Bernard Manin's analysis of the changes that have been taking place in all modern political parties ('The metamorphoses of representative government', *Economy and Society* 23/2, May 1994, pp. 133–71) is the most perceptive known to me, although his model of the latest incarnation of representative government (party as a 'tribunal of the public') is distinctly idealised.
51. Antonio Polito, *Cool Britannia: Gli Inglezi (E Gli Italiani) Visti di Londra* (Donzelli, 1998), cited in Eric Hobsbawm, 'The death of neo-liberalism', *Marxism Today*, November–December 1998, pp. 4–8.
52. Bruce I. Newman (ed.), *Handbook of Political Marketing* (Sage, 1999), pp. xiii–xiv.
53. *Guardian*, 30 April 1998. If Mandelson was joking it is not recorded that his audience noticed it. The previous year, just after the election, he had told a meeting in Germany that 'ballot boxes and Parliaments were elitist relics' and that people wanted to be more 'involved in government'

through 'the far superior instruments of plebiscites, focus groups and the internet. . . . It may be that the era of pure representative democracy is coming to an end.' The Germans were not amused (Nick Cohen, 'New Labour . . . in focus, on message, out of control', *Observer*, 28 November 1999).

54. It should be noted that thanks to outsourcing and spending cuts elsewhere, as well as to higher unemployment, an ageing population, and other changes in demand, social security spending nonetheless rose as a proportion of government spending from just over 20 per cent in 1980 to nearly 40 per cent in 1999, offering an ever larger target.

55. Nick Cohen, 'Cowards' way', *Observer*, 30 July 2000. Cohen observes that ironically enough it was Margaret Thatcher who in 1960 had promoted the law that opened councils up to public scrutiny, as a means of limiting corruption, real or alleged, in Labour-controlled councils. The difference forty years had made to both parties' attitudes to democracy is instructive.

56. Stuart Weir and Wendy Hall (eds), *EGO Trip: Extra-Governmental Organisations in the United Kingdom and Their Accountability* (The Scarman Trust for Democratic Audit, 1994); and Wendy Hall and Stuart Weir, *The Untouchables: Power and Accountability in the Quango State* (The Scarman Trust, 1996).

57. Quango appointments were now advertised, but the appointments process itself remained secret and unaccountable. 'Dissidents' were not encouraged.

58. Michael Power, *The Audit Society: Rituals of Verification* (Oxford University Press, 1997), p. 3.

59. 'Auditing is a process of operationalising the accountability of an agent to a principal where the principal can't do it alone and where trust is lacking. . . . Much of the audit explosion presumes that teachers, social workers, etc. can't be trusted – with often, or sometimes, perverse effects. . . . Audits [can] create the distrust they presuppose and . . . this in turn leads to various organisational pathologies. . . . Where the solution to these pathologies of distrust is yet more and better auditing, yet more guardians of impersonal trust, then one has the audit society in a nutshell' (ibid., pp. 135–6).

60. The official term used in relation to 'failing schools' was to subject them to 'special measures', the expression also used by the Health Minister Alan Milburn in describing plans for hospitals (*Guardian*, 1 July 2000). In 2000 the Labour government also announced the first invitation to the private sector to take over the management of a public prison, Brixton, apparently as a way of overcoming what looked like intransigent racism on the part of the staff (*Guardian*, 7 July 2000).

61. The Labour leadership clearly regretted its election promise to create an elected upper house. In January 2000 a Commission chaired by Lord

Wakeham recommended a second chamber still called the House of Lords, with a majority appointed by an independent commission and a minority elected by proportional representation on a regional basis. No one liked the report and the plan to remit it to a joint House of Commons/House of Lords committee was put on hold. On the other hand the House of Lords as then constituted, with its remaining 92 hereditary peers, still had a large conservative (with a small 'c') majority (only 33 new life peers were created in the months immediately following the reform, in spite of the fact that only 233 peers out of a total of 694 accepted the Labour whip) and seemed rather more apt than the old one to challenge government legislation.

62. Ken Livingstone, the former Leader of the Greater London Council (abolished by Mrs Thatcher in 1997), now a Labour MP, was the popular favourite to become Mayor. Blair and the modernisers were determined to prevent this, having identified him as the embodiment of the 'old' Labour socialist values they were dedicated to exorcising. They rigged the nomination procedure so transparently that when Livingstone decided to run as an independent candidate public sympathy carried him to victory with 58 per cent of the final (run-off) votes cast.

63. Labour won 34 per cent of the final vote, and 56 seats out of a total of 129, in Scotland; and 35 per cent of the vote, and 28 out of 60 seats, in Wales. The Scottish National Party won 27 per cent of the final vote and 35 seats in Scotland. Plaid Cymru (the Welsh National Party) won 30.5 per cent of the final vote and 17 seats in Wales.

64. An issue that threatened to do this was the failure of the Treasury to provide 'matching' funds for Wales, which would have triggered a development grant of £1.2 million from the European Commission. Alun Michael, who had been imposed by Blair as leader of the Welsh Labour Party, was forced to resign and was replaced by his deputy, Rhodri Morgan, an 'old Labour' politician popular in Wales whom Blair had been determined to exclude. In office, however, Morgan avoided conflict with Downing Street.

65. Cf. e.g. Peter Mandelson and Roger Liddle, *The Blair Revolution: Can New Labour Deliver?* (Faber and Faber, 1996), pp. 4–8.

66. *Social Justice: Strategies for National Renewal*, Report of the Commission on Social Justice (The Borrie Report), 1994, chapter 1. The secretary to the Commission, David Miliband, subsequently became head of policy in Blair's office.

67. Department of Social Security data reported in the *Guardian*, 14 July 2000.

68. A total of 166,760 households were recognised as homeless by local authorities in England. Shelter estimated that this represented over 400,000 people, not counting 41,000 who were living in squats and 78,000 couples and lone parents sharing accommodation.

69. Notifiable offences in England and Wales rose from about sixty per thousand population in 1980 to about eighty-five per thousand in 1998–99 (*Social Trends 30*, p. 150).

70. The average prison sentence rose from 17 months in the early 1980s to 23.6 months in 1998 (*Social Trends 30*, p. 160).

71. The Social Justice Commission did briefly (pp. 51–2) discuss racial discrimination, as a product of racism, but not racism itself – its causes or the steps needed to combat it. The MacPherson inquiry into the racist murder of Stephen Lawrence, a black student, in 1993, eventually concluded that the Metropolitan Police force was saturated with racism ('institutional racism'). For electoral reasons Blair opted for what he called 'very tough measures on asylum and crime' – code-words for conciliating the racist right (*Guardian*, 18 July 2000).

72. The Institute for Fiscal Studies pointed out in 1999 that average real earnings had not risen by the official figure of 30 per cent over the years since 1978, but by more like 20 per cent, when account is taken of the fact that workers who had dropped out of employment altogether during this period were disproportionately low-wage workers ('Wages and work-force composition', *IFS Update* Issue 2: 1999, p. 8). By 1999 the average chief executive's salary and bonus package was worth eighteen times the average worker's and in that year average CEO's pay rose by 17.6 per cent, compared with a 5 per cent increase in average earnings (Charlotte Denny, '1 chief executive = 5 roadsweepers', *Guardian*, 5 July 2000).

73. The number of pensioners living below the poverty line rose from 2 million to 2.4 million in the two years 1998–2000 (*Guardian*, 14 July 2000, citing Department of Social Security data). In spite of strenuous efforts by the leadership to prevent it, the Labour Party conference in October 2000 passed a resolution calling for the state pension to be relinked to average earnings. The Chancellor, Gordon Brown, immediately declared he would not be bound by this decision.

74. *Social Justice*, p. 379.

75. *A Fresh Start: Improving Literacy and Numeracy for Adults* (Department for Education and Employment, 1999), p. 4.

76. Like many parts of the public service, under constant pressure for improved performance and demands for more accountability, the police were suffering from large numbers of early retirements. The New Labour government promised to increase recruitment by 3,000 a year to raise total numbers to the peak level of 128,000 last reached under the Conservatives in 1993.

77. Philip Gould, *The Unfinished Revolution: How the Modernisers Saved the Labour Party* (Abacus, 1999), p. 243. New Labour's reliance on Gould's thinking, as revealed in his book, deserves attention. Gould brought to 'the project' a single-minded commitment to make Labour appealing to

the legitimate aspirations of intelligent victims of secondary modern schooling (of whom he was one), no matter what it cost in pandering to their racist and socially authoritarian prejudices. The attempt by Anthony Giddens and others to elevate 'New' Labour practice into a philosophy under the rubric of a 'third way' was widely judged to be unsuccessful. For a definitive discussion see Alan Zuege, 'The chimera of the third way', in Leo Panitch and Colin Leys (eds), *Global Capitalism Versus Democracy: Socialist Register 2000* (Merlin Press, 1999), pp. 87–114.

78. Polly Toynbee's comment summed up what it took the Hatfield rail crash to make the public grasp: 'All "privatisation" of publicly financed services – hospitals or trains – makes profit straight from the public purse. The idea that their superior efficiency earns those profits is a fairytale that died at Hatfield' (*Guardian*, 15 November 2000).

79. The government's case was further weakened when it emerged that the consortia bidding for the contract had not been able to convince private investors that their contracts would be profitable enough, obliging the government to get the European Investment Bank, underwritten by the EU governments, to back the bids of three of them with a loan of nearly £1 billion.

80. As public outrage rose a number of Conservatives (and notably the Shadow Chancellor of the Exchequer, Michael Portillo) began dissociating themselves from rail privatisation, and one Conservative columnist openly called for re-nationalisation.

81. The 'soft' or conditional nature of public support was also revealed in September 2000 when lorry drivers blockaded oil refineries to force the government to cut the tax on diesel fuel; Conservative opinion poll support momentarily converged on Labour's for the first time since 1997.

82. Kevin Brown, 'Big companies hit at Blair', *Financial Times*, 26 September 2000. The responses were from 210 chairmen or chief executives of companies with 200 or more employees. The poll was conducted before the oil lorry drivers' blockade of refineries earlier that month.

83. Riddell, *Honest Opportunism*, p. 271.

4 Markets, commodities and commodification

1. The French economist Leon Walras proposed the fiction of an imaginary auctioneer constantly at work clearing the frictionless markets of marginalist economics.

2. Barbara Harriss-White remarks that in mainstream economics the definition of markets is 'so remote from experience that "market" has no entry at all in *Palgrave's Dictionary of Economics*, despite appearing in the text thousands of times' ('Free Market Romanticism in an Era of Deregulation', *Oxford Development Studies* 24/1, 1996, p. 29). For a seminal discus-

sion of markets see Geoffrey M. Hodgson, *Economics and Institutions* (Polity, 1988), chapter 8, esp. p. 174: 'We shall here define the market as a set of social institutions in which a large number of commodity exchanges of a a specific type regularly take place, and to some extent are facilitated and structured by those institutions. Exchange . . . involves contractual agreement and the exchange of property rights, and the market consists in part of mechanisms to structure, organise and legitimate those activities. Markets, in short, are organised and institutionalised exchange.' Harriss-White cites a definition by von Fourie that improves on Hodgson by referring to the conflictual aspect of market behaviour: '. . . economically purposeful interchange of commodities on the basis of quid pro quo obligations at a mutually agreed upon exchange rate . . . in a cluster of exchange rivalry relations' ('Free Market Romanticism', p. 29).

3. See chapter 2, p. 18.
4. Russell Mokhiber and Robert Weissman, 'The Insanity Defence', corpfocus@essential.org, 18 January 1999. On the Brusssels lobby see Justin Greenwood, Jürgen R. Grote and Karsten Ronit (eds), *Organized Interests and the European Community* (Sage, 1992).
5. John Kay, *Why Firms Succeed* (Oxford University Press, 1995).
6. Mark Granovetter, 'Economic action and social structure: the problem of embeddedness', *American Journal of Sociology* 91/3, 1985, pp. 481–510.
7. *Non-rivalrous* – one person's consumption of the good or service – e.g. the security afforded by police patrols, or a television broadcast – does not take it away from anyone else. *Non-excludable* – no one can be prevented from using or enjoying it.
8. Gordon White, 'Towards a Political analysis of markets', *IDS Bulletin* 24/3, 1993, pp. 4–11. The summary offered here does not do justice to White's powerful analysis. The examples given are deliberately 'northern', whereas White's analysis is general, but directed more towards the 'south'.
9. This can cut both ways. The 'lumpiness' of resource requirements has been used by successive British governments to justify relying on private capital markets for infrastructural investments, from the Channel Tunnel to hospitals and the London Underground.
10. See, e.g., Raphael Kaplinsky with Anne Posthuma, *Easternisation: The Spread of Japanese Management Techniques to Developing Countries* (Cass, 1994), esp. chapter 1.
11. Benjamin Coriat, 'Globalization, variety, and mass production: the metamorphosis of mass production in the new competitive age', in J. Rogers Hollingsworth and Robert Boyer (eds), *Contemporary Capitalism: The Embeddedness of Institutions* (Cambridge University Press, 1997), pp. 243–6.
12. Theodore Levitt, 'The globalization of markets', in H. Vernon-Wirtzel

and Laurence H. Wirtzel (eds), *Global Strategic Management*, 2nd edn (Wiley, 1990), p. 310.

13. For a balanced conclusion on this question see Andrew Sayer and Richard Walker, *The New Social Economy: Reworking the Division of Labour* (Blackwell, 1992), pp. 191–223.

14. The impact of computers and telecommunications on the division of labour has been extensively explored since the early 1980s by Ursula Huws, to whom I am also indebted for an introduction to the work of Jonathan Gershuny on which some of hers was initially founded. See, e.g., Huws, 'Telework:Projections', *Futures*, January/February 1991, pp. 19–30; and 'The making of a cybertariat? Virtual work in a real world', in Leo Panitch and Colin Leys (eds), *Working Classes, Global Realities: Socialist Register 2000* (Merlin Press, 2000), pp. 1–23. There is a slight difference of terminology here: I see the conversion of services into goods as a normal consequence of the commodification of services, meaning by 'commodification' only finding a way to standardise and price a service and make a profit from employing people to provide it – e.g. laundry services; whereas for Huws, the replacement of services by the sale of goods that enable the function to be performed by the consumer is the essence of commodification (see, e.g., Huws, 'Consuming fashions', *New Statesman and Nation*, 19 August 1988, p. 32).

15. William J. Baumol and William G. Bowen, *Performing Arts: The Economic Dilemma* (Twentieth Century Fund, 1966), p. 164. This book was published exactly 100 years after Marx observed, that 'types of work that are consumed as services and not in products separable from the worker . . . but capable of being directly exploited in *capitalist* terms are of microscopic significance [i.e. for capital accumulation] when compared with the mass of capitalist production . . .' ('Results of the immediate process of production', in *Capital*, Vol. I [Penguin, 1976 (1867)], pp. 1044–5, 1047–8). Marx may have been wrong about the importance of services but his discussion of the production of artistic products like books and pictures is nonetheless relevant to the political economy of the media in general, and is discussed by Nicholas Garnham in *Capitalism and Communication: Global Culture and the Economics of Information* (Sage, 1990), pp. 38–40.

16. W. J. Baumol and W. E. Oates, 'The cost disease of the personal services and the quality of life', *Skandinaviska Enskilda Banken Quarterly Review* 2, 1972, pp. 44–54, reprinted in Ruth Towse (ed.), *Baumol's Cost Disease: The Arts and Other Victims* (Edward Elgar, 1997), pp. 82–91; and William J. Baumol, 'Health care, education and the cost disease: A looming crisis for public choice', *Public Choice* 77, 1993, pp. 17–28, reprinted in Towse (ed.), *Baumol's Cost Disease*, pp. 510–21. The first article refers to 'elementary and higher education, medical services, the handicrafts, the live performance of music, drama and dance, libraries and cuisine: in short

many of the things which we associate with a vital and attractive civilization' (Towse [ed.], *Baumol's Cost Disease*, p. 83); in the second article Baumol's and Bowen's original analysis is said to apply to 'a special class of economic activities that includes the live performing arts, automotive repair, health care, education, postal services, automotive and accident insurance and care of the indigent' (ibid., p. 510).

17. 'Health care, education and the cost disease', in Towse (ed.), *Baumol's Cost Disease*, p. 513. It is curious that Baumol seems to assume that all three kinds of professional reduce their inputs voluntarily, in their own self-interest. This might apply to American doctors who are mostly self-employed small businessmen, but not to teachers or policemen, nor to salaried doctors.

18. 'The cost disease of the personal services', in Towse (ed.), *Baumol's Cost Disease*, p. 84.

19. The costs of services do also fall thanks to productivity increases in other sectors, such as transport, which are inputs into service provision.

20. 'The cost disease of the personal services', in Towse (ed.), *Baumol's Cost Disease*, p. 86.

21. Jonathan Gershuny, *After Industrial Society? The Emerging Self-Service Economy* (Humanities Press, 1978), p. 90. The lobbies Gershuny presumably had in mind would be the medical professions. See also his *Social Innovation and the Division of Labour* (Oxford University Press, 1983), pp. 166–8.

22. Hilda Baumol and William J. Baumol, 'The mass media and the cost disease', in William S. Hendon, Douglas V. Shaw and Nancy K. Grant (eds), *Economics of Cultural Industries* (Association for Cultural Economics, 1984), pp. 109–23, reproduced in Towse (ed.), *Baumol's Cost Disease*, pp. 180–94.

23. Richard Collins, Nicholas Garnham and Gareth Locksley, *The Economics of Television: The UK Case* (Sage, 1988), p. 18.

24. Jonathan Burston, 'Spectacle, synergy and megamusicals: the global-industrialisation of the live-entertainment industry', in James Curran (ed.), *Media Organisations and Society* (Arnold, 2000), pp. 69–85. The quotation from Steve Williams, of Industrial Light and Magic, is cited from K. Mazurkewich, 'The Great Canadian Cartoon Conspiracy', *Take One* (Canada), Winter 1995, pp. 4–11.

25. Perhaps most fields seem more complex than others to those most closely involved in them. In his study of BSkyB Mathew Horsman quotes David Elstein's reasons for thinking that Kelvin Mackenzie's unsuccessful period in the company was due to his being unprepared for the complexity of satellite television, compared with running a newspaper: 'It's not that surprising because it's a very difficult business to understand and every different facet of it is perplexing. You know, piracy – what do we do? The studios – what do we do? Rights – what do we do? There's a

zillion things that can go wrong with Sky and when you bump into one for the first time you think, "What's this coming down?" ' (Mathew Horsman, *Sky High: The Amazing Story of BSkyB – and the Egos, Deals and Ambitions that Revolutionised TV Broadcasting* [Orion, 1997], p. 124).

26. This discussion is drawn from Bernard Miège, *The Capitalization of Cultural Production*, (International General, 1989), pp. 20–50; Collins et al., *The Economics of Television*, pp. 1–19; Garnham, *Capitalism and Communication*, especially chapters 1, 8 and 10; Tim Congdon, Brian Sturgess, NERA, William B. Shrew, Andrew Graham and Gavyn Davies, *Paying for Broadcasting: The Handbook* (Routledge, 1992); and Andrew Graham and Gavyn Davies, *Broadcasting, Society and Policy in the Multimedia Age* (Luton University Press, 1997).

27. Garnham, *Capitalism and Communication*, p. 122.

28. Pirate or private copying of audio- and video-tapes and CDs, or their diffusion via the internet, tends to make these products a bit like public goods; it is hard for producers to realise their investment unless they have unchallenged control over the initial distribution – another push towards monopoly.

29. Another example encountered in the television literature is 'existence value', i.e. the value people place on having something available that they may not want most of the time, like news services at a regular hour.

30. Graham and Davies, *Broadcasting, Society and Policy in the Multimedia Age*, p. 23. Commenting on the situation in countries with mainly commercial broadcasting systems, they add (pp. 23–4): 'Other countries with a low element of public service broadcasting typically display poor quality, concentration of ownership plus frequent battles over ownership, flouting of regulators' rules and more or less subtle forms of government interference.' They note that in France between 1983 and 1988 the number of game shows screened jumped from four or five to fifteen or sixteen a week, the amount of light entertainment doubled and the number of feature films almost quadrupled. 'The *Financial Times* described the effects of deregulation on French television as having heralded "an anarchic scenario of dozens of different channels pumping out soft porn and pulp programming punctuated by virtually unrestricted advertising". . . . While the USA market undoubtedly offers considerable choice few would say that it offers television of such high quality as that of the UK, Australia or Canada, where there has been a much stronger contribution by PSBs [Public Service Broadcasters].'

31. Christian Koboldt, Sarah Hogg and Bill Robinson, 'The implications of funding for broadcasting output', in Andrew Graham et al., *Public Purposes in Broadcasting: Funding the BBC* (University of Luton Press, 1999), p. 64. I would argue that the concept of a 'merit good' smuggles a social policy objective into the discourse of public choice economics. The authors' distinction between the effects of different kinds of fund-

ing on social policy objectives and 'merit goods' is not clarified in the text.

32. In 1992 only Spain, Ireland, New Zealand, Portugal and Greece spent less than the UK.

33. Cam Donaldson and Karen Gerard, *Economics of Health Care Financing: The Visible Hand* (Macmillan, 1992), p. 153.

34. This is welfare economics applied to health care, associated in Britain especially with the work of A. J. Culyer (notably his 'The nature of the commodity "health care" and its efficient allocation', *Oxford Economic Papers* 23/2, 1971, pp. 189–211) and summarised by Donaldson and Gerard in *Economics of Health Care Financing*, on which this section relies heavily.

35. Self-insurance schemes exist but are prohibitively expensive for all but the rich; see Alan L. Sorkin, *Health Economics: An Introduction*, 3rd edn (Lexington Books, 1992), p. 169.

36. This seems a slight exaggeration. One can think of others, such as information technology provision.

37. Donaldson and Gerard, *Economics of Health Care Financing*, p. 27.

38. In 1996 infant mortality per 1000 live births was 6.1 in the UK and 7.8 in the USA (OECD *Health Statistics* 1997). In 1992 the USA ranked eighteenth in the world in terms of life expectancy at birth for females, and twenty-third for males (David A. Kindig, *Purchasing Population Health: Paying for Results* [University of Michigan Press, 1997], p. 17).

39. Ida Hellander, David U. Himmelstein, Steffie Woolhandler and Sidney Wolfe, 'Health care paper chase: the cost to the nation, the states and the District of Columbia', *International Journal of Health Services* 24/1, 1994, pp. 1–9; see also Donaldson and Gerard, *Economics of Health Care Financing*, p. 30. After the internal market was introduced in Britain administration costs rose to over 11 per cent of total spending – see chapter 6 below.

40. Sorkin, *Health Economics*, pp. 174–5: 'Several factors are responsible for the growth in the uninsured population [down to 1988]. These include the severe recession of 1981–82 and its reduction of employment; erosion of the Medicaid program's coverage of the poor; to some extent, shifts of workers to industries less likely to offer health insurance; and finally, increased health care insurance costs that have outpaced growth in incomes.'

41. Kindig, *Purchasing Population Health*, pp. 80–1.

42. Allyson M. Pollock and Charlene Harrington, 'What can the UK learn from the US about funding Healthcare?', unpublished paper, Health Policy and Health Services Research Unit, School of Public Policy, University College London, 1999.

43. According to the Health Policy Network the FBI estimated that in the years 1990–95 health-care fraud in the USA totalled $418 billion (*Health*

Care – Private Corporations or Public Service? The Americanisation of the NHS,
Third report of the Health Policy Network, London, 1996, pp. 29–32).
Billing fraud is particularly easy to do and expensive to control in
marketised health care, as the Audit Commission found in the early days
of the NHS internal market. One US company, Tenet, with a stake in
sixty-seven nursing homes in the UK, was convicted in the USA in 1993
of billing frauds totalling $380 million. Another, Columbia-HCA, which
in 1998 co-owned the fourth largest number of acute hospital beds in
the UK, made an agreed settlement in 2000 of $745 million with the US
Department of Justice for fraud and abuse of the Medicare programme
(Howard Berliner, 'Health booty', *Health Service Journal,* 6 July 2000,
p. 34). On fraud in long-term care in the USA see John Braithwaite, 'The
nursing home industry', in Michael Tonry and Albert J. Reiss (eds),
Beyond the Law: Crime in Complex Organizations (University of Chicago
Press, 1993), pp. 13–15.

44. Donaldson and Gerard, *Economics of Health Care Financing,* p. 97.
45. Sorkin, *Health Economics,* p. 179; Donaldson and Gerard, *Economics of
    Health Care Financing,* pp. 128–9 and 137–8.
46. Donaldson and Gerard, *Economics of Health Care Financing,* p. 99.
47. Ibid., p. 129. Moreover, while only 3 per cent of all hospital costs are
    paid for by patients (the bulk being covered by insurance or public
    funds), patients pay for 37 per cent of nursing home costs (Kindig,
    Purchasing Population Health, p. 27).
48. Steven R. Eastaugh, *Health Economics: Efficiency, Quality and Equity*
    (Auburn House, 1992), pp. 356–7.
49. Kindig, *Purchasing Population Health,* pp. 30–2, and Sorkin, *Health Econom-
    ics,* pp. 58–60. There is general agreement that before the advent of
    'managed care' doctors' fee-for-service charges were driving up medical
    costs, but that this was because they were giving more (and/or more
    expensive) treatments to offset lower volumes, not because their produc-
    tivity was stagnant relative to professionals working in industry (though it
    could have been).

5 Public service television

1. Michael Tracey, *The Decline and Fall of Public Service Broadcasting* (Oxford
   University Press, 1998), p. vii.
2. The need to make public service broadcasting a constitutional issue was
   well expressed by Brian Winston in 'Public service in the "new broadcasting age"', in Stuart Hood (ed.), *Behind the Screens: The Structure of British
   Television* (Lawrence and Wishart, 1994), pp. 20–42. For concrete proposals that could well be given constitutional expression see James Curran,
   'Mass media and democracy revisited', in James Curran and Michael

Gurevitch (eds), *Mass Media and Society*, 2nd edn (Arnold, 1996), pp. 81–119.

3. The phrase is Paul Styles', at KPMG. Raymond Williams' prescient analysis of 'flow' is in *Television: Technology and Cultural Form* (Routledge, 1990 [1975]), chapter 4.

4. Guy Debord, *The Society of the Spectacle* (Zone Books, 1994 [1967]), p. 12.

5. Jay G. Blumler, 'Elections, the media and the modern publicity process', in Marjorie Ferguson (ed.), *Public Communication: The New Imperatives* (Sage, 1990), p. 133.

6. *Media Pocket Book 1999* (The Advertising Association/NTC Publications, 1999).

7. Jeremy Tunstall and David Machin, *The Anglo-American Media Connection* (Oxford University Press, 1999), p. 34. The three most watched channels had over 50 per cent between them.

8. *Broadcast*, 26 November 1999. BBC channels 1 and 2 accounted for 26.6 per cent, commercial terrestrial TV for 37.2 per cent and BSkyB for 10.8 per cent. At this stage about a third of all homes had satellite dishes or cable connections.

9. Curran, 'Mass media and democracy revisited'.

10. Parliamentary scrutiny only became regular – though still retrospective – with the creation in 1992 of a more specialised Select Committee on the National Heritage.

11. The BBC and the ITV companies also operated what was in effect a buyers' cartel to keep down the costs of 'acquired' programming, refraining from competition for foreign films or television series.

12. The phrase 'the main formative conversations of society' is from James Curran, 'Media soundings', *Soundings* 5, 1997, p. 132.

13. Tunstall and Machin, *The Anglo-American Media Connection*, p. 131. Twenty per cent was regarded as normal.

14. The concept of 'micro-structures of accumulation' is adapted from the broader one developed in David M. Kotz, Terence McDonough and Michael Reich (eds), *Social Structures of Accumulation* (Cambridge University Press, 1994).

15. New programming is distinguished from 'acquired programming', i.e. already existing programmes bought in.

16. Sylvia Harvey, 'Channel 4 Television: from Annan to Grade', in Hood (ed.), *Behind the Screens*, p. 125. In 1998 the figure was 465 (PACT, *Annual Report and Accounts*, 1999, p. 6).

17. Gillian Ursell, 'Television production: issues of exploitation, commodification and subjectivity in UK television markets', unpublished paper, November 1999, p. 5; for slightly different earlier estimates see Peter Goodwin, *Television Under the Tories: Broadcasting Policy 1979–97* (British Film Institute, 1998), pp. 158–9. The BBC data include staff working in radio and non-'home' services. The BBC's cuts were bigger than else-

where in Europe, where the average job loss in public service broadcasting between 1988 and 1994 was 12.9 per cent, according to the European Broadcasting Union (Tracey, *The Decline and Fall,* p. 267).

18. In 1998 Skillset found that 66 per cent of the workforce were either 'freelance' (39 per cent) or on contracts of less than a year (27 per cent) (*Freelance Employment and Training Needs: A Follow-up Survey,* December 1998, p. 11). A previous study carried out for Skillset (*An Occupational Map of the Broadcast, Film and Video Industry,* January 1997, p. 2) stated that by 1996 'six out of ten (and rising) [were] working as freelances'.

19. *Report of the Committee on the Financing of the BBC,* London: HMSO, Cmnd 9824, 1986, p. 133. For an analysis of the work of the Committee see Tom O'Malley, *Closedown: The BBC and Government Broadcasting Policy, 1979–92* (Pluto, 1994), chapter 6.

20. The franchise auction, held in 1991, involved sealed bids of sums to be paid annually to the government for the licences. The size of the bids was in theory the maximum the bidding company thought it would be able to afford after meeting all costs and paying dividends. The winning bids varied from Carlton's £43.14 million a year for the London licence, to Scottish Television's £2,000 a year for the main Scotland licence – the latter being a famously successful gamble on there being no other serious bidder.

21. Andrew Graham and Gavyn Davies, 'The public funding of broadcasting', in Tim Congdon, Brian Sturges, NERA, William B. Shrew, Andrew Graham and Gavyn Davies, *Paying for Broadcasting: The Handbook* (Routledge, 1992), p. 206.

22. Goodwin, *Television Under the Tories,* p. 137.

23. For a succinct account of Producer Choice see Peter Cloot, *BBC Producer Choice: A Case Study* (Major Projects Association, 1994). See also Martin Harris and Victoria Wegg-Prosser, 'Producer Choice: The Rhetoric and Reality of Change Management at the BBC', paper presented to the 3rd International Conference on Organizational Discourse, King's College, London, 29–31 July 1998. Dr Wegg-Prosser was closely involved in the implementation of Producer Choice and I am indebted to her for guidance on the subject.

24. Goodwin, *Television Under the Tories,* pp. 62–6. In 1990 cables had been laid past only 828,000 homes (less than 4 per cent) of which only 149,000 were subscribers (less than 1 per cent of all homes). By the end of 1995 6.1 million homes had been passed, with 1.3 million subscribers. By the end of 1998 the figures were 11.9 million homes and 3.8 million subscribers (*Media Pocket Book 1999*).

25. The best account of both the cable and the satellite stories is in Goodwin, *Television Under the Tories,* chapters 4 and 5.

26. BSB developed a rectangular receiver in an effort to overcome aesthetic

objections to the proliferation of the large reception dishes originally needed for signals from medium-powered satellites.

27. Mathew Horsman, *Sky High: The Amazing Story of BSkyB – and the Egos, Deals and Ambitions that Revolutionised TV Broadcasting* (Orion, 1997), pp. 46, 67–84.

28. Ibid., pp. xvii and 121.

29. *Review of Commercial Television Qualifying Revenue: Five Years to September 1998* (ITC, 1999), p. 3.

30. Channel 4 was required to share any advertising revenue over 14 per cent of the total 50–50 with the ITV companies, in return for being guaranteed a minimum of 14 per cent if it failed to earn as much as that – a provision designed to prevent it from feeling too much financial pressure to maintain its ratings, and to give the ITV companies some stake in its continued success. This provision too, however, was removed in stages under a new Broadcasting Act passed in 1996. The 1990 Act also made Channel 4 into an independent company, though its directors continued to be appointed by the ITC.

31. Viewing figure for 1999 from *Broadcast*, 26 November 1999; share of advertising revenue from ITC, *Review*, p. 3.

32. In 1995 Havas had revenues of $8.7 billion and Bertelsmann $14.3 billion (Steve Peak and Paul Fisher [eds], *The Media Guide 1999* [Fourth Estate, 1998], p. 11).

33. A few smaller companies remained outside, but dependent on, the big three: Scottish Television (which also took over Grampian, the north of Scotland franchise), Border Television, Channel Television and UTV (Ulster).

34. The new rules meant that neither Murdoch's News Corporation nor the Mirror Group of newspapers, each of which had a market share of over 20 per cent, could own a terrestrial television franchise. The owner of a local newspaper was likewise barred from owning the local television franchise if the paper had over 20 per cent of the local market.

35. *The Future Funding of the BBC: Report of the Independent Review Panel*, Chairman, Gavyn Davies, July 1999 (Department for Culture, Media and Sport, 1999).

36. In 1993 BBC1 and 2 between them were putting out 150 minutes per week of promotion-time, i.e. 'several hundred short trails and pro-motions' (Jeremy Tunstall, *Television Producers* [Routledge 1993], p. 196).

37. Greg Dyke, *A Time for Change*, MacTaggart Lecture, Guardian Edinburgh Television Festival, 25 August 2000, p. 7.

38. A poll conducted by MORI for the Davies Panel found that 54 per cent of respondents were 'fairly satisfied overall' with the BBC and 16 per cent were 'very satisfied'. A *Guardian* poll published on 17 August 1999, in the context of the Davies proposal to raise a digital supplement on the licence fee, reported that 65 per cent of the sample – and 73 per

cent of 18- to 24-year-olds – thought the BBC 'should accept some advertising', and that 45 per cent thought the quality of BBC programmes had got worse over the previous five years, compared with only 8 per cent who thought they had got better.

39. This is a perennial problem. The people who watch most television are older and poorer than the population as a whole; the people who watch it least are the relatively young upper-income earners whose purchasing patterns are not yet set and whom advertisers are keenest to reach.

40. John Hardie, Marketing and Commercial Director, *Network Centre Annual Review* 1997, p. 11.

41. *Who Wants To Be a Millionaire?* was screened nightly in prime time towards the end of the year.

42. Their combined total audience share might just fall within the permitted limit of 15 per cent, but their combined share of net advertising revenue (36 per cent) clearly did not (by an agreement made with the ITC in 1994 this limit was 25 per cent). These limits were, however, already under review by the ITC; Carlton's Chief Executive Michael Green and UN&M's Lord Hollick gave out that they had 'sounded out' the directors of the ITC, the Office of Fair Trading and the Minister for Culture, Media and Sport and, implicitly, felt encouraged to go ahead (*Financial Times*, 27/8 November 1999).

43. *'Public Interest Broadcasting: A New Approach*, the 1999 James MacTaggart Memorial Lecture (ITV Network Ltd, 1999), p. 8.

44. Significantly, City analysts estimated that removing its public service obligations would increase its value dramatically.

45. PACT, *Annual Report and Accounts*, 1999, p. 6.

46. The estimated breakdown was: BBC1 £121 million; BBC2 – £95 million; ITV – £151 million; Channel 4 – £299 million; Channel 5 – £77 million; non-terrestrial £49 million (PACT, *Annual Report and Accounts*, 2000, p. 18). In addition to PACT's 579 producer companies there were 44 production financing and distribution companies, 31 production facilities companies, and 382 'affiliates'.

47. *Production 95: The Results of the 1995 Price Waterhouse/PACT Survey of UK Independent Production Companies* (PACT, 1995), pp. 5 and 13.

48. Channel 4 (which accounted for another quarter of the 'indies' output) paid £92,000 per hour, Channel 5 £61,000 per hour, the BBC £135,000 and ITV £170,000 (PACT, *Annual Report and Accounts*, 2000, p. 18).

49. The seminal discussion of the 'indies' is Kevin Robins and James Cornford, 'What is flexible about independent producers?', *Screen*, 33/2, 1992, pp. 190–200. I am also indebted to Anne Priestley Hill, who kindly made available her dissertation, 'What's independent about independent producers?', Goldsmiths College, 1998, and gave me valuable guidance.

50. Skillset, *An Occupational Map*. These estimates were very rough. Skillset was working on a more accurate survey, due in 2000–01.

51. PACT's 1998 document, *The Courage to Compete*, makes interesting reading. It argued in effect that the broadcasters' oligopsony power was allowing them to buy cheap and sell dear and should be countered by forcing them to buy more programming from independent producers and pay them more – in the name of market efficiency.

52. Peak and Fisher (eds), *The Media Guide 1999*, p. 193.

53. Airey would appear to have said Channel 5 was about more than these three things, but neither she nor her then boss, David Elstein, seemed unambiguously keen to be dissociated from such a quotable phrase (see *Observer*, 9 January 2000).

54. ITV's evening audiences recovered from 1997–99 as noted, but its overall share of viewing continued to decline. It should be noted also that for technical reasons Channel 5 could only be received by 70 per cent of households, so its share of total viewing was more impressive than the absolute figure sugggested.

55. Tunstall and Machin, *The Anglo-American Media Connection*, p. 178.

56. For details of their finances see *Guardian*, 8 and 11 August 2000.

57. These figures (from *Broadcast*, 26 November 1999) are for satellite and cable homes combined and may understate the viewing share of non-terrestrial programmes in households with satellite services.

58. Horsman, *Sky High*, pp. 228–9.

59. The BBC bought the rights to screen recorded match highlights on its *Match of the Day* evening programme. Besides adding to the financial package BSkyB could offer for the live television broadcast rights in competition with the ITV companies, the BBC's involvement offered the football clubs and especially their sponsors exposure to the BBC's much larger audiences. Had the BBC not done this deal, ITV would probably have won the rights – it had had exclusive rights to First Division football since 1988 – and the BBC would have lost still more audience share to ITV. On the other hand helping BSkyB to win the exclusive rights, which would be available only to BSkyB subscribers for a premium price, accelerated the escalation of sports rights costs that had already ended the BBC's pre-eminence in sports broadcasting and could even pose a threat to its survival in the long term.

60. Mark Granovetter and Patrick McGuire, 'The making of an industry: electricity in the United States', in Michel Callon (ed.), *The Laws of the Markets* (Blackwell, 1998), pp. 148 and 166–7.

61. City analysts correctly predicted a high failure rate for new technology ventures: 'Only a few "cyberbrands" will succeed in the long run as the majority are swept up in a backlash as traditional off-line giants play catch-up' (Lisa Buckingham, quoting Shailendra Kumar, associate director of Interbrand, *Guardian*, 22 November 1999).

62. One estimate for the British press, based on predicted US figures, estimated that £140 million worth of classified advertisements could be

lost, mainly by the broadsheets, by the year 2003 (Simon Waldman, 'Classified information', *Guardian*, 19 July 1999). For a balanced discussion of the allegedly impending demise of newspapers see Ian Katz, 'Final edition', *Guardian*, 13 December 1999.

63. For an excellent account of the first few years of the restructuring process, primarily in the USA, see Edward S. Herman and Robert W. McChesney, *The Global Media: The New Missionaries of Corporate Capitalism* (Cassell, 1997), chapters 3 and 4. A summary of US developments from 1995 to 1997 is given by Tunstall and Machin in *The Anglo-American Media Connection*, pp. 53–67. See also Andrew Graham and Gavyn Davies, *Broadcasting, Society and Policy in the Multimedia Age* (University of Luton Press, 1997), p. 13.

64. The combined company had 35.8 per cent of the market; AT&T had 44.5 per cent.

65. 'Weakened by competition, threatened by the new media revolution, battered by soaring production costs, squeezed by advertisers and criticised for dated programming, [the three major US television networks] are no longer able to ignore the pressure from parent companies tired of watching their profits disappear' (*Observer*, 6 June 1999).

66. *New York Times*, 11 October 1999.

67. *Financial Times*, 13/14 November 1999.

68. An earlier attempt by Murdoch to buy a controlling interest in Manchester United was blocked by the Monopolies and Mergers Commission on conflict of interest grounds.

69. *Guardian*, 13 October 1999.

70. Raymond Snoddy, however, the chronicler of Michael Green's rise to power in Carlton, believes this strategy was deliberate and states that in 1995 Green was 'increasingly convinced that technologies such as video-on-demand are not about to sweep away the world of the traditional media. . . . There seem to be limits to how much people will pay for extra convenience and choice' (*Greenfinger: The Rise of Michael Green and Carlton Communications* [Faber, 1996], p. 273).

71. David Birch, 'Why content isn't king', *Guardian*, 3 February 2000.

72. Piers Morgan, 'Keep reading all about it', *Guardian*, 6 December 1999.

73. The predictions of Investec Henderson Crosthwaite Securities were that 50 per cent of homes would be multi-channel by 2003, but only 40 per cent (about 10 million) would be on-line (Mathew Horsman, personal communication).

74. Interview in the *Daily Telegraph* quoted in Steven Barnett and Andrew Curry, *The Battle for the BBC: A British Broadcasting Conspiracy?* (Arum Press, 1994), p. 249. *World in Action* had been responsible for a number of such cases, including the 'Birmingham Four', wrongly imprisoned for alleged involvement in an IRA bombing.

75. *Production 95*, p. 19.

76. On the logic of this see Christian Kobboldt, Sarah Hogg and Bill
    Robinson, 'The implications of funding for broadcasting output', in
    Andrew Graham et al., *Public Purposes in Broadcasting: Funding the BBC*
    (University of Luton Press, 1999), esp. pp. 63–71.
77. Tunstall and Machin, *The Anglo-American Media Connection*, p. 37.
78. Horsman, *Sky High*, p. 121.
79. Ibid., p. 160.
80. Tunstall, *Television Producers*, pp. 113–14. Tunstall's treatment of 'soaps',
    describing the industrial character of their production, is one of the
    highlights of an exceptionally perceptive book.
81. Richard Collins, Nicholas Garnham and Gareth Locksley, *The Economics
    of Television: The UK Case* (Sage, 1988), p. 56.
82. Tunstall, *Television Producers*, p. 109.
83. Gillian Ursell, 'Labour flexibility in the UK commercial television sector',
    Media, Culture and Society 20/1, January 1998, pp. 143–4.
84. Christopher Hird, Fulcrum Productions, interview, 6 September 2000.
85. It would have been closer to £1.4 billion if the Premier League clubs had
    not sold NTL the pay-per-view rights to forty matches a year for three
    years for £328 million, which analysts thought a bad deal for both sides.
86. Figures from an internal BBC report submitted to the government,
    reported in the *Observer*, 9 January 2000. This represented a dramatic
    acceleration of inflation in these genres; for the years 1989/90 to 1996/
    97 the BBC calculated the rate of inflation of talent and rights approxi-
    mately as follows: sitcoms 18 per cent, sport 14 per cent, drama 13 per
    cent, features 10 per cent, comedy/variety 7 per cent, 'other' 2 per cent
    (cited in David Currie and Martin Siner, 'The BBC: balancing public and
    commercial purpose', in Graham et al., *Public Purposes in Broadcasting*,
    p. 81).
87. *The Future Funding of the BBC*, pp. 48–9.
88. Gavyn Davies asserted in his Panel's report that 'some of the BBC's
    digital offerings have been distinctly threadbare, and they have taken
    vital funds away from the analogue services, which have suffered as a
    result', adding that: 'The BBC has managed to maintain its share of the
    audience to a much greater extent than was expected some years ago. It
    is hard to avoid the suspicion that this has been done by cheapening or
    "dumbing down" the product – a process which the BBC assures us will
    now be reversed' ibid., pp. 17–18).
89. The new media promised opportunities to take this approach further.
    Paul Styles, a media expert at KPMG, foresaw that 'in time you're ...
    likely to get an elite form of subscription emerging, for people who'll
    pay for optimised services. ... [This] can be done for special pro-
    gramming ... you'll get more of those kinds of services. They'll never be
    on the same scale as some of the mass channels but like other forms of
    life you'll get that kind of tiering' (interview, 7 September 2000).

90. These events are summarised in Colin Sparks, 'Independent production', in Hood (ed.), *Behind the Screens*, pp. 141–2.

91. Tunstall, *Television Producers*, pp. 203–4.

92. Ursell, 'Television production', p. 16. Her data on freelance wages are given in 'Turning a way of life into a business: an account and critique of the transformation of British television from public service to commercial enterprise', unpublished paper 1999, p. 22. I am grateful to Dr Ursell for making this and other papers available to me.

93. Barnett and Curry, *The Battle for the BBC*, p. 189.

94. Horsman, *Sky High*, pp. 74–6. The suspicions were also fuelled by the fact that Thatcher had refused to refer Murdoch's takeover of the *Times* and *Sunday Times* newspapers to the Monopolies Commission although it clearly breached the anti-monopoly rules (see Brian McNair, *News and News Journalism in the UK* [Routledge, 1994], p. 126).

95. Goodwin, *Television Under the Tories*, pp. 110–16.

96. The most notorious case was Central Television's prize-winning 1998 documentary *The Connection*, in which several sequences proved to have been faked. The ITC could have fined Central £8 million (3 per cent of its turnover); the fine imposed was £2 million, the largest in the ITC's short history.

97. Interview, 17 November 1999.

98. Barnett and Curry, *The Battle for the BBC*, pp. 217–18. Figures for broadcast hours exclude World Service broadcasts, which were paid for by a separate grant from the Foreign Office.

99. The figure for the BBC is derived from the total expenditure on television, as opposed to radio, including a share of overheads proportionate to the ratio of television to radio operating costs (75 per cent) (BBC *Report and Accounts 1994/95*, p. 81); the ITV figure is derived from the *ITC Annual Report and Accounts 1995*, p. 11.

100. Barnett and Curry, *The Battle for the BBC*, pp. 188–9.

101. An extended statement of this view is *The BBC's Public Service Obligations & Commercial Activities: An ITV Analysis* (ITV, 2000). In practice, BBC successes are always attacked as constituting unfair competition with commercial operators. The logic of the critique is, sometimes explicitly, that the BBC should not be allowed to do anything from which commercial broadcasters can make a profit.

102. See for example Currie and Siner, 'The BBC'.

103. Barnett and Curry, *The Battle for the BBC*, pp. 257–8.

104. David Goldberg, Tony Prosser and Stefaan Verhulst (eds), *Regulating the Changing Media: A Comparative Study* (Clarendon Press, 1998), chapter 5.

105. Graham Murdock and Peter Golding, 'Common markets: corporate ambitions and communication trends in the UK and Europe', *Journal of Media Economics* 12/2, 1999, pp. 117–32.

106. Criticisms of the commodification of the BBC under Birt were voiced by

some senior serving and former BBC producers and journalists, such as
John Tusa and Mark Tully, and occasionally by sympathetic press journalists, as well as by academics and others, such as those in the Campaign
for Press and Broadcasting Freedom. For commentaries of a kind all too
rare in the previous decade see Will Hutton, 'How the Naked Chef killed
Panorama', and Chris Horrie, 'Bong! Greg Utd 1, ITV 0', both in the
Observer, 8 October 2000.
107. Jay G. Blumler, 'Meshing money with mission: purity versus pragmatism
in public broadcasting', *European Journal of Communication*, 8, 1993,
p. 405.
108. E.g. Tunstall and Machin, *The Anglo-American Media Connection*, p. 177.
109. Steven Barnett and Emily Seymour, '*A Shrinking Iceberg Travelling South*':
*Changing Trends in British Television: A Case Study of Drama and Current
Affairs*, a Report for the Campaign for Quality in Television Ltd, London,
September 1999. The title is taken from one of the interviews quoted in
the report (p. 69): 'There's no long-term commitment to anything – no
Lew Grade type character developing great pools of talent, nowhere for
writers and directors to grow up. The quality end is a shrinking iceberg
travelling south.'
110. Ibid., p. 5. The share of peak time devoted to current affairs had actually
risen sharply between 1977–78 and 1987–88 but fell back again by
1997–98.
111. On 15 February 2001 the *Guardian* reported that research commissioned
by the ITC showed that both BBC1 and ITV 'relied upon a narrow range
of shows. Over the past 25 years on BBC 1 and ITV together, soaps have
increased by 150%. Drama on BBC1 has halved to 11%, replaced by
"hobbies and leisure, quiz shows and features" which have shot up from
3% in the 1970s to 27% last November.'
112. Golding showed that at the end of the 1980s the government had
become the biggest advertiser in Britain and employed a staff of 800 in
the Central Office of Information and 700 press and information officers
in fourteen departments ('Political communication and citizenship: the
media and democracy in an inegalitarian social order', in Ferguson,
[ed.] *Public Communication*, p. 95). The 1980s growth rates for PR personnel are drawn from Aeron Davis, 'Public relations, news production and
changing patterns of source access in the British national media', *Media,
Culture and Society* 22/1, January 2000, pp. 39–59. Fifteen per cent of the
PR workforce were employed by government, 28 per cent by companies,
53 per cent by consultancies and 5 per cent by non-profit agencies.
113. An ITV advertising executive quoted in '*A Shrinking Iceberg*', p. 31. How
industry members see these questions is vividly illustrated by the numerous extracts from interviews in the report.
114. Interview, ITV Network Centre Executive, 9 December 1999.
115. Snoddy, *Greenfinger*, pp. 214–15.

116. For a discussion of these processes at work in the USA see Graham
     Murdock, 'Large corporations and the control of the communications
     industries', in Michael Gurevitch, Tony Bennett, James Curran and Janet
     Woollacott (eds), *Culture, Society and the Media* (Routledge 1982),
     pp. 145–47. For British examples see Granville Williams, *Britain's Media –
     How They Are Related: Media Ownership and Democracy*, 2nd edn (Campaign
     for Press and Broadcasting Freedom, 1996), p. 24. Christopher Hird
     argues convincingly that if advertisers became more dependent on
     sponsorship as a means of reaching mass audiences than they are now –
     for example, if TiVO technology (a US-made device for preselecting and
     recording television programmes) resulted in more and more viewers
     skipping spot advertisements – then even controversial programmes
     would find sponsors who for business reasons saw controversy as some-
     thing they would like to be identified with. Such is not yet the situation,
     however.

117. Antenna UK 96, *The Television Sponsorship Report* (Antenna Publications,
     1996), p. 56.

118. Ibid., p. 30.

119. Cf. Richard Maxwell, 'Out of kindness and into difference: the value of
     global market research', *Media, Culture and Society* 18, 1996, p. 110:
     '. . . information produced from personal data collected in Spain by Alef
     [a Spanish market research company] will be incorporated into a num-
     ber of the products sold in Spain. . . . Alef sells information about
     cultural differences in Spain so that a foreign client's products appear as
     local goods. . . .'

120. '*A Shrinking Iceberg*', p. 60.

121. Ibid., p. 57.

122. Lord Reith, who as Director of the pre-Charter BBC denied both the
     Labour Party leader, Ramsay MacDonald, and the Archbishop of Canter-
     bury the opportunity to broadcast during the 1925–26 General Strike,
     noted that the government could trust him 'not to be impartial'.

123. For a series of cases in point see Barnett and Curry, *The Battle for the BBC*,
     pp. 29–34, 162–3 and 169–71; see also Williams, *Britain's Media*,
     pp. 22–3. For a succinct analysis of how 'the always fragile BBC myth of
     independence was drained of potency' see Winston, 'Public service in
     the "new broadcasting age" ' (see note 2), pp. 35–8.

124. Steven Barnett and Emily Seymour, *From Callaghan to Kosovo: Changing
     Trends in British Television News 1975–1999* (University of Westminster,
     2000). The study was financed by the BBC and the ITC.

125. See, e.g., Steve Barnett, 'Not the Nine O'Clock News is not the end of
     the world', *Observer*, 15 October 2000. And what about the BBC's plans
     for one-minute news bulletins on its new youth channel, BBC3?

126. Matt Wells, 'BBC 1's new chief stands up for populism', *Guardian*, 15
     September 2000.

127. Chris Smith (Secretary of State for Culture, Media and Sport), 'Right balance', *Guardian*, 18 December 2000.
128. Interview, 6 December 1999.
129. Interview, 17 December 1999.
130. Christopher Hird, Fulcrum Productions, interview, 2 December 1999.
131. Shelley McLachlan and Peter Golding, '"Tabloidization" in the British press: a quantitative investigation into changes within British newspapers from 1952–1997', unpublished paper, Communication Research Centre, Loughborough University, 1999.
132. Peter Stothard, 'The times they aren't changing', *Guardian*, 16 June 1997, cited in McLachlan and Golding, '"Tabloidization"', p. 3.
133. Matt Wells, David Teather, Dan Milmo and Maggie Brown, 'Great white hope'. *Guardian*, 20 November 2000. Even this perceptive comment is, significantly, framed in the language of consumption – what pensioners and others will want but won't be able to get – rather than in the language of democratic principle – what democratic politics needs.
134. Peter Goodwin, 'Public service broadcasting and new media technology: what the BBC has done and what it should have done', *The Public* 4/4, 1997, p. 73. There was also the fact that the BBC was delivering some of its new services, such as UK Gold (mainly BBC archive material), on subscription-only channels, and to that extent was no longer providing universal access in spite of being financed by a universal tax.
135. Cf. Golding, 'Political communication and citizenship', p. 100: 'We urgently require a philosophy of communications which locates and understands the role of communications processes in the public sphere. What is the nature of the goods produced by broadcasting and other communications services? Without an answer to this question the response to much communications research must indeed be "So what?"'
136. *Public Interest Broadcasting*, p. 8.
137. Horsman, *Sky High*, p. 257.
138. For comparisons with the press in Britain see Curran, 'Mass media and democracy revisited', *Mass Media and Society*, pp. 88–90; for comparisons with other countries see Graham and Davies, *Broadcasting, Society and Policy in the Multimedia Age*, pp. 23–5; with France, Michael Scriven and Monica Lecomte (eds), *Television Broadcasting in Contemporary France and Britain* (Berghahn, 1999).

6 The national health service

1. For country comparisons see, e.g., Julian Tudor Hart, *Feasible Socialism: The National Health Service, Past, Present and Future* (Socialist Health Association, 1994), pp. 23. Hart comments (p. 77): 'Britain (before NHS "reform") seems to be the only country so far studied where cholecystec-

tomy [surgical removal of gallstones] rates correlate rationally with local prevalence of gallstones.'

2. In 1996 infant mortality per 1,000 live births was 6.0 in Canada, 6.1 in the UK and 7.8 in the USA (*OECD Health Data 1998*, [OECD, 1998]). Life expectancy for males was 74.3 in the UK and 72.5 in the USA.

3. In 1996 health-care expenditure per head in purchasing power parity dollars was: UK $1,317, Canada $2,065, USA $3,898 (ibid.).

4. Health Policy Network, *Health Care: Private Corporations or Public Service? The Americanisation of the NHS* (Public Health Alliance, NHS Support Federation, NHS Consultants' Association, 1996), pp. 28–9.

5. For a summary of the opposition and how it was overcome see Charles Webster, *The National Health Service: A Political History* (Oxford University Press, 1998), pp. 25–8. On Bevan's famous remark and what he in fact gave the consultants, see 'Note on "stuffing their mouths with gold" ', in Charles Webster (ed.), *Aneurin Bevan on the National Health Service* (University of Oxford Wellcome Unit for the Study of Medicine, 1991), pp. 219–22.

6. Webster, *The National Health Service*, p. 144

7. Ibid., chapter 3. Thatcher's declaration (at the Conservative Party Conference on 8 October 1982) is more often than not misquoted as 'safe in our hands'.

8. John Mohan, *A National Health Service? The Restructuring of Health Care in Britain Since 1979* (Macmillan, 1995), pp. 10–22, and Webster, *The National Health Service*, p. 151.

9. For a collection of stories exemplifying this see Peter Bruggen, *Who Cares? True Stories of the NHS Reforms* (John Carpenter, 1997). The book is mainly focused on the 1990s but a number of the cases it recounts are from the 1980s.

10. *Compendium of Health Statistics*, 1999 (Office of Health Economics 2000), figure 3.5.

11. John Yates, *Private Eye, Heart and Hip: Surgical Consultants, the National Health Service and Private Medicine* (Churchill Livingstone, 1995), pp. 128 and 133.

12. *Laing's Healthcare Market Review*, 1999–2000 (Laing and Buisson, 1999), table 3.1, p. 99. Company-paid PMI has always accounted for more than half of all those covered.

13. *Laing's Review of Private Healthcare*, 1996 (Laing and Buisson, 1996), pp. 103 and 125.

14. The biggest opportunities were enjoyed by surgeons. In 1992 four out of five NHS consultants engaged in some private practice. Of these, most made between £10,000 and, £100,000 a year on top of their NHS salaries; 1,300 made between £100,000 and £300,000; 90 made more than £300,000 (*Laing's Review of Private Healthcare*, 1995 [Laing and Buisson,

1995], p. 120, citing a study by the Monopolies and Mergers Commission).

15. Alain Enthoven, *Reflections on the Management of the NHS* (Nuffield Provincial Hospitals Trust, 1985). For a caustic comment on Enthoven's qualifications and logic, see Hart, *Feasible Socialism*, pp. 56 and 58–61. For slightly conflicting accounts of the genesis of the reforms, and Mrs Thatcher's role in them, see Mohan, *A National Health Service?*, pp. 65–7; Webster, *The National Health Service*, pp. 182–92; Peter West, *Understanding the National Health Service Reforms: The Creation of Incentives?* (Open University Press, 1997), pp. 18–22.

16. West, *Understanding the National Health Service Reforms*, chapter 5.

17. Initially residents in long-term residential care had to dispose of all assets above £8,000 to pay for their care before the full costs would be met by the local authority. The figure was later increased to £16,000.

18. The distribution of the total of 554,100 places for elderly, chronically ill and physically and mentally disabled people in the UK in 1999 was: for-profit 69 per cent; voluntary sector 12 per cent; NHS and local authority combined, 19 per cent (*Laing's Healthcare Market Review*, 1999–2000, table 6.2).

19. Cf. Radical Statistics Group, 'NHS "indicators of success": what do they tell us?', *BMJ* 310, 1995, pp. 1045–50; Ray Robinson and Julian Le Grand, (eds), *Evaluating the NHS Reforms* (The King's Fund, 1993); West, *Understanding the National Health Service Reforms*.

20. Estimates vary but Webster accepts that down to the 1980s administrative costs were 5 per cent of total NHS spending and that by 1997 they were 12 per cent, while 'managers talk of 17 percent as an eventual target', compared with over 20 per cent in the USA (Webster, *The National Health Service*, p. 203).

21. I ignore for present purposes 'extra-contractual referrals', which provided a limited safety valve for the pressures this created.

22. Nick Goodwin, 'GP fundholding: a review of the evidence', in Anthony Harrison (ed.), *Health Care UK 1995/96* (The King's Fund, 1996), pp. 116–30.

23. Few people believed that the change would save many administrative costs in practice, and one study thought these costs might even rise (see Bronwyn Croxson, *Organisational Costs in the New NHS* [Office of Health Education, 1999]).

24. Referring to public sector workers, Blair told the British Venture Capital Association in July 1999 that he 'bore the scars' inflicted by a group of people resisting change. The Health Secretary, Frank Dobson, tried to correct the impression that this applied to nurses, but did not exclude doctors (Mick McKeown and Dave Mercer, 'A touch of the blues', *Health Service Journal*, 10 February 2000, p. 30).

25. *The New NHS: Modern and Dependable*, Cm. 3807 (The Stationery Office, 1997).
26. Boards were to consist of four to seven GPs, one or two community or practice nurses, one social services nominee, one lay member appointed by the health authority, a representative of the health authority and the PCG Chief Executive (Azeem Majeed, 'Primary care groups: a short summary of key facts', paper presented to a workshop on Primary Care at the School of Public Policy, University College London, January 1999).
27. Unless otherwise stated the data in this section are drawn from the *Compendium of Health Statistics*, 1999.
28. Private work by GPs amounted to less than 3 per cent of all GP consultations, mostly by about 200 GPs working in the Harley Street area of central London (*Laing's Healthcare Market Review*, 1999–2000, p. 138).
29. Allyson Pollock, Stewart Player and Sylvia Godden, 'GPs' surgeries turn a profit', *Public Finance*, 26 November–2 December 1999, pp. 26–8.
30. The data in this section are drawn from *UK Dental Care Market Sector Report*, 1999 (Laing and Buisson, 1999).
31. The total value of dentists' earnings in 1999 was about £2.6 billion. Of this, just under £1 billion represented fees for private work; a further £0.5 billion consisted of the charges (co-payments) that adult patients now had to pay for NHS-funded dentistry; the balance of £1.1 billion came from the NHS budget.
32. Bruggen, *Who Cares?*, p. 155.
33. The market-oriented literature describes this as a 'sector', implying that the NHS is only another 'sector' of a single 'industry', rather than a public service under siege by market forces. Calling the private hospital industry a 'sector' also tends to obscure its dependence on NHS clinicians and NHS private beds, as well as on increasing amounts of public funding.
34. *Laing's Healthcare Market Review* 1999–2000, p. 48. Except where otherwise noted, this and the following two sections are drawn from the relevant chapters of the *Review*.
35. Ibid., p. 75.
36. Over half of all elective surgery performed in private sector hospitals in 1997–98 was day surgery, compared with a quarter of all operations in the NHS (ibid., p. 87).
37. Ibid., p. 74.
38. Vertical integration by BUPA encountered serious resistance from the Office of Fair Trading on competition grounds (ibid., p. 123), unintentionally highlighting the advantages of public provision.
39. For a detailed survey of the sector see Stewart Player and Allyson Pollock, 'Long-term care: from public responsibility to private good', *Critical Social Policy* 21/2, 2001, pp. 205–29.
40. *Laing's Healthcare Market Review* 1999–2000, p. 179.

41. Unless otherwise noted the data in this section are drawn from *Pharma Facts and Figures* (Association of the British Pharmaceutical Industry, 2000).

42. Ibid., p. 45.

43. Anne Mason, Adrian Towse and Michael Drummond, *Disease Management, the NHS and the Pharmaceutical Industry* (Office of Health Economics,1999). The main limits laid down in 1996 were that any disease management joint venture scheme with the private sector must demonstrate that it was clinically beneficial, had cost benefits for the NHS and protected patients' interests. It also had to be monitored and evaluated and the health authority was accountable for it.

44. David Gilbert and Andrew Chetley, 'New trends in drug promotion', *Consumer Policy Review* 6/5, 1996, pp. 162–7. SmithKline Beecham's successful exploitation of groups representing people with genetic disorders, by manipulating their umbrella organisation, the Genetic Interest Group, to support its campaign to get the European Parliament to legalise the patenting of genes, is described by George Monbiot in *Captive State: The Corporate Takeover of Britain*, (Macmillan, 2000), pp. 257–60.

45. On the financing of medical conferences and payments to doctors to promote particular drugs see Sarah Boseley, 'Warning signs on the doctors' roadshow', *Guardian*, 15 February 2001.

46. Julie Froude and Jean Shaoul, 'Appraising and evaluating PFI for hospitals', paper presented to the CIMA Public Sector Accounting Workshop, University of Edinburgh, 24–5 September, 1998.

47. For example, 'In New York State, since laparoscopic cholecystectomy was introduced in 1988, the complication rate for endoscopic surgery was fifteen times higher than for open surgery' (Hart, *Feasible Socialism*, p. 76).

48. Mainly because of the extra costs involved in transferring patients from their homes to hospital in the cases where this became necessary (Andrew Wilson et al., 'Randomised controlled trial of effectiveness of Leicester hospital at home scheme compared with hospital care', *BMJ* 319, 1999, pp. 1542–6; Jeremy Jones et al., 'Economic Evaluation of hospital at home versus hospital care: cost minimisation analysis of data from randomised controlled trial', *BMJ* 319, 1999, pp. 1547–50).

49. The definitive work on NHS financing and the PFI/PPP programme is by Allyson Pollock, Declan Gaffney, David Price, Jean Shaoul and Matthew Dunnigan, summarised in four articles in the *BMJ* 319, 1999.

50. See Chau Shum et al., 'Nurse management of patients with minor illnesses in general practice: multicentre, randomised controlled trial', *BMJ* 320, 2000, pp. 1038–43; P. Venning et al., 'Randomised controlled trial comparing cost effectiveness of general practitioners and nurse practitioners in primary care', *BMJ* 320, 2000, pp. 1048–53.

51. See Katherine Pearce and Rebecca Rosen, *NHS Direct: Learning from the London Experience* (The King's Fund, 2000); and A. O'Cathain et al., 'How

helpful is NHS direct? Postal survey of callers', *BMJ* 320, 2000, p. 1035. The early evidence suggested that it relieved some of the pressure on GPs but did not save money.

52. Karin Janzon, Stella Law, Chris Watts and Allyson Pollock, 'Lost and confused', *Health Service Journal*, 9 November 2000, p. 26.
53. Pat Armstrong and Hugh Armstrong, *Universal Health Care* (New Press, 1998), p. 1.
54. Ingrid Mcleod-Dick, *Health Care Reform in Ontario Hospitals During 1994 to 1996* (Schulich School of Business, York University), 1997.
55. According to Kirsty Milne ('Caring but sharing', *New Statesman and Society*, 26 February 1995), a majority of GP fundholders polled in 1995 were actually opposed to the 'reforms'.
56. Roger Jowell, Alison Park, Lindsay Brook, Katarina Thomson and Caroline Bryson (eds) *British Social Attitudes: The 14th Report: The End of Conservative Values?* (Ashgate, 1997), p. 53.
57. Hart, *Feasible Socialism*, p. 32.
58. See, e.g., Sarah Boseley, 'Medical profession struggles to survive', *Guardian*, 13 May 2000, and Walter Ellis, 'Is there something rotten at the heart of the medical profession?', *Independent on Sunday*, 18 June 2000.
59. Roy Lilley, cited in Health Policy Network, *In Practice: The NHS Market* (National Health Service Consultants' Association, 1995), p. 13.
60. Audit Commission, *The Doctors' Tale: The Work of Hospital Doctors in England and Wales* (HMSO, 1995); Yates, *Private Eye, Heart and Hip*, pp. 18–22 and 31–3.
61. John Yates, in evidence given to the House of Commons Select Committee on Health, and personal communication; Anthony Browne, 'Top doctors prescribe themselves £1m salaries', *Observer*, 8 October 2000. Surgeons operating on private patients in NHS theatres might earn as much as £1,500 for half a day's work, on top of their NHS salaries, while the theatre nurses were NHS staff working for their NHS salaries.
62. Janet Snell, 'When the going gets tough', *Health Service Journal*, 26 February 1998, pp. 28–30. The shortage of full-time staff was made up by importing nurses from abroad, chiefly English-speaking countries with lower wages such as India, Jamaica and Nigeria. In 1999 3.5 per cent of all nurses in England, and 31 per cent in inner London, had been trained abroad (James Buchan, 'Abroad minded', *Health Service Journal*, 6 January 2000, pp. 20–1).
63. *Laing's Review of Private Healthcare*, 1995, p. 116.
64. Mark Lattimer, *The Gift of Health: The NHS, Charity and the Mixed Economy of Healthcare*, (Directory of Social Change, 1996), pp. 73–89.
65. For the practical problems involved in this see David Heald and David A. Scott, 'NHS capital charging after five years', in Harrison (ed.), *Health Care UK 1995/96*, pp. 131–40. For the political dimension of the way the NHS hospitals were obliged to amortise their imputed debt on private

sector terms, even though their other operations were controlled in such a way as to make them unable to meet those terms, see Jean Shaoul, 'A capital way of accounting', unpublished paper, Department of Accounting and Finance, University of Manchester, 1996.

66. On the higher cost of PFI financing relative to the public sector see Declan Gaffney, Allyson M. Pollock, David Price and Jean Shaoul, 'NHS capital expenditure and the private finance initiative – expansion or contraction?', *BMJ* 319, 1999, pp. 48–51; on risk transfer see Allyson Pollock and Neil Vickers, 'Private pie in the sky', *Public Finance*, 14 April 2000, pp. 22–3.

67. This was foreseen quite early on by one of the government's external advisers: 'The private finance initiative is ... beginning to affect the mainstream of NHS provision ... as lawyers, financial advisers, and consultants search for creative solutions as they scent the prospect of profits from the increasing commercialisation of health care. Those providing private finance and putting their investment at risk will not expect to play a passive part in the management of services, and they will no doubt take a close interest in the appointment and performance of trust managers' (Chris Ham, 'Profiting from the NHS', *BMJ* 310, 1995, pp. 415–16).

68. Declan Gaffney, Allyson M. Pollock, David Price and Jean Shaoul, 'The politics of the private finance initiative and the new NHS', *BMJ* 319, 1999, p. 252.

69. John G. R. Howie et al., 'Quality at general practice consultations: cross sectional survey', *BMJ* 319, 1999, pp. 738–43.

70. Alex Waghorn and Martin McKee, 'Surgical outpatient clinics: are we allowing enough time?', *International Journal for Quality in Health Care* 11/3, June 1999, pp 215–19; Anthony Harrison and Bill New, *Access to Elective Care: What Should Really Be Done About Waiting Lists*, (The King's Fund, 2000), pp. 24 and 27.

71. Gaffney et al., 'NHS Capital expenditure', p. 48.

72. *Turning Your Back on Us: Older People and the NHS* (Age Concern, May 2000).

73. The practice came to public attention through the case of Jill Baker, a 67-year-old woman, in April 2000.

74. Penelope M. Mullen, 'Is it necessary to ration health care?', *Public Money and Management* 18/1, 1998, pp. 52–8. Mullen comments (p. 56): 'It may well be that no society can, or would wish to, provide absolutely every medical intervention and form of care that are conceivably possible (but not necessarily needed or even demanded). On the other hand, rationing/priority setting in the presence of a generous resource allocation, *mutatis mutandis*, is likely to be far less painful – will need fewer "hard choices" – than rationing/priority setting in the face of severely constrained resources.'

75. Judy Jones, 'Government announces army of 133 to rescue England's NHS', *BMJ* 320, 2000, p. 1027.
76. The facts appear to be that Tim Evans, the IHA's top PR executive, extracted an 'unequivocal' declaration from Blair on *Newsnight* that he had no ideological objection to cooperation between the NHS and the private health-care sector, and informed him afterwards about the spare capacity in the private sector and Dobson's instruction not to use it except as a last resort (interview with Peter Fermoy, IHA, 6 September 2000). According to the *Guardian* (28 July 2000), Blair later confirmed Evans' statements through a chance meeting with a journalist after dinner at a restaurant and took a personal interest in the policy change that followed.
77. The IHA claimed that there were 800 'critical care' beds available in private hospitals, but like 'intermediate care' this term had no established meaning, evidently falling between 'intensive care' and normal 'acute care'.
78. Janzon et al., 'Lost and confused.' The government stated that 'Before Mr Milburn [the Health Secretary] sanctions NHS funds going to private nursing or residential homes he will also expect them to replace ... "the missing component of care" – the hands-on work needed to get an elderly patient back at home after a stay of up to three months' (*Guardian*, 2 May 2000).
79. Department of Health/Independent Healthcare Association, *For the Benefit of Patients: A Concordat with the Private and Voluntary Health Care Provider Sector* (Department of Health, 2000); italics added.
80. *The NHS Plan: A Plan for Investment and Reform*, Cm 4818-I (The Stationery Office, 2000), p. 98.
81. Anthony Browne, 'Last chance for a cure', *Observer*, 26 March 2000.
82. Quoted in ibid.
83. *Laing's Healthcare Market Review* 1999–2000, p. 67.
84. Seamus Ward, 'New horizons: not just acute idea', *Health Service Journal*, 7 September 2000; Allyson M. Pollock, 'Will primary care trusts lead to US-style health care?'; Allyson M. Pollock, Stewart Player and Sylvia Godden, 'How private finance has triggered the entry of for-profit corporations into primary care'; and Sylvia Godden and Allyson M. Pollock, 'Financing of primary care premises', all forthcoming in *BMJ*, 2001.
85. In 1998/99 NHS trusts paid £1 billion in legal claims – almost 2 per cent of the total NHS budget, although not all of this was for medical 'malpractice', while in 1999 £77 million was paid in compensation by the doctors' Medical Defence Union.
86. Estimates derived from *Laing's Healthcare Market Review* 1999–2000, tables 1.1, 1.2 and 6.2.
87. *NHS Plan*, p. 66. The New Labour-oriented Institute of Public Policy

Research was said to be considering proposals 'to hand over the running of NHS hospitals to the private sector as an experiment to see if commercial firms can deliver better value for money and more effective care than the public sector' (*Guardian*, 17 October 2000).

88. Interview, 31 July 2000. For an early forecast of the trend see Sally Ruane, 'Public-private boundaries and the transformation of the NHS', *Critical Social Policy* 27/2, 1997, pp. 52–77.

89. See especially *Inequalities in Health: Report of a Research Working Group* (The Black Report: Department of Health and Social Security, 1980).

90. See Colin Leys, 'Intellectual mercenaries and the public interest: management consultancies and the NHS', *Politics and Policy* 27/4, 1999, pp. 447–65.

91. David Price, Allyson Pollock and Jean Shaoul, 'How the World Trade Organisation is shaping domestic policies in health care', *The Lancet* 354, 1999, p. 1890.

92. Karen Stocker, Howard Waitzkin and Celia Iriart, 'The exportation of managed care to Latin America', *New England Journal of Medicine* 340/14, 1999, pp. 1131–6. The authors note that HMO executives rarely claimed that they would improve disease prevention or the quality of services, but emphasised the profits to be made in Latin America, particularly stressing 'the importance of access to the social security funds of those countries' (p. 1132).

93. Inward FDI in health services to the USA expanded tenfold between 1990 and 1997, while outward health services FDI from the USA barely increased (Padma Mallampally and Zbigniew Zimny, 'Foreign direct investment in services', in Yair Aharoni and Lilach Nachum [eds], *Globalization of Services: Some Implications for Theory and Practice* [Routledge, 2000]), pp. 35–6).

94. Price et al., 'How the World Trade Organisation is shaping domestic policies in health care', p. 1890.

95. For an analysis of the threat to higher education see *The Threat to Higher Education: A Briefing on Current World Trade Organisation Negotiations* (People and Planet, 2000).

96. Allyson M. Pollock and David Price, 'Rewriting the regulations: how the World Trade Organisation could accelerate privatisation in health-care systems', *Lancet* 356, 2000, p. 1998.

97. Ibid., pp. 1998–9.

7 Market-driven Politics versus the Public Interest

1. Mikhail Lermontov, *A Hero of Our Time* (Ardis, 1988 [1848]), author's preface, p. 2.

2. David Marquand, *The Progressive Dilemma: From Lloyd George to Blair*, 2nd edn (Phoenix, 2000), p. 254. In the USA, of course, doctors do sell

medical services, and at many prestigious American universities students
– or their parents – are indeed customers.

3. Survey data collected in Anne Oakley, *Housewife* (Allen Lane, 1974),
cited in Ursula Huws, 'New technology and domestic labour' (CSE
Microprocessors Group, 1979).

4. Karl Marx, Preface to the First Edition of *Capital* (Penguin, 1973 [1867]),
p. 90.

5. The weakness of opposition to the effects of market-driven politics calls
for a major study of its own. A valuable survey of the failure to resist PFI
in the NHS is Sally Ruane, 'Acquiescence and opposition: the private
finance initiative in the National Health Service', Policy and Politics 28/
3, 2000, pp. 411–24, which stresses the discipline enforced on Labour
backbenchers after 1997, as well as on NHS officials; the fact that new
hospitals were so badly needed, setting up a competition for the only
funding that was on offer – a competition from which local Labour MPs
and councillors found it impossible to stand aloof; and the difficulty
UNISON, the main NHS trade union, experienced in finding allies who
understood the long-term implications of PFI.

6. It might even be considered a defining characteristic of socialism. Marx
famously saw the benefits of rising productivity in production as consisting in the expansion of leisure, in which he included the 'artistic,
scientific etc. development of the individuals in the time set free' – which
certainly includes education and would surely have included health care
had it really existed in 1858 (Karl Marx, *Grundrisse* (Penguin, 1973
[1858], 706).

7. William J. Baumol, 'Health care, education and the cost disease: a
looming crisis for public choice', *Public Choice* 77, 1993, pp. 17–28,
reprinted in Ruth Towse (ed.), *Baumol's Cost Disease: The Arts and Other
Vitims*, (Edward Elgar, 1997), pp. 510–21.

8. Ursula Huws, 'Consuming fashions', *New Statesman and Society*, 19 August
1988, p. 33. She added: 'And perhaps our children could do with more
teachers as well as more computers.' Direct public involvement in such
choices is surely the only way support can be obtained for the rising rate
of taxation that will be needed to sustain public services.

9. André Gorz made this point in 1967: 'Expansion of the socialized sector,
or the satisfactory operation of the already existing social services, can be
obtained only by continually restricting the private sector . . . by limiting
capital's sphere of autonomy and counteracting its logic, by restraining
its field of action . . . the socialist sector must take control of the
industries it depends on . . . or else it will be nibbled away and exploited
by the private sector . . .' (André Gorz, *Strategy for Labor* [Beacon Press,
1967], pp. 97–8).

Index